ITALIAN COOKING

ITALIAN COOKING

Robin Howe

PARK LANE PRESS

First published in 1979 by Park Lane Press,
36 Park Street, London W1Y 4DE

Text: © Robin Howe 1979

Editor: Fiona Roxburgh
Consultant editor: Mary Anne Sanders
Designer: Gail Engert
Series designer: Rod Springett Associates
Photographer: Paul Kemp
Props research: Penny Markham
Diagrams: Marion Appleton
Production: Georgina Ewer

Text set by SX Composing Ltd., Rayleigh, England
Printed by Chromoworks Ltd., Nottingham, England
Bound by Dorstel Press Ltd., Harlow, England

Contents

Notes

The symbol 🦐 denotes that the recipe is a more glamorous and ambitious dish and suitable for special occasions; it may therefore require more preparation as well as possible extra expense.

When preparing a dish that includes wine, try to use Italian wine. Ideally you should use the type of wine produced in the district where the dish originates. This applies also to olive oil, used throughout Italian cooking, and often to other ingredients as well. For further details on the important use of herbs and flavourings in Italian cooking *see pages* 212–217.

Italian sugar is already fine and so castor sugar should be used unless otherwise stated in the ingredients.

All spoon measures are level unless otherwise stated.

Plain flour should be used unless otherwise stated in the ingredients.

Egg sizes are specified only where exact quantities are vital to the recipe.

Introduction

For those to whom other people's cooking is an adventure and a new experience, then the cooking of Italy with its variety and its originality will come as a joy. And what better way could there be to understand this diversity and flavour of Italian cooking than to take a leisurely tour of this lovely country, from the Alps in the north to the islands of Sicily and Sardinia in the south. As the landscape changes so does the cooking, in accordance with local tastes, climate and tradition.

For the visitor to Italy one of the pleasures is the discovery of the passionate devotion to genuine food by the people; they are for ever wandering through the hills in search of herbs, wild asparagus, and strange-looking mushrooms, or visiting olive oil mills to find the finest oil of the first cold pressing. Amateurs of water go to the local fountains where spring water spouts, and all Italians have a favourite wine supplier.

The Italians have much to be grateful for in their country; forests still stocked with game, hills cloaked in vines and olive trees, plains that are vast vegetable gardens, and seas and lakes filled with fish. It is no wonder that Italians are not only devoted to good eating but, it seems, to the endless discussion of food. This impression is strengthened when you begin to count the hundreds of *sagre* (food festivals) held throughout the country, or consider the large number of cooking magazines. Italians like to eat in the way their parents and grandparents did, retaining ancient traditions. Where else would you find it said seriously, 'our recipes are an ancestral message?' as they do in Apulia, or find a soup made with seven different types of vegetables, seven different types of meat, and claimed to be made 'only by a truly virtuous girl?'

Italian cooking is both rustic and sophisticated and this makes it easy to do for the non-Italian. A recipe may seem long, even complicated at first sight, but once the dish is simmering on top of the stove, or baking in the oven, the Italians leave it there while they get on with other chores. Slow aromatic cooking is the Italian housewife's axiom.

Some people are inclined to think that Italian cooking is highly spiced, which it certainly is not. In Basilicata they like to use a lot of ginger, locally known as *forte*, which means strong, but it is not used anywhere else in the country. Nutmeg is used in large quantities and every kitchen boasts its grater, used only for nutmeg. No Italian woman would use other than freshly grated nutmeg, or for that matter freshly grated pepper. Salt too, is usually natural salt from the sea. Garlic is used in discreet quantities in most recipes. Cheese, although used a great deal in Italian dishes, should never be used excessively; too much, say the Italians, 'spoils the touch of the food on the tongue.'

An Italian luncheon usually begins with an antipasto followed by a dish of pasta with a sauce, while dinner begins with a soup. The main course is usually of meat, fish or poultry. On the whole vegetables are served as a separate course and usually there is a salad of some kind which will arrive at the same time as the main course. Desserts are not general, cheese or fruit being preferred to finish the meal. However, on Sundays and festive occasions a tart would be offered.

Buon appetito.

Robin Howe

The author's home in Imperia, Liguria

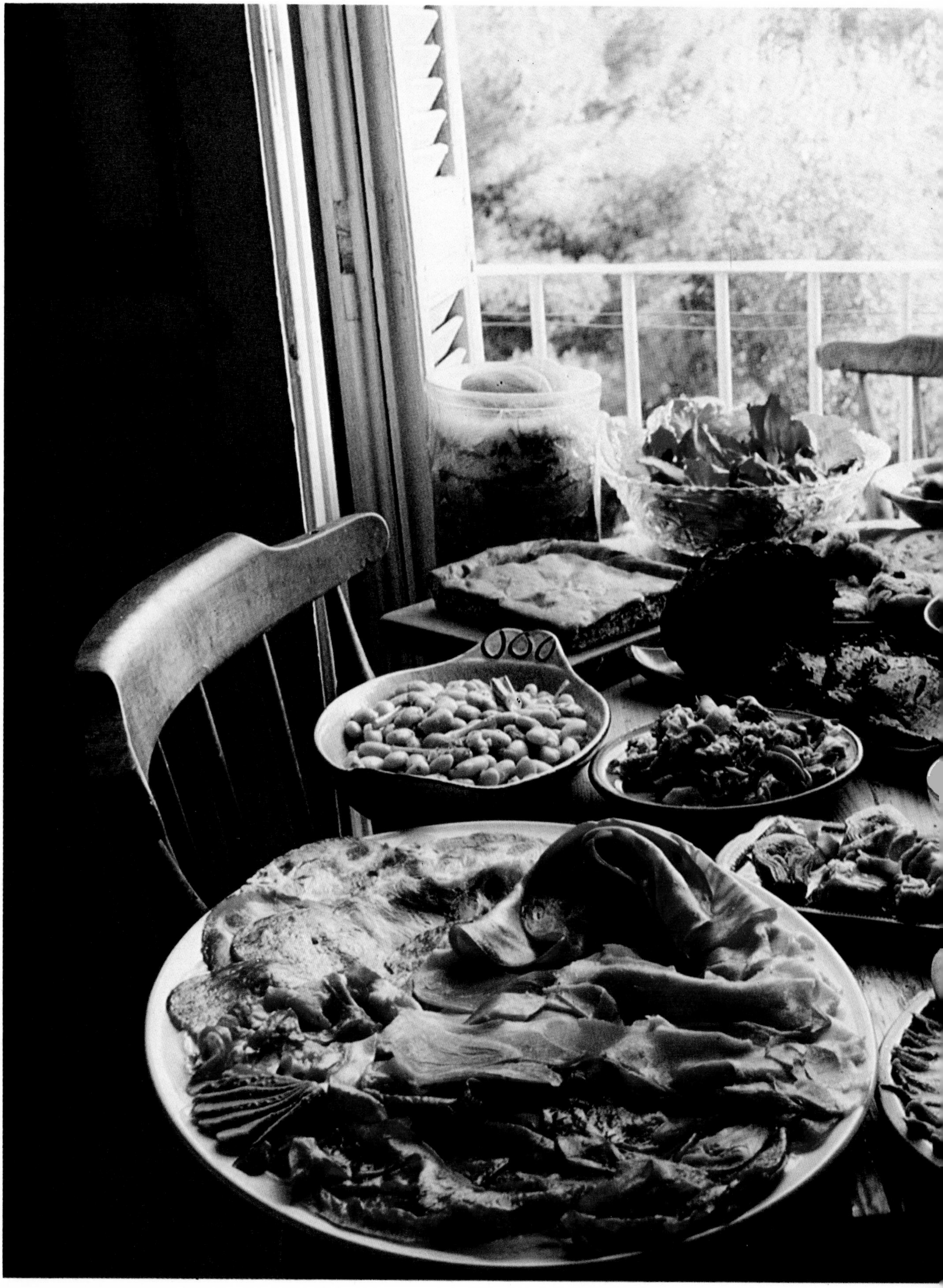

Antipasti

This is an important course, and very much an introduction to the Italian culinary scene. As its name suggests, it is served before the main course and, while it is designed to whet the appetite, never to drown it, it can nevertheless reach monster proportions. It should prepare the stomach for what it is about to receive and the discerning Italian gastronome will not choose his main dish until he has selected his antipasto.

The variety of dishes contained in Italian antipasto is almost legendary. It can be two or three simple items, or trolleys positively groaning under the weight of dishes. Many of these dishes are classic, such as *antipasto misto all'italiana,* which usually includes a plate of wafer-thin slices of smoked and boiled ham and salami which will vary throughout the country. In some areas Parma ham will be chosen, in others the fine San Daniele or the Casentino ham; the Tuscans prefer their own mountain hams, hand-cut on the bone. Another interesting thinly sliced meat is the *Bresaola della Valtellina,* a lean beef salted, spiced and smoked in rafters for sixty days and served in an olive oil and lemon dressing. There will also be a slice of mortadella – the best, it is claimed, comes from Bologna, but it is a matter of taste; the Sardinians prefer their own wild boar mortadella just as they prefer their wild boar ham, fine and brittle, smoked in flitches in darkened cellars until almost black. In Umbria the hams, salami and sausages come from Norcia, which is also a black truffle area. In Rome the Norcia pork products are rated so highly that a pork butcher is called a *norcina.*

There is not one type of salame but dozens, all regional. For example, in Tuscany they are flavoured with fennel seeds, and along the Po Valley red wine finds its way into the mixture. Sardinia makes a salame from wild boar, while in the south of Italy a salame called *luganega* is produced, one well known to the ancient Romans as *lucanica.* Milan has a vast selection of salami and many Italians consider these to be the best. Real salami connoisseurs find their way into the hills where the peasants still make salami, hams and sausages according to ancient traditions. Not quite a salame but in a similar class are Modena *zampone,* stuffed pig's trotters, and *cotechini,* fat pork-stuffed sausages.

Italian sausages equally are numerous and varied in their fillings, flavourings and shapes. Some are for boiling, others for frying, others are eaten raw, some are large, some minute. Sometimes they are kept for weeks; some are separated, others one feels should be sold by the metre. All find their place on the antipasto list, especially so in mountain areas.

With Italy's long coastline it is not surprising that there are a multitude of fish or *magro antipasto* dishes. Fish specialities appear according to the season; grilled swordfish is a favourite in Sicily and Liguria; mussels, clams and oysters further south, are often served raw on a bed of seaweed. Venice serves scampi, all members of the prawn family and other shellfish. Liguria has whitebait and *gianchetti,* tiny, boneless fish fry. Fresh sardines, which are delicious grilled or stuffed are a general favourite everywhere, so are fresh anchovies, which have a unique flavour, especially when served, as in Liguria, cleaned and filleted but uncooked and marinated in a simple dressing. There are numerous fish salads which usually include octopus and squid with a few shrimps for good measure. In Livorno and Liguria grilled small red mullet are served. Sicily has a fondness for sea urchins, *ricci di mare,* which are bothersome to prepare but good to eat.

But not all antipasti, whether fish or meat, are cold. In many regions small squares of the local type of pizza are served; in Naples miniature round pizzas are served and in Liguria *focaccia* or the *torta verde,* the latter a covered spinach or chard pie that started life as an Easter pie but is now prepared almost all the year round. Vegetables are favourite antipasto items, especially raw mushrooms, marinated in a dressing for some hours; there are also pickled gherkins, tiny pickled onions, black and green olives, and also so-called white olives from Gaeta. In

Sicily large olives are fried stuffed with meat. Fried or marinated baby artichokes are everywhere a favourite, so are large artichokes served hot with a butter sauce; tomatoes are cut into wedges, served sprinkled with chopped herbs, basil or parsley depending on the region, while red peppers are served in oil. Beans, both fresh and dried, are served cold with a dressing; melon and figs are served together with thin slices of ham. In the Ligurian hills a goat cheese can be found flavoured with garlic and chilli peppers and preserved in jars covered with olive oil. In many country areas you will be offered goat or sheep cheese, often served with very young, raw broad beans still in their pods which you can peel yourself. Quite a number of salads also appear as antipasto.

There are favourite hot antipasto items such as cauliflower fritters and sardine butter grills, which consist of filleted canned sardines mixed to a paste with lemon juice, brandy, paprika pepper and tomato juice and quickly grilled on a piece of toast. There are also stuffed courgette flowers, and Gorgonzola toast.

Add to this formidable collection the meat loaves, such as *cima* from Genoa, cold stuffed veal, the Venetian meat loaf, made from a mixture of tongue, pork and mortadella; the thinly sliced cold meats, such as beef, pork or veal, or Piedmont's minced or sliced raw veal served with a dressing, and it comes as something of a surprise that the antipasto is considered only as an appetite whetter.

1. Prosciutto di Parma
2. Mortadella
3. Cotechino
4. Salametto
5. Peperoni
6. Salame genovese
7. Salame milanese

Prosciutto con fichi

Smoked ham with figs

TO SERVE FOUR

INGREDIENTS

8–12 ripe fresh figs, green or purple
100 g (4 oz) Italian smoked ham

It is important that the figs be fresh and very ripe. They can be served, peeled or unpeeled, but it makes for easier eating if they are peeled first. They should be slit open on one side to expose their bright flesh. Serve the ham and figs on the same plates but separately.

Prosciutto con melone

Smoked ham with melon

TO SERVE FOUR

INGREDIENTS

1 medium-sized sweet melon
100 g (4 oz) Italian smoked ham

The ham must be sliced paper-thin. 100 g (4 oz) should give 8 to 12 slices.

Peel the melon, cut into four wedges and remove all the seeds. The ham can be served wrapped around the melon, or the two ingredients served separately on the same plate. In Tuscany, the ham and melon are served on separate plates.

Prosciutto con fichi; prosciutto con melone

Fondi di carciofi in salsa

Artichoke hearts in sauce

TO SERVE FOUR

INGREDIENTS
2 400-g (14-oz) tins
   artichoke hearts –
   450 g (1 lb) drained
   weight
juice of 1 lemon
2 tablespoons olive oil
salt and pepper
1 teaspoon fresh
   marjoram, finely
   chopped or ½ teaspoon
   dried

Drain the artichokes. Combine together the remaining ingredients and marinate the artichokes in this for an hour or so. Turn occasionally to make sure they are coated with the marinade. Serve the artichokes in their marinade as part of a general plate of antipasto.

Cappelle di funghi farcite

Baked stuffed mushroom caps

TO SERVE FOUR

INGREDIENTS
12 large mushrooms
40 g (1½ oz) butter or
   margarine
3 tablespoons olive oil
1 clove garlic, crushed
2–3 shallots or spring
   onions, finely chopped
25 g (1 oz) soft
   breadcrumbs
50 g (2 oz) grated cheese,
   preferably Parmesan
2–3 leaves fresh basil,
   finely chopped or ½
   teaspoon dried
salt and freshly ground
   pepper

The original recipe uses the Italian funghi, *porcini,* or edible boletus. However, any large firm and fresh mushrooms can be used instead.

Wash the mushrooms, separate the stems and the caps. Dry the caps carefully. Squeeze the stems dry and chop finely. Heat 25 g (1 oz) of the butter and 1 tablespoon of oil in a small pan. Add the garlic and shallots, stir well, then add the chopped stems and fry over a moderate heat for 5–10 minutes until dry. Preheat the oven to 180°C, 350°F, Gas Mark 4. Stir the stems gently, take from the heat and mix with the breadcrumbs, cheese and basil. Rub a shallow oven-to-table baking dish with the remaining oil, place the caps in this and put some of the filling into each one. Sprinkle lightly with salt and pepper and top each mushroom with a sliver of the remaining butter. Bake in the oven for 15–20 minutes or until just tender.

Funghi marinati

Marinated mushrooms

TO SERVE FOUR

INGREDIENTS
450 g (1 lb) fresh firm
   mushrooms
150 ml (¼ pint) white wine
   vinegar
6 black peppercorns
2 cloves garlic, crushed
75 ml (3 fl oz) each olive
   oil and water
1 teaspoon salt
1 bayleaf

Top to bottom : fondi di carciofi in salsa; cappelle di funghi farcite; funghi marinati

This is a particularly popular antipasto, and to obtain the full flavour of the marinade it should be prepared two days in advance. It can be made with almost any type of small firm mushroom.

Wash the mushrooms and discard their stems. Pat the caps dry but do not peel them. Combine the remaining ingredients, put into a shallow pan and bring to a gentle boil. Lower the heat and cook for 15 minutes; add the mushrooms and continue simmering for 5 minutes. Take from the heat and let the mushrooms cool in the pan, put into a bowl and leave in the refrigerator for a couple of days in the marinade in order to absorb its full flavour. Then drain and serve.

Funghi alla salamoia

Pickled mushrooms

TO SERVE FOUR

INGREDIENTS
Method 1
450 g (1 lb) mushrooms
1 teaspoon dried oregano
 (optional)
1 tablespoon capers
1 clove garlic, sliced
good pinch of salt
2–3 tablespoons water
Method 2
450 g (1 lb) mushrooms
1 teaspoon peppercorns
1 clove garlic, sliced
good pinch of salt
1 blade mace
red wine vinegar, enough
 to cover

Method 1
Wash the mushrooms, do not peel but take off the stems (these can be used to flavour a soup). Put the caps with the remaining ingredients into a pan and cook slowly for about 10 minutes. Cool and serve as part of a general plate of antipasto.

Method 2
Wash the mushrooms, remove the stems and wipe the caps dry on a cloth. Pack the mushroom caps into a glass jar, add the remaining ingredients, covering the caps completely. Leave for a couple of days in the refrigerator, drain and serve.

Melanzane a funghetti

Aubergines cooked as mushrooms

TO SERVE FOUR

INGREDIENTS
900 g (2 lb) aubergines
275 ml (½ pint) olive oil
2–3 cloves of garlic,
 chopped
2–3 tablespoons finely
 chopped parsley
1 teaspoon dried oregano
pinch of salt

This dish can be served either hot or cold but if cold, the oil must be olive oil as this never congeals.

Peel the aubergines and slice thinly. Heat the oil in a frying pan or shallow pan, add the aubergines, garlic and parsley. Cover and cook slowly until tender and a golden brown. As aubergines absorb oil you may find it necessary to add a little more during cooking. After about 10 minutes cooking sprinkle with oregano and salt. Continue cooking for a further 10 minutes. Drain and serve.

Fiori di zucchini ripieni

Stuffed courgette flowers

TO SERVE FOUR–SIX

INGREDIENTS
1 small courgette
100 g (¼ lb) green beans
1 small floury potato
1 egg, well beaten
1–2 tablespoons grated
 Parmesan cheese
25 g (1 oz) butter
1 tablespoon oil
3–6 cloves garlic, crushed
2–3 leaves fresh basil,
 finely chopped
salt and pepper
20 courgette flowers

This is a Ligurian recipe which is extremely good and much more simple to prepare than would seem at first sight. The plants begin to produce flowers in August–September and only the male flowers should be used, otherwise you will lose your crop. Marrow and pumpkin flowers can be prepared in the same way.

Wash and slice the courgette; top, tail and trim the beans; peel and quarter the potato. Cook these together in salted water until tender. Drain and rub through a coarse sieve. Put the vegetables into a bowl, and add the egg and cheese. Soften the butter, combine with 1 tablespoon of oil and add to the mixture together with the garlic, basil, salt and pepper. Preheat the oven to 220°C, 425°F, Gas Mark 7. Open up the flowers and carefully remove the stamens. Fill each flower with a little of the vegetable mixture, then carefully cover over the petals to enclose the stuffing and lightly rub with oil. Put the stuffed flowers into a well oiled baking tin and cook in the oven for about 20 minutes until they become quite brown. They can be served hot or cold but are better hot.

Fiori di zucchini ripieni

Zucchini alla salamoia

Pickled courgettes

TO SERVE FOUR

INGREDIENTS
4 medium-sized
  courgettes
5 tablespoons olive oil
2 cloves garlic, chopped
good pinch of salt
½ teaspoon dried oregano
1 bayleaf
white wine vinegar

Wash the courgettes, wipe them dry and cut into thick slices. Heat 3–4 tablespoons of the olive oil, add the courgettes and cook gently until tender, for about 20 minutes. Drain, cool and put them into a glass jar. Add 1 tablespoon of olive oil, the garlic, salt, oregano, bayleaf and enough vinegar to cover. Seal and turn the jar round and round in order to thoroughly mix the contents but do not shake or the courgettes will break up. Keep for 2–3 days in the refrigerator before serving cold.

Zucchini dorati

Fried courgettes

TO SERVE FOUR

INGREDIENTS
900 g (2 lb) medium-sized
  courgettes
2 eggs, well beaten
2 tablespoons grated
  Parmesan cheese
flour for coating
150 ml (¼ pint) olive oil

Wash the courgettes, wipe them dry and cut into thick round slices. Combine the eggs and cheese. Lightly coat the courgettes with flour, then dip into the egg and cheese mixture. Heat the oil in a frying pan until very hot. Fry the courgette slices, a few at a time, until brown. Take them out with a perforated spoon, drain and keep warm in the oven. When all the slices are browned, serve hot.

They can also be served cold, provided the frying has been done in olive oil.

Top : funghi alla salamoia;
zucchini alla salamoia;
bottom : melanzane a funghetti;
zucchini dorati

Bruschetta

Garlic toast

TO SERVE FOUR

INGREDIENTS
4 thick slices toasted bread
4–8 cloves garlic, crushed
olive oil
salt and black pepper

This speciality of Umbria should be made with a coarse type of bread and grilled over charcoal. Failing charcoal, I get the best results by toasting the bread on a griddle pan, although ordinary grilling is quite adequate. Do not stint on the garlic as this is not a dish for refined palates; it goes well with a strong red table wine. The time for eating bruschetta in Umbria is during the olive gathering and in Spello, in the province of Perugia, there is a *sagra della bruschetta,* or a garlic toast festival, on the last Sunday in March.

Spread the toasted bread while still hot with garlic and oil and sprinkle with salt and freshly ground black pepper.

Crostini alla fiorentina

Chicken livers on fried bread

TO SERVE FOUR

INGREDIENTS
225 g (½ lb) chicken livers
1 tablespoon each olive oil and butter
1 very small onion, grated
1 sprig parsley
3–4 anchovy fillets
150 ml (¼ pint) dry white wine
pinch of salt
a few drops of lemon juice
4 slices day-old bread
oil and butter mixed for frying the bread
grated Parmesan cheese

Trim and chop the livers. Heat 1 tablespoon each of oil and butter, add the onion and fry until a golden brown – it must not become dark. Add the livers and the parsley, anchovies and wine, sprinkle lightly with salt and cook gently for 10 minutes. Sprinkle with the lemon juice.

While the livers are cooking, fry the bread in further oil and butter or if preferred, the bread can be toasted. Discard the parsley. Spread the livers on top of the fried bread or toast, sprinkle with cheese and serve at once.

Top to bottom : bruschetta; crostini alla fiorentina; toast al Gorgonzola

Toast al Gorgonzola

Gorgonzola 'Rabbit'

TO SERVE FOUR

INGREDIENTS
1 small stalk celery
3 egg yolks
100 g (4 oz) Gorgonzola
2 tablespoons double or single cream
salt and pepper
butter
4 large thick slices bread

If available, mild Gorgonzola (in Italy called *dolce* or sweet) is better in this dish. If using a sharp Gorgonzola, test for saltiness, as it may have sufficient salt already.

First prepare the 'rabbit'; very finely chop the celery, beat the egg yolks and mash the Gorgonzola. Combine these ingredients with the cream, add salt and pepper and mix until smooth. Heat the grill. Generously butter one side of the bread and grill on this side until a light brown. Take from the grill, spread with the Gorgonzola mixture and then grill until the top is well browned. The bread is definitely toasted on one side only in the Italian way.

Formaggio con le olive

Mixed cheeses with green olives

TO SERVE FOUR–SIX

INGREDIENTS
50 g (2 oz) butter
350 g (12 oz) Ricotta
225 g (8 oz) mild
  Gorgonzola
salt and white pepper
1–2 cloves garlic, crushed
2 sprigs parsley, finely
  chopped
100 g (4 oz) green olives,
  pitted

Soften the butter and beat it until light. Rub the Ricotta through a sieve and combine with the butter. Beat well. Add the Gorgonzola and thoroughly blend into the butter-Ricotta mixture, then add salt, pepper, garlic and parsley. Chop half of the olives finely and mix these into the cheese mixture and beat until it is creamy. Shape into a square or oblong, or put it into a lightly oiled mould. Cover and keep in the refrigerator for 3–4 hours. Serve garnished with the remainder of the green olives. Serve either as a pâté or as a cheese with bread.

Mozzarella in carrozza

Fried Mozzarella sandwiches

TO SERVE FOUR

INGREDIENTS
1 small day-old sandwich
  loaf
1 large Mozzarella cheese,
  about 200 g (7 oz)
1 egg (size 2)
pinch of salt
150 ml ($\frac{1}{4}$ pint) milk
flour for coating
olive oil for deep frying
fine breadcrumbs
fresh parsley for garnishing

The literal translation of this recipe is Mozzarella in a carriage and it originated in the Campania-Naples region.

Cut the bread into eight equal slices. Cut eight equal slices from the Mozzarella and put a slice on to each slice of bread. Cut the bread to almost the same shape as the cheese but just a scrap larger all round. Beat the egg in a bowl, add the salt, then the milk. Beat well. Dip a slice of bread into the egg-and-milk mixture, then place on a large flat plate. Repeat this with the remaining slices. Take the Mozzarella, slice by slice, coat with flour, then dip into the egg-milk mixture. Place the Mozzarella slices on the bread and leave to rest for 30 minutes. Prepare a pan with plenty of oil for deep frying. Sprinkle each slice of bread and Mozzarella generously with breadcrumbs and, when the oil is very hot, fry them until a golden brown. Drain thoroughly on kitchen paper and serve at once on a hot platter garnished with sprigs of fresh parsley.

Peperoni alla bagna cauda
Sweet peppers with bagna cauda sauce

TO SERVE FOUR

INGREDIENTS
2 large sweet peppers
4 large tomatoes, not too ripe
3–4 anchovy fillets
2 cloves garlic, thinly sliced and soaked in a little milk
bagna cauda sauce (*page* 181)

Wipe the peppers with a damp cloth, cut into halves and remove the seeds and cores. Roast over a flame on the end of a long fork until they are blistered black, or roast in a hot oven. Cool, then pull or scrape off the outer skin and slice the flesh into thin strips. Put these into a fairly deep serving dish. Peel the tomatoes and slice them thinly. Spread these over the peppers, add the anchovy fillets and finally the drained garlic. Immediately before serving, pour the hot *bagna cauda* sauce over the top.

Try to keep everything as warm as possible. This dish is also much improved if slivers of white truffle are sprinkled on top of the sauce.

Top: peperoni alla bagna cauda; *bottom*: sardine sott'olio

Sardine sott'olio
Sardines in tomato sauce

TO SERVE FOUR

INGREDIENTS
400 g (14 oz) sardines in oil
50 g (2 oz) butter
1–2 cloves garlic, finely chopped
2–3 sage leaves, chopped or ½ teaspoon dried
100 g (4 oz) tomato purée
1–2 sweet peppers
2 hard-boiled eggs
100 g (4 oz) pickles

The type of pickles used in this recipe are tiny gherkins, baby onions, or else artichoke hearts.

Drain and carefully fillet the sardines. Arrange the fillets in a shallow serving dish. Heat the butter in a pan, add the garlic, sage and tomato purée and cook for about 10 minutes; leave until quite cold. Grill or roast the peppers until they are burned black. Cool, peel off the thin outer skin and cut into strips. Cut the eggs into quarters. When ready to serve, pour the cold tomato sauce over the sardines and garnish with the pickles, peppers and eggs around the side of the plate.

18

Caponata
Aubergine salad with a sweet-sour sauce

TO SERVE FOUR–SIX

INGREDIENTS
450 g (1 lb) aubergines
olive oil for frying
3 stalks of celery
1 medium-sized onion, sliced
225 g (8 oz) ripe tomatoes
1 tablespoon sugar
150 ml (¼ pint) red wine vinegar
1 tablespoon pine-nuts (optional)
1 tablespoon sultanas
50 g (2 oz) large green olives
1 tablespoon capers
salt and pepper

It is important for this Sicilian salad that a good quality wine vinegar is used, as an inferior quality would spoil the flavour. It should also be realised that the sauce is more sour than sweet.

Wash the aubergines and cut into rather large dice without peeling them. Sprinkle with salt and leave in a colander or tilted plate with a weight over them for about 1 hour to drain off their bitter juices. Wash well and thoroughly dry. Heat plenty of oil and fry the aubergines until brown. Drain on kitchen paper. Cut the celery stalks into short lengths and fry until crisp in the same oil. Take from the pan and put aside with the aubergines. Take a ladleful of the oil from the pan, put into another pan and add the onion and tomatoes, stir well, then add the remaining ingredients, aubergines and celery and cook gently for 10 minutes. Take from the stove, arrange on a plate and leave until quite cold, before serving.

Variations of this recipe include adding 2–3 tablespoons of grated bitter chocolate or a large quantity of finely chopped basil with the remaining ingredients. Strips of sweet pepper, fried separately like the aubergines and celery, can also be added as a garnish.

Insalata di cavolo
Cabbage salad

TO SERVE FOUR–SIX

INGREDIENTS
1 small white cabbage
1 clove garlic, crushed
3 tablespoons olive oil
1 tablespoon vinegar
salt and black pepper
2 eggs, well beaten
150 ml (¼ pint) single cream
anchovies for garnishing

Wash the cabbage, trim off any thick stalks and shred finely. Cook whole in lightly salted water until just tender, and keep hot. Put into a salad bowl and mix in the garlic. Combine the oil, vinegar, salt and pepper. Gradually beat in the eggs and cream. Put into the top of a double boiler and cook, stirring all the time, over hot but not boiling water. As soon as the sauce thickens, take it from the stove and pour while still hot over the cabbage. Garnish with anchovies.

This dish can be served at once or left until cold but do not chill.

Pomodori alla salsa verde

Tomatoes with a green sauce

TO SERVE FOUR

INGREDIENTS
salsa verde (*page* 183)
4–6 large ripe but firm
  tomatoes

First prepare the sauce. Wash or wipe the tomatoes, cut off the stem ends and cut each one into 2–3 thick slices. Arrange these on a plate and place about 1 teaspoon of green sauce on top of each. Chill in the refrigerator before serving.

Condijon

Mixed vegetable salad

TO SERVE FOUR

INGREDIENTS
1 small cucumber – Italian
  cucumbers are short and
  stubby
½ yellow sweet pepper or
  1 whole small one
450 g (1 lb) tomatoes
a few small onions or
  spring onions
a few filleted salted
  anchovies
1 clove garlic, chopped
salt to taste
6 fresh basil leaves or
  ½ teaspoon dried
handful black olives, pitted
olive oil for the dressing

There are several recipes and names for this particular salad (it is also called *condion* or *condigion*). It is, I think, the origin of the so-called *salade niçoise*. This is not surprising, for the Ligurians held the coast around what is now Nice for centuries and left many of their recipes behind, including their version of the pizza, the focaccia (*see page* 61).

The tomatoes used in the salad should not be too ripe, Italians preferring green ones for their salads.

Peel and chop the cucumber. Wash the pepper, discard the core and seeds and cut away thick pith. Quarter the tomatoes, cut the pepper into thin strips, thinly slice the onions and cut the anchovies into pieces. Put all these ingredients into a salad bowl, add garlic, salt, basil (if large basil leaves are used chop them roughly) and olives and dress with olive oil.

Insalata di frutta alla menta
Orange salad with mint

TO SERVE FOUR–SIX

INGREDIENTS
3–4 large ripe oranges
1–2 grapefruit
castor sugar
1 head of lettuce
4–6 mint leaves, coarsely
   chopped

Peel the fruit, discard all the pith and separate the flesh into segments; pull off all the thin skin and discard the pips. Combine the segments in a bowl, sprinkle with sugar and put into the refrigerator. In the meantime wash the lettuce, discard the broken leaves, gently dry the rest and line a deep salad bowl with it. Arrange the fruit in the middle and sprinkle with fresh mint leaves, coarsely chopped.

Top : insalata di frutta alla menta;
bottom : insalata di fagiolini

Insalata di fagiolini
Bean salad

TO SERVE FOUR

INGREDIENTS
225 g (8 oz) dried white
   beans
2–3 tablespoons olive oil
1 tablespoon vinegar
1–2 cloves garlic, crushed
salt and pepper
1 small onion, finely sliced
150 g (5 oz) tuna fish,
   tinned
2–4 anchovy fillets
coarsely chopped green
   herbs for garnishing

This is a very robust dish from Tuscany but particularly popular in Florence. Good quality tinned white beans can be used in the same way.

Soak the beans overnight in plenty of cold water. Next day drain and put them into a large pan with fresh cold, unsalted water. Bring to a rapid boil, lower the heat and cook the beans until tender, for about 2½ hours. Mix the oil and vinegar together in a salad bowl, add garlic, salt, pepper and onion (putting aside some rings to use as a garnish). When the beans are tender, drain well, add to the salad bowl, stirring them well until coated with the dressing. Cover and leave until cool. When ready to serve, break the tuna fish into fairly large chunks, add to the beans, mixing them in carefully. Garnish with the anchovy fillets, the remaining onion rings and herbs – parsley, basil or sage is the usual Italian choice.

Insalata di mare

Mixed fish salad

This consists of a rich mixture of cooked fish of all kinds: tiny inkfish or squid, baby octopus, shellfish such as clams and small mussels, the odd prawn or so and, in Liguria, *gianchetti* (tiny boneless fishbait) are often added. It is usually served cold in an oil and lemon or vinegar dressing. It is not often made in the home although it is possible to ask the fishmonger for a mixture of such fish to make it yourself.

It is a favourite restaurant salad, served all along the coast of Italy, the ingredients varying according to region and availability of certain fish, and of course the time of the year.

Insalata di funghi e formaggio

Mushroom and cheese salad

TO SERVE FOUR

INGREDIENTS
450 g (1 lb) mushrooms
olive oil for coating
225 g (8 oz) firm cheese
  such as Gruyère or
  Cheddar
salt and pepper

Wash the mushrooms, take off the stems (these can be used in a soup or sauce), pat the caps dry and slice rather thinly. Put into a bowl and add enough oil to coat the caps thoroughly; cut the cheese into large dice, add to the bowl, mix well, add salt and pepper and serve.

If you do not want to serve the salad immediately, leave the mushrooms in the oil and add the cheese later.

Insalata di patate

Potato salad

TO SERVE FOUR

INGREDIENTS
675 g (1½ lb) waxy
  potatoes
salt
Dressing
1 tablespoon anchovy paste
4–6 anchovy fillets
½ small onion, finely
  chopped
1 tablespoon capers
1–2 cloves garlic, chopped
150 ml (¼ pint) white wine

Wash the potatoes and cook them in their skins in boiling salted water over a moderate heat until tender. Do not let them break. Meanwhile put the anchovy paste into a small bowl, add the anchovies with their oil and mix well; add the onion, capers, garlic and wine. When the potatoes are tender, drain well, cool, peel and cut them into medium-sized cubes. Put them into a salad bowl and while still warm cover with the dressing. Mix gently so that all the potatoes are well coated, taste before adding salt for the anchovies are probably salty enough, and leave for 10–15 minutes before serving.

Left : insalata di patate agrodolce;
right : insalata di patate

Insalata di patate agrodolce

Sweet-sour potato salad

TO SERVE FOUR-SIX

INGREDIENTS
4–6 large potatoes
1 medium-sized onion,
  finely chopped
1 stalk celery, chopped into
  small rounds
2 hard-boiled eggs,
  chopped
1 small gherkin, sliced
1 good sprig parsley, finely
  chopped
150 ml (¼ pint) tarragon
  vinegar
2 eggs, well beaten
50 g (2 oz) sugar
salt and pepper
½ teaspoon dry mustard
2–3 tablespoons olive oil
2–3 rashers fat bacon,
  chopped

Wash the potatoes and cook them in their skins until tender. Cool, peel and cut into thick slices or cubes. Mix with the onion, celery, hard-boiled eggs, gherkins and parsley in a salad bowl. Beat the vinegar into the beaten eggs, add half a cup of water, beat well, add the sugar, salt, pepper and mustard. Heat the oil in a small pan, add the bacon and fry until this is crisp and brown, then add the egg and vinegar mixture and stir well. Now cook over hot water until the mixture thickens, stirring all the while to prevent curdling. While it is still hot pour this dressing over the potato salad. Toss lightly and serve.

23

Panzanella
Bread salad

TO SERVE FOUR

INGREDIENTS
3 slices coarse white
  bread, 2 days old
2–3 sprigs fresh basil or
  parsley, chopped or
  ½ teaspoon dried
1 tablespoon capers
salt and black pepper
olive oil
tarragon vinegar
Dressing
2 cloves garlic
3–4 anchovies
2 small chilli peppers,
  chopped

This very Tuscan speciality is reminiscent of the Lebanese bread salad *fattoush*. It may seem unusual at first sight but is really good. Obviously any type of bread may be used but the less refined the better.

Soak the bread in water, squeeze it dry and crumble well. Mix together with the basil or parsley, capers, salt, pepper and just enough oil and vinegar to moisten. Put aside while making the dressing. Pound the garlic to a paste, add the anchovies and peppers and continue pounding until the paste is smooth. Work in some vinegar until it is still creamy but fairly thin. Arrange the bread mixture on a plate, pour the dressing over the top, chill and serve.

Sliced or quartered tomatoes, sliced hard-boiled egg, or onions are often added as a garnish.

Insalata di pomodori al basilico
Tomato salad

TO SERVE FOUR–SIX

INGREDIENTS
1 clove garlic, halved
4–5 large firm tomatoes
  (Mediterranean variety)
salt and pepper
2 sprigs fresh basil or
  ½ teaspoon dried
pinch of dried oregano
5 tablespoons olive oil

Italians usually choose rather green tomatoes for their salads; they are, however, ready for eating. This salad can be prepared with ripe tomatoes, provided they are firm.

Rub a large shallow salad bowl with garlic. Wash, dry and thickly slice the tomatoes, discard their seeds, sprinkle lightly with salt and leave on a plate or small tray to drain off their liquid (this should take about 10–15 minutes.
  Meanwhile put the basil, oregano and freshly ground black pepper into the salad bowl, add the olive oil and stir well. Add the sliced tomatoes, stir them gently into the dressing and leave to rest for 10 minutes, preferably in the refrigerator, to chill slightly before serving.

Peperoni arrostiti
Sweet pepper salad

TO SERVE FOUR–SIX

INGREDIENTS
4–6 yellow and green
    sweet peppers
salt
2 cloves garlic, crushed
2–3 sprigs parsley, finely
    chopped
olive oil

First grill the peppers either under a medium heat, or bake in a hot oven, or stick on a long fork and hold over a gas flame until their skins are burnt and can be pulled off easily.

When the peppers are ready, prick each one with a fork to eliminate any natural moisture. Peel them, and cut into wide strips, discarding the seeds and cutting away any thick pith. Arrange the strips in a shallow dish, sprinkle with salt, add the garlic and parsley and completely cover with oil, but without drowning the strips.

The peppers are ready to be eaten as soon as they are cold but will keep for several days, if well covered with oil.

Insalata di sedano
Celery salad

TO SERVE FOUR–SIX

INGREDIENTS
1 head celery
olive oil
Dressing
5 tablespoons olive oil
3 tablespoons wine vinegar
1 tablespoon mostarda di
    Cremona (*see recipe*)
2–3 sprigs parsley, finely
    chopped
salt and pepper to taste

This is an unusual salad. The original recipe calls for balsam-flavoured vinegar but any other herb vinegar such as tarragon may be substituted.

Mostarda di Cremona is a mixture of candied fruit and mild mustard in a sweet syrup, obtainable from Italian delicatessans; if not available, a sweet chutney could be used as a substitute.

Wash the celery, pull off any coarse strings and cut into short lengths. Heat some oil in a frying pan and fry the celery for a few minutes. Drain on kitchen paper and leave until quite cold. Put into a salad bowl. Combine the dressing ingredients and beat with a fork until well amalgamated. Pour the dressing over the celery and leave for 2 hours or so, turning it from time to time.

Top : peperoni arrostiti;
insalata di sedano;
bottom : insalata di
pomodori al basilico

Pasta, rice, polenta and gnocchi

Pasta

Pasta has been known in Italy since the days of the Etruscans, as reliefs dating from the fourth century BC show. Therefore, it is not surprising that Italians resent being told that Marco Polo brought the secret of pasta-making with him from China when he returned from his travels there. They agree that the Chinese were making pasta before the Italians, but they vehemently disagree that the Italians learned the art from them.

Throughout history Italian pasta has been called by many names: macaroni, lasagne, fideli, vermicelli, etc. But for Italians today all shapes are pasta. For many foreigners spaghetti is the only pasta they know, although this misconception is being corrected with the increasing interest in pasta cooking throughout the world. Many non-Italians are inclined to think that macaroni is always a short tubular shape, but in Naples we find long macaroni. Indeed, macaroni come in a vast number of short fat shapes. The name spaghetti comes from *spago*, meaning string and we should treat the word spaghetti as plural, as do the Italians.

The Ligurians have a strong if not undisputed claim to have been the first to manufacture pasta on a commercial scale in Italy, but the Neapolitans then took over as being the largest consumers of pasta, thus losing their earlier nickname of 'leaf-eaters' because of their fondness for cabbage and being called instead 'the macaroni-eaters'.

1. Tagliatelle
2. Capelli d'angelo in nidi
3. Capelli d'angelo
4. Fettuccine in nidi
5. Paglia e fieno
6. Spaghetti
7. Lasagnette verdi in nidi
8. Reginette
9. Lasagne verdi
10. Lasagne
11. Chifferotti
12. Tortiglioni
13. Pagliacci
14. Mezze maniche rigate
15. Fusilli
16. Abissini
17. Rotelle
18. Ditalini
19. Pipette
20. Farfalle
21. Canestrini
22. Penne
23. Agnelli

In Italy good commercial pasta should by law be made from durum wheat which contains gluten and a vegetable protein and best qualities of pasta contain as much as 14–15 per cent protein. Pasta is accused of causing weight gain but this is disputed by manufacturers.

Most Italians, especially in the north, eat pasta with a fork without the aid of a spoon – never, but never, with a knife. The most efficient manner in which to eat spaghetti is to wind the strands round the prongs of a fork, not too many at a time. It is permissible to twist them against the inside of your plate, which should have a sloping edge, like a shallow soup plate. Pasta should always be served hot and on hot plates. Cold or tepid pasta is a sin in the eyes of a connoisseur. When using left-over pasta and a recipe calls for 225 g (8 oz), this means cooked weight.

Pasta shapes

Commercially made pasta, *pasta asciutta*, comes in a bewildering number of shapes. There are claims that there are over a thousand different shapes throughout the country, but this is not so. Certainly there are some 200 different shapes with maybe 600 other different names, since pasta manufacturers give the pasta shapes pet names culled from their fertile imaginations. Among the shapes of the large spaghetti family, for there is not one size spaghetti but many, there are such names as *linguine*, and *bucatini*. In the vermicelli family there are the long fine shapes, down to the so-called angel's hair, *capelli d'angelo*, almost as thin as thread which comes in strands like hanks of wool. Among the macaroni shapes are long and short tubes, some plain, others ribbed, and finally we get the flat squares and oblongs and even frilled lasagne for casserole dishes.

Commercially made pasta, made from pure durum wheat, does not require eggs in the mixture, the wheat being sufficiently glutinous and binding. But in recent years it has become fashionable to add eggs to the pasta dough and many manufacturers are compelled because of popular demand to add eggs to what is essentially an adequate mixture. However, home-made pasta, because it is made with ordinary wheat flour, must be made with eggs. Good quality commercially made pasta without eggs will keep for months, even up to five years and longer. It should not be exposed to the light but stored covered, preferably not in those attractive glass jars sold especially for the purpose of storing pasta. Green pasta, if kept exposed, will lose its colour in time. When a packet of pasta has been opened, provided it is kept in a dry and dark place with the top closed, will keep for quite a long time.

Although all pasta is made from the same type of dough, in the shapes there appears a subtle difference in the flavour. This is important in Italy where many people eat pasta almost every day of their lives and need to ring the changes in the shapes. However, it should be noted that, although a recipe calls for a particular shape, almost all pasta shapes can be used in the same manner. Spaghetti, noodles, trenette, tagliatelle are all interchangeable as far as their sauces are concerned.

Cooking pasta

The Italians cook their pasta until it is cooked to the state where you can actually feel your teeth biting into it or *al dente*. To be *al dente*, the pasta must be neither too soft nor too hard. It is usual for pasta manufacturers to state on the packets just how long their particular product should be cooked, and this should be followed faithfully.

Different shapes and qualities of pasta take different times to cook. The tubular shapes, such as macaroni or canneloni, take less time than the thick spaghetti shapes as the boiling water runs through the tubes, thus hastening cooking. Cooking time is determined by the thickness of pasta and some of the small but thick shapes can take a longer time to cook than the long and thin shapes. Also, pastina shapes used in soups take longer to cook in stock than in water. One small word of caution – cooking times can be affected by such things as hard water, height above sea level, and the diversity of stoves.

Here are two methods of cooking pasta, Method 1 which could be called the classic method, and Method 2 which its creator likes to call the 'revolutionary method'. Depending on whether it is eaten as a main dish or antipasto, 450 g (1 lb) pasta will serve four-six.

Milanese ladies eating pasta in 1827

Method 1
This method applies to both commercially produced and home-made pasta. Remember that home-made pasta takes a far shorter time to cook than commercially produced pasta, between 6–10 minutes.
1. Use a very large tall pan.
2. Fill the pan with water – if pasta is cooked in too little water it will stick. Bring the water to a rapid bubbling boil, then add 1 tablespoon of salt.
3. Add the pasta all at once. If using long pasta, such as spaghetti, do not break it but fan it out and slowly ease it into the pan. Stir with a long fork if using long pasta, a shorter one for small shapes. Cover the pan and let the water come again to the boil, remove the lid, stir the pasta and continue cooking rapidly for the time indicated on the packet. Stir from time to time.
4. As soon as cooking time is reached, take the pasta from the heat and drain at once in a colander. Do not drain too thoroughly for, as they say in Italy, pasta is greedy for water and should always remain a little moist – not though swimming in water. This moisture, which is like a thin film over the pasta, is soon absorbed.
5. Do not on any account rinse pasta in cold water unless it is to be made into a casserole dish when it must be rinsed in order to stop it cooking. Except in salads pasta is always served hot.
6. Immediately after draining, turn the pasta into a hot serving dish, add the sauce, stir it in well and serve at once.

Method 2
This method was evolved by Eva Agnesi, daughter of one of Italy's leading pasta manufacturers and is the method I always use. It economizes on heat and prevents soggy or over-cooked pasta. Do not cook home-made pasta this way.
1. Prepare a large pan of bubbling, boiling, salted water, allowing 1 tablespoon of salt to every 450 g (1 lb) of pasta.
2. Add the pasta, stir well, then bring back to the boil and boil – allowing 2 minutes for thin shapes, 3 minutes for the thicker ones. Wrap the lid of the pan in a cloth and cover tightly. Immediately turn off the heat and leave the pasta for the exact cooking time given on the packet.
3. Drain, but not too well – pasta should always have a thin film of water on it.
4. Dress with the chosen sauce and serve at once. If using electric heat which takes time to cool down, take the pan from the ring as soon as the lid is clamped on and put it on the side of the stove, otherwise it will go on boiling too fast and the pasta will overcook.

Pasta gialla
Home-made pasta dough

TO SERVE FOUR–SIX

INGREDIENTS
450 g (1 lb) flour
salt
4 eggs (size 2)

Home-made pasta is lighter in texture and rather more delicate in flavour than commercially made pasta. There was a time not long ago when the average Italian housewife made her own pasta, but now many Italian housewives go out to work and have no time to make pasta at home, and fewer and fewer households can boast a cook. Today when freshly made pasta appears on the Italian table, more than likely it has come from the nearby shop that makes and sells fresh pasta, from noodles to stuffed ravioli, every day.

Making pasta dough is not difficult but it can be tedious unless one has a passion for pastry making. However, with the rising cost of commercially produced pasta, the Italian housewife is beginning to think again of making her own pasta. In this she is being assisted by excellent pasta-making gadgets which are great time and effort savers. Some of these are simple in the extreme and have been on the market for some years. For example, there is a ravioli cutter which is simply a metal sheet with evenly distributed small wells, like patty pans but with sharp edges. A sheet of rolled-out dough is placed over this, small indents are made over the 'wells' into which is put a blob of filling. Over this is spread another sheet of rolled pastry and a rolling pin rolled over the top, thus automatically cutting out the ravioli. But there are other more sophisticated gadgets available, into which, for example, you can put your dough and filling, turn a handle and out come strips of perfectly made perforated ravioli.

This dough is used for making ravioli, lasagne, tagliatelle, fettuccine, canneloni and other flat shapes.

Sieve the flour with a good pinch of salt on to a pastry board. Make a well in the centre and break in the eggs, with a fork (1). Work the flour from the outside of the mound into the middle and over the eggs (2). Work this well to a smooth dough, then knead until it is smooth and firm to the touch (3). After 10 minutes kneading the dough should be elastic and shiny. Dip a cloth in warm water, wring it out until almost dry and wrap the ball of dough in it. Leave for 30 minutes to rest.

To use the dough, break it into two pieces, roll out into very thin sheets, using as little pressure as possible, and sprinkle lightly with flour to prevent sticking. At this stage the dough can be cut into the desired shapes or left to dry for 10 minutes. (See individual recipes.)

To make tagliatelle or fettuccine, which are flat noodles, roll the sheets of dough as you might a Swiss roll and cut into narrow strips (4). Gently unroll with a slight tossing movement to avoid the strips sticking together. Place the strips on a floured board and let them dry for 10 minutes. Home-made noodles may be used immediately or, when making a large quantity, can be kept in a refrigerator for 24 hours if carefully wrapped in foil. Home-made pasta freezes well.

Pasta verde
Green pasta

TO SERVE SIX

INGREDIENTS
100 g (4 oz) spinach
4 eggs, lightly beaten
450 g (1 lb) flour

Wash the spinach, cut off the poor leaves and thick stalks and cook until very soft without adding water to the pan. Drain thoroughly, squeezing out all the liquid; chop and rub through a sieve or mouli-légumes. Mix the spinach and eggs, then gradually add the flour to make a firm dough. A little more or less flour may be required than indicated, depending on the dryness of the spinach. Cook as for normal pasta (see page 30).

Pasta rosa (Rose-coloured pasta)
This is prepared as above but with 2 tablespoons of tomato concentrate used instead of spinach.

Bucatini all'amatriciana

Spaghetti amatriciana

TO SERVE FOUR–SIX

INGREDIENTS

450 g (1 lb) ripe tomatoes
1 small sweet pepper
225 g (8 oz) lean bacon
2 tablespoons olive oil or other fat
1 small onion, finely chopped
1–2 cloves garlic, halved
salt and pepper to taste
450 g (1 lb) bucatini or spaghetti
75 g (3 oz) grated Pecorino cheese

A classic recipe which has been adopted by the Romans and locally called 'the dish of the 5 'P's, that is, *pancetta* (bacon), *pomodori* (tomatoes), *pecorino* (sheeps' cheese), *peperoncini* (small peppers) and pasta. The original version, which came from the town of Amatrice in the Sabine Hills, used bucatini, a thick type of spaghetti, and purists claim that tomatoes properly do not belong and were probably added by the Romans. If Pecorino is not available, use Parmesan or a mixture perhaps of Parmesan and another hard, sharp-flavoured cheese such as Cheddar.

Blanch and peel the tomatoes, squeeze out the seeds and chop the flesh. Dice the sweet pepper, discarding the core and seeds. Cut the bacon into thin strips. Heat the oil, add the bacon and fry until it is crisp and brown. Take from the pan, put aside but keep hot. Add the onion, garlic and sweet pepper and fry until brown. Discard the garlic. Add the tomatoes, salt and plenty of black pepper or a good pinch of cayenne pepper. (Many of the trattoria proprietors in Rome pride themselves on the pepper hotness of this dish.) Cook for about 30 minutes. Cook the pasta until *al dente* (*see page* 30). Drain and turn into a hot deep serving dish. Mix the bacon with the pasta and add the sauce, pouring it straight from the pan into the pasta. Either stir well but gently and sprinkle with cheese, or stir the cheese into the pasta and sprinkle slivers of butter on top.

Fettuccine al burro

Noodles with butter

TO SERVE FOUR–SIX

INGREDIENTS

450 g (1 lb) flat noodles
butter
grated Parmesan cheese

This is a favourite Roman recipe, fettuccine being the name used in Rome for the more common name of tagliatelle.

Cook the pasta until *al dente* (*see page* 30). Drain well, turn into a very hot, deep serving dish and add plenty of butter and Parmesan cheese. Other pasta, such as spaghetti or many of the small shapes, can be served in the same way.

Top : bucatini all'amatriciana;
bottom : fettuccine al burro

Lasagne al forno

Baked lasagne

TO SERVE FOUR–SIX

INGREDIENTS
3 tablespoons olive oil
450 g (1 lb) minced meat
1 onion, finely chopped
1 clove garlic, peeled and
  halved
3–4 tablespoons tomato
  concentrate
575 ml (1 pint) water
salt and pepper to taste
225 g (8 oz) lasagne
350 g (12 oz) soft slicing
  cheese such as Bel Paese
  or Fontina
butter for greasing
grated Parmesan cheese to
  taste

Lasagne con la ricotta
450 g (1 lb) Ricotta cheese
225 g (8 oz) grated cheese,
  preferably Parmesan
salt and pepper
3 eggs, well beaten
225 g (8 oz) lasagne
50 g (2 oz) butter or
  margarine
finely chopped parsley or
  dill to taste

Either commercially or home-made lasagne pieces, 5 × 8 cm (2 × 3 in), may be used. If making the lasagne at home, use the pasta dough recipe described on page 31. Either green or white lasagne may be used, or a mixture of both, or else there is a frilled variety which gives the finished dish a pleasing effect. The meat should be raw pork or beef or a mixture of both. The size of the onion is a matter of taste.

First prepare the filling or sauce for the lasagne. Heat 2 tablespoons of oil, add the meat, onion and garlic, stir well and fry gently until the meat is brown. Discard the garlic. Dilute the tomato concentrate with the water, add to the meat, stir again, add salt and pepper, cover and simmer for 1 hour. Prepare a large pan with plenty of boiling salted water. Add the remaining 1 tablespoon of oil. Thoroughly wet a clean white cloth with warm water, then squeeze until it is just damp. Spread this over the kitchen table. When the water is at a bubbling boil, drop in 3–4 lasagne oblongs – you can cook more at one time if your pan is extra large but take care as over-crowding often results in the pasta pieces sticking together. The time of cooking depends on the type of pasta used. Home-made pasta cooks in about 5 minutes; as soon as it rises to the surface and floats, the pasta is ready. Commercially-made pasta takes between 10–15 minutes, so consult the instructions on the packet. Preheat the oven to 180°C, 350°F,

Gas Mark 4. When the lasagne is cooked, take the pieces out carefully with a perforated spoon and place each one separately on the damp cloth to drain. Slice the cheese as thinly as possible. Rub an oblong baking dish with butter. Arrange a layer of lasagne at the bottom, spread this with a layer of meat sauce and one of sliced cheese. Repeat this until all the ingredients are used up, with a final or top layer of meat sauce and sliced cheese. Sprinkle this with grated cheese and bake in the oven for 30–45 minutes.

Instead of using sliced cheese, a thick béchamel sauce may be used, spreading it across the meat in the same way. If using green and white lasagne, use them in alternate layers. In Piedmont slivered white truffles are sprinkled on top just before serving.

Lasagne con la ricotta (Lasagne and cream cheese)
Rub the Ricotta through a sieve, mix in the grated cheese, salt and pepper and finally the eggs. Beat the mixture until smooth and put aside. If the Ricotta is a little dry, a few tablespoons of milk or cream can be added. Cook the lasagne (*see above*) and drain. Rub a baking dish with butter. Place a layer of lasagne along the bottom, spread this with some of the cream mixture and continue until all the ingredients are used up with creamed cheese being the top layer. Sprinkle with parsley and dot with the remaining butter. Cook as above.

Pappardelle con la salsa di lepre

Noodles with a hare sauce

TO SERVE FOUR–SIX

INGREDIENTS

legs and back of a hare
50 g (2 oz) butter
2 tablespoons olive oil
2–3 rashers streaky bacon, diced
1 small onion, finely chopped
1 stalk celery, finely chopped
salt and pepper to taste
2–3 sprigs fresh thyme, finely chopped or ½ teaspoon dried
1 tablespoon flour
275 ml (½ pint) red wine
575 ml (1 pint) meat stock
450 g (1 lb) wide noodles
grated Parmesan cheese

This is a very special dish from Tuscany.

Take off the meat from the hare and cut into small pieces. Heat the butter and oil together in a large pan, add the bacon and fry until its fat begins to run, then add the onion and celery and cook gently until brown. Add salt, pepper, thyme and finally the pieces of meat and cook until brown; sprinkle with flour and stir well to avoid lumps. Add the wine, stir again and cook over a low heat until the wine has been reduced by half. Add the stock, cover the pan and cook over a low heat for about 2 hours. About 15–20 minutes before the sauce is ready, cook the noodles (*see page* 30). Drain and drop them into the sauce. Toss gently and serve in a hot dish. Serve the cheese separately.

Maccheroni o fettuccine alla chitarra

This is a regional speciality from Abruzzo-Molise and is one of the most ancient household methods of cutting pasta in thin strips. It takes its name from the so-called guitar, or *chitarra*, on which the pasta is rolled. This is a wooden frame with guitar-like strings of steel wire strung over the top over which the prepared dough is rolled with a rolling pin and the dough forced through or cut by the strings into narrow ribbons of pastry. Many families in the Abruzzo-Molise region still have and use these guitar-like instruments, although similar shapes are produced commercially today.

Prepare the pasta (*see page* 31) and serve with traditional sauces; one of these is an equal mixture of Bolognese sauce (*see page* 185) and Amatriciana (*see page* 32), sprinkled with slivers of butter and grated Parmesan cheese, or with grated Provola or Scamorza cheese (*see page* 207).

Maccheroni con salsa di sarde

Macaroni with a sardine and garlic sauce

TO SERVE FOUR—SIX

INGREDIENTS
450 g (1 lb) macaroni
150 ml (¼ pint) olive oil
50 g (2 oz) butter
2 large cloves garlic, coarsely chopped
100 g (4 oz) tinned sardines, drained and filleted
4 tablespoons fresh parsley, finely chopped
275 ml (½ pint) dry white wine, cider or lager
a little ground pepper and grated nutmeg
3 tablespoons fine grated breadcrumbs

The usual pasta shape used in this recipe is one the Italians call *lumaconi*, or snails. However, it can be made with any other short, stubby pasta shape, and in particular with cannelloni.

Cook the macaroni (*see page* 30). While it is cooking, make the sauce. Heat the oil and butter together in a large pan, add the garlic, sardines and parsley, break up the fish and cook gently for 5 minutes. Drain the macaroni in a colander and rinse swiftly in cold water. Add to the sauce, stir well, add the wine, a good sprinkling of pepper and nutmeg and the breadcrumbs and stir with a fork until the macaroni is completely covered with the sauce. Then serve at once.

Paglia e fieno

'Straw and hay'

TO SERVE FOUR—SIX

INGREDIENTS
225 g (8 oz) plain noodles
225 g (8 oz) green noodles
75 g (3 oz) butter
1 teaspoon flour
275 ml (½ pint) single cream
4 tablespoons grated cheese

Top: maccheroni con salsa di sarde; *bottom*: paglia e fieno

Fettuccine are narrow flat noodles. In this Roman speciality two varieties are used, the plain which represents straw, and green which represents hay.

Cook all the noodles in the same pan (*see page* 30). While they are cooking, prepare the sauce. Heat half the butter in a small pan, add the flour and cook until smooth, stirring all the time. Add the cream slowly and continue cooking and stirring over a low heat for 3 minutes. Drain the noodles, turn into a deep hot serving dish, add the sauce, the remaining butter, the cheese, stir well and serve at once.

Penne all'arrabbiata

Macaroni with a hot pepper sauce

TO SERVE FOUR–SIX

INGREDIENTS

450 g (1 lb) ripe tomatoes
450 g (1 lb) penne (quill-
shaped macaroni)
25 g (1 oz) butter
1 small onion, finely
chopped
1–2 cloves garlic, finely
chopped
100 g (4 oz) streaky bacon,
finely chopped
1–2 small hot peppers,
left whole
50 g (2 oz) grated Pecorino

Although Pecorino cheese is used in this dish, many Italians nevertheless prefer to use Parmesan, but almost any piquant hard cheese may be substituted. The tiny hot peppers used, called *peperoncini*, are very hot. They may be chopped or left whole, depending entirely on how peppery-hot the sauce is to be. However, since the name of this dish means angry or enraged, the sauce should not be too mild. Any type of short macaroni may be used in this recipe instead of penne.

Blanch, peel and chop the tomatoes discarding their seeds. Heat the butter in a frying pan, add the onion and garlic, stir well, then add the bacon. Fry this until its fat runs freely, then add the tomatoes and finally the pepper. Continue cooking gently, adding about half the cheese. Stir well from time to time and continue cooking for about 35–40 minutes until the sauce is thick. Ten minutes before the sauce is ready cook the macaroni (*see page* 30). Drain the pasta, turn it out into a hot serving dish, add the sauce, stir most of it into the dish but leave some as a garnish on top, and serve at once, with a separate bowl of grated cheese.

Top: penne all'arrabbiata;
bottom: penne al forno ai tre colori

Penne al forno ai tre colori

Baked macaroni

TO SERVE SIX

INGREDIENTS

350 g (12 oz) penne
450 g (1 lb) ripe tomatoes
olive oil
225 g (8 oz) courgettes
salt to taste
2–3 sprigs fresh oregano,
finely chopped or
½ teaspoon dried
225 g (8 oz) Mozzarella or
Bel Paese
butter

Penne are shaped like old-fashioned pen nibs or quills but can be replaced by almost any of the short macaroni shapes. Instead of oregano, another green, well-flavoured herb may be substituted.

Cook the pasta (*see page* 30) until almost *al dente*. Blanch, peel and purée the tomatoes and mix with a little oil. Thinly slice the courgettes. Heat 3–4 tablespoons of oil and lightly fry the courgettes until they are a golden brown. Add salt and oregano. Preheat the oven to 180°C, 350°F, Gas Mark 4. Thinly slice the Mozzarella.

Rub a baking dish with butter. Drain the pasta into a colander and quickly rinse in cold water. Place a third of the pasta in a layer on the bottom of the dish, cover this with a layer of tomato purée, then the Mozzarella. Add a second layer of pasta and one of tomato and Mozzarella and all the courgettes, with the oil and oregano. Cover with the remaining pasta, spread with the rest of the tomato purée and Mozzarella. Sprinkle lightly with oil and bake in the oven for about 20 minutes, by which time the Mozzarella will have melted and spread over the top.

Ravioli

TO SERVE SIX

INGREDIENTS
pasta dough (*page* 31)
grated Parmesan cheese
tomato sauce (*page* 184)

Meat filling
150 g (6 oz) lean meat
50 g (2 oz) butter
stock or water
1 slice bread
150 ml (¼ pint) red wine
100 g (4 oz) cooked spinach
50 g (2 oz) Parmesan
 cheese, grated
1 small onion, grated
salt and pepper
2 eggs, well beaten

Ricotta filling
25 g (1 oz) butter
1 egg yolk
200 g (7 oz) Ricotta
1 heaped tablespoon
 chopped parsley
50 g (2 oz) Parmesan
 cheese, grated
salt and pepper

Spinach filling
225 g (8 oz) hot cooked
 spinach
25 g (1 oz) butter
50 g (2 oz) Parmesan
 cheese, grated
salt and pepper
freshly grated nutmeg
1 egg, well beaten

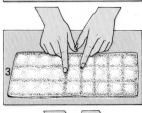

This recipe makes about 60 ravioli.

Prepare the pasta dough. Using a long rolling pin, roll it out into 4 equal very thin oblongs. On one sheet drop tiny mounds of filling 4 cm (1½ in) apart in straight lines. Dip a pastry brush into cold water and brush it in straight lines between the mounds (1). Place a sheet of dough evenly over the top (2). Work quickly in order that the dough remains pliable, otherwise it will crack. Firmly press down with the fingers between each mound of filling along the wetted line to form 5 cm (2 in) squares (3) and cut the pasta into squares with a pastry cutter or wheel (4). Separate the squares and put them aside on a floured teacloth.

Prepare a very large, wide pan with plenty of rapidly boiling salted water and drop in the ravioli. Stir gently with a wooden spoon and boil until tender, for 6–8 minutes, during which time the ravioli will rise to the surface of the water. Remove them carefully with a perforated spoon and place on a hot serving dish. Sprinkle lightly with tomato sauce and cheese, or simply with melted butter and cheese, or with a cream sauce.

Ravioli di carne (Meat filling)
Italians would use veal in this recipe, but chicken or pork can be used instead.

Failing Parmesan, use another hard, piquant cheese.

Cut the meat into cubes. Heat the butter, add the meat, brown, and then add enough stock to cover the bottom of the pan. Simmer for 15 minutes. Soak the bread in water and squeeze dry. After the meat has been cooking for 15 minutes add the wine and continue to cook until the meat is tender. Cool and pass through a mincer, adding the spinach, cheese, onion, bread, salt and pepper. Knead the mixture well and bind with the eggs. Drop in small heaps on to the prepared ravioli pastry.

Ravioli di Ricotta (Ricotta filling)
If Ricotta is not available, use a dry cottage cheese, not one with cream.

Soften the butter and beat until soft. Add the egg yolk, beat this well into the butter, then beat into the Ricotta and continue beating until the mixture is smooth. Add the Parmesan, parsley and seasonings and drop the mixture into small heaps on to the prepared ravioli pastry.

Ravioli di spinaci (Spinach filling)
While the spinach is still hot, add the butter and beat it well into the spinach. Add the cheese, salt, pepper and nutmeg to taste and finally the egg. Mix well and drop in small heaps on to the prepared pastry.

Spaghetti all'aglio ed olio

Spaghetti with garlic and oil

TO SERVE FOUR–SIX

INGREDIENTS
450 g (1 lb) spaghetti
150 ml (¼ pint) olive oil
2–3 cloves garlic, crushed

This is a dish from Campania.

Cook the spaghetti (*see page* 30). Meanwhile make the sauce. Heat the oil in a small pan until it is just warm, add the garlic and leave over a low heat for a minute or so. Drain the spaghetti, turn it into a hot deep serving dish, add the sauce and stir it well into the spaghetti and serve at once.

In some areas finely chopped parsley is added to the sauce at the end when the dish becomes *spaghetti all'aglio ed olio e prezzemolo*. In Abruzzo finely chopped hot peppers are added to the sauce, thus making it very fiery indeed. Some cooks do not heat the oil at all, while finally there is a version in which the garlic is finely chopped and even allowed to slightly brown in the oil, giving it a slightly bitter flavour. Cheese is not then served with this type of sauce.

Spaghetti alla carbonara

Spaghetti with bacon and egg sauce

TO SERVE FOUR–SIX

INGREDIENTS
450 g (1 lb) spaghetti
100 g (4 oz) streaky bacon
1 tablespoon olive oil
4 egg yolks
2 tablespoons single cream
50 g (2 oz) grated
  Parmesan cheese
salt and black pepper

more liquid !

Alla carbonara means charcoal burner's style and is a Roman favourite with almost every trattoria in the capital serving it, and claiming a 'secret' recipe. However, like all traditional recipes it has variations.

Cook the spaghetti (*see page* 30). Meanwhile cut the bacon into thin strips. Put the oil into a large pan and fry the bacon until its fat runs freely. Put the pan aside but keep it hot. Beat the egg yolks in a bowl, add the cream, half the cheese, salt and a good sprinkling of freshly ground pepper. Return the pan to the stove over a minimum heat. Drain the spaghetti, stir it rapidly into the pan with the oil and bacon. Immediately add the egg and cheese mixture. The eggs will cook immediately they are mixed into the hot spaghetti. Do not on any account allow the spaghetti to cook after the egg mixture has been added. Serve at once on hot plates – this is important in this dish – with the rest of the cheese separately.

Spaghetti al Gorgonzola

Spaghetti with Gorgonzola

TO SERVE FOUR–SIX

INGREDIENTS
450 g (1 lb) spaghetti
25 g (1 oz) butter
275 ml ($\frac{1}{2}$ pint) single cream
75 g (3 oz) Gorgonzola, crumbled
pinch of salt
2–3 fresh sage leaves or $\frac{1}{2}$ teaspoon dried
white peppercorns

Left: spaghetti all'aglio ed olio; *right*: spaghetti al Gorgonzola

'Sweet' or piquant Gorgonzola may be used in this recipe but if the latter go easy on the salt as it is salty already.

Cook the spaghetti (*see page* 30). Meanwhile melt the butter in a small pan, add the cream, Gorgonzola, salt and sage. Cook slowly taking care not to boil, stirring all the time until the mixture is a sauce.

Take the pan from the heat, put aside but keep hot. Drain the spaghetti, turn into a hot serving dish, add the Gorgonzola sauce and stir it gently but firmly. Discard the sage leaves. Serve at once, sprinkled with freshly ground white peppercorns.

Spaghetti con salsa cruda

Spaghetti with uncooked tomato sauce

TO SERVE FOUR–SIX

INGREDIENTS
450 g (1 lb) spaghetti
450 g (1 lb) ripe tomatoes, peeled
1–2 cloves garlic, peeled and slivered
salt, pepper and sugar to taste
mixed green herbs to taste
4 tablespoons olive oil

Cook the spaghetti (*see page* 30) until *al dente*. Meanwhile whirl the rest of the ingredients, except the oil, either in an electric liquidizer until smooth, or put into a cocktail shaker and shake well. Add the oil little by little, as for making mayonnaise. When the spaghetti is cooked, turn it into a deep serving dish, add the sauce, mix well and serve at once.

Tagliatelle alla bolognese

Noodles with Bolognese sauce

TO SERVE FOUR–SIX

INGREDIENTS
575 ml (1 pint) Bolognese sauce (*page* 185)
450 g (1 lb) tagliatelle
a few slivers butter
50 g (2 oz) grated Parmesan cheese

Among the many Bolognese culinary claims is one that they make the finest tagliatelle, a claim hotly disputed by the Piedmontese. For this dish, home-made noodles should be used but commercially produced pasta can also be cooked in the same manner.

Make the sauce. Cook the tagliatelle until *al dente* (*see page* 30). Turn into a hot serving dish, sprinkle with butter add half the sauce and half the cheese, mix well and quickly, and serve immediately. Serve the rest of the sauce and cheese separately.

Timballo di maccheroni

Macaroni and bacon casserole

TO SERVE FOUR

INGREDIENTS
225 g (8 oz) macaroni
575 ml (1 pint) fresh tomato juice made from 900 g (2 lb) ripe tomatoes
1 large onion, finely grated
salt and pepper
¼ teaspoon caraway seeds
4–6 strips bacon, diced
100 g (4 oz) grated cheese

Choose any of the short, stubby macaroni shapes for this recipe.

Cook the macaroni (*see page* 30). Meanwhile prepare the sauce. Combine the fresh tomato juice, onion, salt, pepper and caraway seeds in a flameproof casserole and bring slowly to a simmer. In another pan fry the bacon in its own fat. Preheat the oven to 200°C, 400°F, Gas Mark 6. Drain the macaroni as soon as it is tender, rinse swiftly in cold water, add to the sauce, add half the cheese and mix well. Add the bacon, sprinkle with the remaining cheese and bake in the oven for about 25 minutes. Serve at once.

Top : tagliatelle alla bolognese;
bottom : timballo di maccheroni

Tortellini alla panna

Tortellini in a cream sauce

TO SERVE FOUR–SIX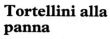

INGREDIENTS
pasta dough (*page* 31)
50 g (2 oz) butter
50 g (2 oz) lean pork, minced
25 g (1 oz) turkey breast, minced
25 g (1 oz) bone marrow – optional
25 g (1 oz) Parma smoked ham, finely chopped
25 g (1 oz) Bologna mortadella, chopped
50 g (2 oz) grated Parmesan cheese
salt, pepper and freshly grated nutmeg
1 egg, well beaten

Tortellini are tiny pasta shapes, folded to resemble a navel. The Bolognese claim to have created this special member of the pasta family and in the city of Bologna there is the Learned Order of the Tortellini with a large and impressive membership all of whom are dedicated to the preservation of the traditional tortellini. At their functions members wear red and gold hats shaped like a tortellini and a ribbon round their necks from which dangles a tortellini made of gold. It is said that when the Bolognese eat their famous *tortellini in brodo*, they never speak a word until the dish is finished, and then only to utter a gentle murmur of appreciation.

Neighbouring Modena, Bologna's fiercest gastronomic rival, also lays claim to the creation of the tortellini, declaring it to be the invention of a local cook who dreamt that he saw Venus rising from the waves, glimpsed her perfect navel and rushed into his kitchen to recreate this perfection in pasta.

Make the pasta dough (*see page* 30). Roll it into a ball and leave for 20 minutes on a floured pastry board covered with a

floured cloth. Meanwhile prepare the filling. Heat the butter in a pan, add the pork, turkey and bone marrow – this is optional. Cook until a golden brown, then mix with the ham and mortadella and put twice through the coarse blade of a mincer. Add the cheese, salt, pepper and nutmeg to taste, mix well, bind with the egg and make sure the mixture is thoroughly blended. Put aside.

Roll out the dough into a very thin sheet. Cut into small rounds, 3–4 cm (1–1½ in), and put a tiny nut of filling in the middle of each round (1). Fold the dough over the filling to make a semi-circle (2). Take this in the right hand and fold it round the left index finger so that the two ends curl round and slightly overlap (3). Press the ends firmly together with the finger so that the ends curl up slightly (4). Spread the tortellini on a dry cloth to dry for 30 minutes.

Prepare a large pan with plenty of boiling salted water. Drop the tortellini into this and cook until tender, for 5–6 minutes. Take from the pan with a perforated spoon and serve, either with a meat sauce (*see page* 185) or a cream sauce (*see page* 182).

Trenette al pesto
Noodles with pesto sauce

TO SERVE FOUR–SIX

INGREDIENTS
225 g (8 oz) potatoes
450 g (1 lb) trenette
100 g (4 oz) pesto sauce
  (*page* 182)
Pecorino or Parmesan
  cheese, grated

This is a typical recipe from Genoa. Trenette are rather narrow flat noodles. If fresh basil is not available for making the pesto sauce, small jars of the sauce can be bought from Italian delicatessens.

Peel the potatoes and cut into thin strips. Have a large pan ready with plenty of vigorously boiling salted water. Add the potatoes, cook for 2 minutes, then add the trenette and cook until *al dente* (*see page* 30). Take 2–3 tablespoons of the cooking liquid and mix into the pesto. Drain the potatoes and trenette, turn into a hot serving bowl, add the pesto and mix well. Serve the cheese separately.

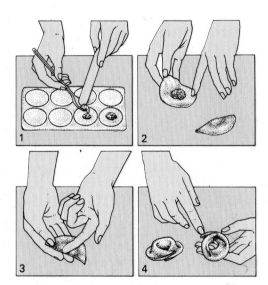

Tortellini alla panna

Rice

There are four main categories of rice used in Italian cooking and, although all of them can be used in most Italian rice dishes, it is probably better to use, where possible, a quality adapted to special dishes. The four categories are: *comune originario*, which can be used for almost any rice dish, in particular for sweet dishes; *semifino*, which is short, finer than the usual Italian types but neither as long nor as fine as Patna rice and which is used in soups and minestrone; *fino* is used for plain boiling (*all' inglese*); finally *arboria, vialone* and *carnaroli* are used exclusively for a risotto.

Despite the many claims among the rice producers in the north of Italy, there is no doubt that Italians as a whole do not look upon this cereal with the same favour as they do pasta. It is useless to point out its merits, higher protein value, being easier on the digestion and this is a point which usually appeals to the Italians – they remain immune. Statistics (1977) show that they eat 4 kilos of rice for every 30 kilos of pasta.

1. Comune originario
2. Semifino
3. Fino
4. Arboria

Riso all' indiana

Indian rice

TO SERVE SIX

INGREDIENTS
450 g (1 lb) Italian fine rice
½ tablespoon salt
butter or margarine

This method of cooking is used by the Italians usually with shellfish or other fish, in a salad, or as an accompaniment to other dishes instead of a vegetable, but I find it excellent with creamed chicken or duck. It has nothing to do with Indian cooking.

Prepare a fairly large pan with plenty of rapidly boiling salted water, dribble in the rice like rain and when it is all in the pan stir well with a wooden spoon. Continue cooking until *al dente*, that is, for about 14 minutes. Preheat the oven to 150°C, 300°F, Gas Mark 2. Drain the rice, put into a sieve, rinse under cold running water, then drain again. Spread a clean kitchen cloth over a baking sheet, add the rice and spread it over the cloth, then fold up the edges of the cloth to make an envelope. Put into the cool oven and leave for 15 minutes, or until the rice is dry and each grain separate. Turn out into a hot buttered vegetable dish and serve at once.

Riso al salto
Fried leftover rice

This is a good way to deal with leftover cooked rice. It can be served with either grated cheese, chicken-liver sauce, bacon, fried sausages, Bolognese sauce (*see page 185*), tomato sauce, or chutney.

Melt a large knob of butter or margarine in a deep frying pan, add the rice and smooth it over the pan with a palette knife. Cook over a moderate heat until a thick brown crust forms underneath. Slide the rice on to a hot plate, then turn it over and brown the other side, or put the pan under a hot grill to brown the top. The rice must be heated through and with a crust on both top and bottom.

Serve like a cake on a hot round plate, cut into portions and accompanied by a bowl of grated Parmesan cheese plus any of the accompaniments mentioned above.

Riso all'indiana con pesce
Indian rice with fish

TO SERVE FOUR–SIX

INGREDIENTS
riso all' indiana (*page 42*)
450 g (1 lb) white fish fillets
50 g (2 oz) butter
1 small onion, finely sliced
salt and pepper
150 g (5 oz) tinned peeled tomatoes
150 ml (¼ pint) white wine
150 ml (¼ pint) single cream

Cook the rice (*see opposite*). While it is drying in the oven, prepare the fish. Heat half the butter, add the onion and fry until soft but not brown. Add a tablespoon of warm water, a pinch of salt, pepper and the tomatoes (smash these with a wooden spoon as you stir). Add the rest of the butter and wine, and stir well. Add the fillets and let them cook gently, basting from time to time with the sauce. When the fillets are cooked, add the cream, stirring this gently into the sauce. Serve the fillets, together with the sauce, on top of the rice.

Riso all'indiana con pesce

43

Risotto

Once the general method has been mastered the preparation of an Italian risotto will not be difficult. However, remember that a risotto is not the same as a pilau. The latter must always be dry, while a risotto on the contrary is exceedingly moist. The connoisseurs say that when served it should be *all'onda*, that is, with the liquid still just bubbling. First the rice is fried in a mixture of onion, garlic, finely chopped parsley and anchovies either in butter or in a mixture of oil and butter, called a *battuto*. This gentle frying gives the rice its flavour, or *insaporito*. When this mixture has been cooking lightly for a few minutes, the rice is added, well stirred with a wooden spoon and cooked for about five minutes. Then a ladleful of hot stock or water is added and cooking continues until the rice begins to swell and the liquid is absorbed. Another ladleful of hot liquid is added and this is repeated until all the liquid has been absorbed and the rice is cooked. It must always remain at simmering point and at no time should it be allowed to dry out. A risotto must be watched all the time it is cooking, and the time to stop adding liquid is when the rice is *al dente*, that is, with a little bite left in it, yet tender and with just enough liquid remaining to be *all'onda*, or 'rippling rice'. A risotto takes between 20–25 minutes to

Top: risotto in bianco;
bottom: risotto alla finanziera

Risotto in bianco

White risotto

TO SERVE SIX

INGREDIENTS
75 g (3 oz) butter
½ a small onion, finely chopped
450 g (1 lb) short round rice
150 ml (¼ pint) dry white wine
salt and white pepper
1.5 litres (2¾ pints) hot white meat stock or water
50 g (2 oz) grated Parmesan cheese

Heat 50 g (2 oz) of the butter in a large heavy pan, add the onion and cook this over a moderate heat until it changes colour. Dribble in the rice and stir it for 5–8 minutes. Add the wine and continue to cook for about 10 minutes over a moderate heat until the wine has completely evaporated. Add salt and white pepper to taste. Add a ladleful of hot stock, cook this until it has been absorbed, then add another ladleful of hot stock and continue until all the stock has been used up and the rice is cooked. At the last moment add the cheese, take the pan from the heat and add the remaining butter.

Serve plain with butter and cheese, with a shrimp or prawn sauce, or with cooked chopped fennel (*see page* 176).

Risotto alla finanziera

Chicken-liver risotto

TO SERVE SIX

INGREDIENTS
100 g (4 oz) butter
1 small onion, thinly sliced
8–10 chicken livers, cleaned and chopped
225 g (8 oz) mushroom caps, thinly sliced
1 small red pepper, cored, seeded and sliced
salt and pepper
1 thin strip lemon rind
450 g (1 lb) short round rice
1.5 litres (2¾ pints) boiling chicken stock
150 ml (¼ pint) dry white wine
50 g (2 oz) grated Parmesan cheese

A dry Marsala wine is suggested instead of dry white wine in some recipes. It creates quite a different flavour but marries well with the chicken livers.

Melt half the butter in a large heavy pan, add the onion and fry until it begins to soften and change colour. Add the livers, mushrooms, red pepper, salt, pepper and lemon rind. Cook over a moderate heat for 5 minutes. Dribble the rice into the pan, stirring well with a wooden spoon, and cook for 5–8 minutes. Add a ladleful of the stock, stir well but gently and continue cooking until this had been absorbed. Continue gradually adding ladlefuls of stock until it has all been absorbed into the rice. Add the wine and continue to cook over a moderate heat until the rice is *al dente*. Take from the heat, discard the lemon rind, add the remaining butter and about half the cheese. Stir, then serve hot with the rest of the cheese served separately.

cook, depending on the heat of the stove, etc. Very frequent stirring is necessary to avoid sticking. When adding the liquid to the hot rice it will sizzle quite alarmingly, but this is normal. Do not strain but let the rice rest for a couple of minutes before serving. 450 g (1 lb) of rice does six generous servings.

It is the slow cooking which gives the risotto its special character with every grain of rice separate and soft yet with a slightly resistant centre.

It is important when adding salt to a risotto to do so with caution, especially when using stock, which might already be salted. As the stock reduces, its salinity is greatly increased, so taste it first.

Risotto in forma
Baked risotto with a tomato sauce

TO SERVE SIX

INGREDIENTS
risotto in bianco (*page* 44)
butter for greasing
a 23-cm (9-in) diameter
  ring mould
Sauce
50 g (2 oz) butter
1 small onion, finely
  chopped
150 g (5 oz) tinned peeled
  tomatoes, preferably
  Italian
225 g (8 oz) tinned peas
2–3 sprigs parsley, finely
  chopped
225 g (8 oz) tinned tuna fish

Preheat the oven to 220°C, 425°F, Gas Mark 7. Meanwhile make the risotto (*see page* 44). Rub a ring mould generously with butter. Turn the risotto into the mould and bake in the oven for 10 minutes. Then prepare the sauce. Heat the butter in a pan, add the onion and fry until it is soft but not brown. Add the tomatoes, break these up in the pan and cook until they are mushy. Drain the peas from their liquid, and add to the sauce together with the parsley. Break up the tuna fish and gently add to the pan. Unmould the risotto on to a hot plate and pour the sauce in the middle. Serve hot.

Risotto al Maso Scari

Risotto with red wine

TO SERVE SIX

INGREDIENTS
100 g (4 oz) butter
150 ml (¼ pint) olive oil
1 small onion, finely
    chopped
575 ml (1 pint) red wine
450 g (1 lb) short round
    rice
1.5 litres (2¾ pints) meat
    stock, boiling
pinch of salt
75 g (3 oz) grated
    Parmesan cheese

This is a recipe given to me by the Baron de Cles whose vineyards stretch along the hills above Trento on the way to the Brenner Pass. He calls for 'alpine fresh' butter, for 'virgin olive oil' and, naturally, for his own Teroldego Rotaliano, called Maso Scari, a ruby coloured wine, as well as for 'old matured grana cheese'. All of this does make this risotto particularly good, but the Baron's recipe is also good without such perfections.

Heat half the butter and all the oil, add the onion and cook gently until it is soft and begins to change colour. Add the wine and cook until it has evaporated. Add the rice and cook this for 5–8 minutes, then add a ladleful of the boiling stock, stir with a wooden spoon and continue adding the stock in this manner until it has all been absorbed. Add the salt, turn off the heat, add the remaining butter and the grated cheese. Leave for 3 minutes to rest and serve at once, naturally, adds the Baron, accompanied by the same type of red wine and extra cheese, served separately.

Risotto alla milanese

TO SERVE SIX

INGREDIENTS
½ small onion
25 g (1 oz) bone marrow
    (optional)
100 g (4 oz) butter
450 g (1 lb) short round
    rice
150 ml (¼ pint) dry white
    wine
1.5 litres (2¾ pints) hot
    meat stock
½ teaspoon saffron
1 teaspoon salt
50 g (2 oz) grated
    Parmesan cheese

This risotto is the pride of Milan and is always served with the equally beloved *ossobuco milanese* (*see page* 132). Although the bone marrow does make a difference to the richness of the rice, not all recipes stipulate that it should be used. Soak the saffron in 2 tablespoons of tepid water for about 10 minutes before using.

Chop the onion and the bone marrow. Heat half the butter in a large, heavy pan, add the onion and bone marrow and cook over a slow heat until the onion changes colour, then pour in the rice 'like rain'. Stir with a wooden spoon and cook the rice gently for 5–8 minutes. Add the wine and continue cooking over a good heat until the wine has evaporated. Add a ladleful of stock. When the stock has been absorbed in the rice, add a second ladleful. Continue until all the stock is finished up. After about 10 minutes cooking, add the saffron-water and mix it well into the rice in order to obtain its characteristic yellow colour and flavour. Add the salt. If all the rice does not become yellow, this is not important, a two-coloured risotto is also considered very Milanese. When the rice is tender but *al dente*, take the pan from the heat, add the cheese and the remaining butter. Serve hot.

Risotto 'alla Sbiraglia'

Chicken risotto

TO SERVE SIX

INGREDIENTS
1 900-g (2-lb) boiling fowl
2 stalks celery
2 carrots
1 large onion, diced
salt and pepper
2 tablespoons olive oil
25 g (1 oz) fat bacon
150 ml (¼ pint) dry white
    wine
1 tablespoon tomato
    concentrate
450 g (1 lb) short round
    rice
50 g (2 oz) grated
    Parmesan cheese
50 g (2 oz) butter

This dish (its name means police or cop's risotto) is considered to be one of Venice's triumphal dishes. As with all traditional dishes it has its variations.

Cut off all the flesh from the chicken and put this aside. Put the carcass into a large pan with 2 litres (3½ pints) of water, 1 stalk of celery, 1 carrot, half the onion, salt to taste and cook gently for about 1½ hours. Meanwhile dice the chicken flesh. Finely chop the remaining carrot, onion and celery. Heat the oil with the bacon, add the vegetables and gently fry until they are a golden brown, then add the diced chicken meat. Let this cook for a while, stirring until the pieces are well coated with fat, then add the wine and continue cooking for about 10 minutes until this evaporates. Add the tomato concentrate and stir again. Sprinkle with salt and pepper and continue cooking for 20 minutes. Strain the stock from the chicken bones and put the stock aside. Add the rice to the chicken and vegetables, stir well and cook for 5 minutes, then add a ladleful of the hot chicken stock, stir again with a wooden spoon and continue cooking until the stock has been absorbed, then add a further ladleful of hot stock. Repeat this until all the stock, about 1.5 litres (2¾ pints), has been used up. When the rice is tender, remove from the heat and add the cheese and butter, cut into slivers.

Top to bottom: risotto al Maso Scari;
risotto alla milanese; risotto 'alla Sbiraglia'

46

Timballo

Rice timbale

INGREDIENTS
risotto in bianco (*page* 44)
butter
fine breadcrumbs
225 g (8 oz) Mozzarella
 cheese, sliced
2 hard-boiled eggs, sliced
grated Parmesan cheese
Filling
15 g ($\frac{1}{2}$ oz) dried
 mushrooms
4–6 chicken livers
1 tablespoon olive oil
1 onion, finely chopped
1 large tomato, peeled and
 chopped
salt and pepper to taste
150 ml ($\frac{1}{4}$ pint) chicken
 stock
150 ml ($\frac{1}{4}$ pint) dry white
 wine

There are so many recipes for this Neapolitan timbale, also called *sartù*, that its preparation is a matter of using one's imagination and also what is around in the kitchen. Sweetbreads, calves' liver and brains are often added to the filling, as are sometimes small meat balls, or shelled peas, even slices of bacon and Italian small sausages. The resulting dish is rich and looks as good as it tastes. The origin of the word *sartù* has been lost over the centuries.

The timbale turns out like a cake, very smooth and giving no suggestion of a filling. It is a dish which appears at first sight to be difficult to make but once mastered can become a party piece. Apart from the rest of the filling being served as a sauce, you can also serve it with a tomato, meat or cream sauce.

First prepare the filling. Soak the mushrooms in tepid water for 20–30 minutes and then drain and chop them. Chop the chicken livers. Heat the oil in a small pan, add the onion and cook until it is soft and a golden brown. Add the tomato, mushrooms, chicken livers, salt and pepper and cook for 5 minutes. Add the chicken stock and wine. Stir well and leave to simmer. Make a *risotto in bianco* (*see page* 44). Preheat the oven to 180°C, 350°F, Gas Mark 4. Rub the inside of an 18-cm (7-in) round cake tin or soufflé dish generously with butter and sprinkle with fine breadcrumbs. Spoon in about two-thirds of the rice, pressing it well down and around the sides to make a well at the bottom. Arrange half the Mozzarella cheese on the bottom, cover with some of the egg slices and sprinkle with cheese. Add about two-thirds of the filling, the rest of the Mozarella, the remaining egg slices, some more Parmesan cheese, if liked, and cover with the rest of the rice. Press it all down fairly firmly and evenly to encase the filling. Sprinkle the top with Parmesan cheese, breadcrumbs and slivers of butter. Bake in the oven for about 1 hour, or until a golden brown crust has been formed. Take from the oven and leave to cool for about 5 minutes. Turn out and serve with Parmesan cheese separately and with the remainder of the filling.

Polenta

Polenta, one of the staple foods of Lombardy and the Veneto, and also the north of Italy generally, is usually made with maize flour, although in some areas it is made from chestnut flour, or ground barley. In some parts of Piedmont, it is made from buckwheat flour. It is variously described as a porridge or even a pudding and is a descendant of the ancient Roman *pulmentum* which was served to the Romans either as a hard cake or as a soft porridge. In Renaissance days ground barley and chestnut flours were used and sometime in the seventeenth century, when a sack of maize flour was unloaded from a ship in Venice, this too was turned into polenta. The maize flour had come from America, but via Turkey and so was called *grano-turco*, or Turkish corn, as it is to this day. In Venice, where polenta is eaten in large quantities, it is often made from white maize flour.

Polenta is prepared and served in a variety of ways, hot, cold, savoury and even sweet. Traditionally it is cooked in a copper pan, not tin-lined, called a *paiolo*, but it can be cooked in any type of large heavy pot. While the polenta is cooking, it is vigorously stirred with a long wooden stick not unlike a very long, thin rolling pin. The length of the stick is important as polenta has a nasty habit of spitting viciously at the cook as he or she stirs. When it is cooked it is placed on a large round wooden board, like a bread board but with a handle, and cut with a wooden knife.

Polenta

TO SERVE SIX

INGREDIENTS
1 litre (1¾ pints) water
2 teaspoons salt
225 g (8 oz) polenta flour

In Venice polenta is served with small grilled birds and also with crisply fried bacon, cheese, or cooked mushrooms, in a sauce. In Piedmont and Liguria polenta is almost always served with game dishes, while the Tuscans serve it, as often as not made with chestnut flour, smothered with mushrooms in a thick and rich sauce, or with Ricotta cheese. They also have an excellent country dish of lamb cooked with plenty of olives and served with polenta. In most mountain areas polenta forms a basis for tomato and other sauces.

Put the water and salt into a large pan and bring to a furious boil. Put the polenta flour into a bowl and then let it dribble slowly like rain into the water, stirring all the time in a clockwise direction with a long wooden spoon until it begins to thicken. The reason for this slow dribbling-in of the polenta is that, if it is added all at once it becomes hard. Keep as far away from the pan as possible to avoid the vicious spitting. When the mixture is smooth and thick cover the pan, lower the heat and continue cooking for 30–40 minutes.

When ready, take a wet spatula and run this round the pan to loosen the polenta from the sides. Turn out on to a wooden board and shape it like a cake, either with a wooden spoon dipped in water or, preferably, with a wooden knife. At this stage the polenta is ready for use. It can be cut into thick slices and served with stews instead of bread.

Polenta has its origins in the ancient Roman *pulmentum* shown being prepared in this stone frieze dating from the third century BC.

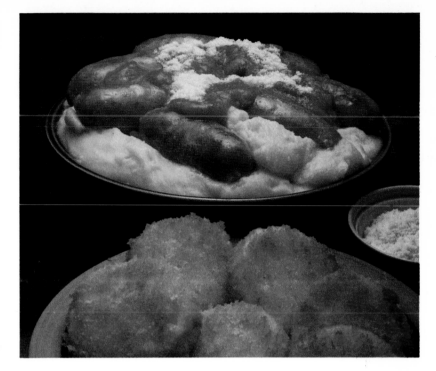

Polenta pasticciata con salsicce

Polenta with sausages

TO SERVE SIX

INGREDIENTS
225 g (8 oz) polenta flour
75 g (3 oz) butter or
  margarine
450 g (1 lb) pork sausages,
  preferably Italian
hot tomato sauce (*page* 184)
salt and pepper
grated Parmesan cheese

Prepare the polenta (*see opposite*). While it is cooking, melt the butter in a frying pan, add the sausages and fry slowly until they are brown all over. Prepare the tomato sauce. When the polenta is thick but still rather soft, turn it out on to a large hot serving dish. Make small wells all over the top into which to put the sausages. Spread with tomato sauce and lightly sprinkle with salt, pepper and cheese.

Some Italian cooks prefer to skin the sausages before cooking and coarsely crumble them over the polenta. Cooking times are obviously shortened by this process and the sausages can be stretched to cater for more people.

Fritelle di polenta alla lodigiana

Polenta fritters

TO SERVE FOUR–SIX

INGREDIENTS
225 g (8 oz) polenta flour
2 eggs, well beaten
breadcrumbs
olive oil for frying
hot tomato sauce (*page* 184)

Cook the polenta (*see opposite*) until very stiff. Turn it out into a mixing bowl, beat until smooth, then spread it on a wooden board. Smooth it down to about 2 cm ($\frac{1}{2}$ in) thick and leave until cold. Cut into rounds with a pastry cutter or rinsed glass. Dip each round into the beaten egg and then roll in breadcrumbs. Heat the oil and fry the polenta rounds, a few at a time, until a golden brown all over. Take from the pan with a perforated spoon and drain on kitchen paper. Serve on a hot dish with the tomato sauce separately.

Gnocchi

Gnocchi are small dumplings, usually made from potatoes, semolina or polenta, but there are also fish and meat gnocchi, and a great favourite is the Umbrian spinach and Ricotta gnocchi. Gnocchi have been part of the Italian cooking scene since the days of the Romans, although Italians suspect that they are a later inheritance taken from the Germanic culinary influence when Italy was part of the Holy Roman Empire. Certainly, between the German and Austrian *Knödel* and the Italian gnocchi there is a family likeness, but who taught who, no one seems certain. Bartolomeo Scappi in his book published in 1570 makes a reference to gnocchi in his pasta section. The book, incidentally, was the first of its kind to have what might be called an early Mrs Beeton approach to comprehensive cooking.

Present-day Romans have a favourite dish of gnocchi called *strozzapreti* or *strangolapreti*, literally meaning 'priest stranglers', suggesting that the Romans produced gnocchi so heavy that they were enough to choke a priest. However, accusations of strangling priests have been levelled at the Tuscans and Venetians for similar dishes, albeit somewhat more kindly, claiming that a priest died of euphoria while eating the local gnocchi.

Gnocchi di patate
Potato dumplings

TO SERVE FOUR–SIX

INGREDIENTS
900 g (2 lb) large floury potatoes
salt and pepper to taste
225 g (8 oz) flour, sieved
melted butter
grated cheese

Wash and peel the potatoes and cook in plenty of boiling salted water until soft. Drain thoroughly – the potatoes must be as dry as possible. Mash until smooth, or pass through a ricer. Put into a mixing bowl, add salt and pepper, beat well, then add the flour, little by little to make a firm dough. A little more flour may be required, depending upon the quality of the potatoes and even of the flour. Knead the dough well for 2–3 minutes, if it seems at all sticky, add just a little more flour, taking care not to add too much. Put the dough on to a floured wooden board and break it into 4–6 pieces. Roll each piece into a cylinder about 1.5 cm ($\frac{1}{2}$ in) thick and cut each cylinder into smaller cylinders 3 cm (1 in) long. Pinch the centre of these between the thumb and forefinger. Sprinkle lightly with flour. Bring a large pan filled with salted water to a gentle boil. Drop about a third of the gnocchi into the water (or all of them together if the pan is big enough) and let them boil rapidly – they are cooked when they rise to the surface and float. Take them out with a perforated spoon and drain at once on a warm dry cloth. When all the gnocchi are ready, put them into a shallow hot serving dish and serve hot, sprinkled with melted butter and grated cheese; you can leave them for a minute or two in a warm oven.

Gnocchi can also be served with a meat sauce and Parmesan cheese, in which case they are called *gnocchi alla romana*, with a cream and butter sauce, or simply with melted butter and grated cheese. In Campania, gnocchi are served with a tomato sauce flavoured with basil. For a Piedmont variation put them on a hot serving dish, cover with sliced Fontina cheese and sprinkle generously with melted butter. Bake for 5 minutes in a hot oven (220°C, 425°F, Gas Mark 7) and serve with grated cheese and a tomato sauce. Another Piedmontese variation, during the truffle season, is to sprinkle gnocchi with slivered truffles before serving.

Gnocchi di Romagna

TO SERVE FOUR–SIX

INGREDIENTS
225 g (8 oz) Ricotta cheese
2 eggs, well beaten
100 g (4 oz) grated Parmesan cheese
100 g (4 oz) flour, sieved
salt, pepper and nutmeg
50 g (2 oz) butter, melted

Rub the Ricotta through a sieve into a mixing bowl. Add the eggs, half the grated cheese, most of the flour, a little salt, pepper and nutmeg to taste and mix thoroughly to a firm dough. Turn this on a floured wooden board and break into two pieces. Roll these into cylinders about 3–4 cm (1–1$\frac{1}{2}$ in) thick, then cut into rounds about 1 cm ($\frac{1}{4}$ in) thick. As you shape the rounds, roll them gently in flour so they will not stick together. Have ready a large pan filled with gently boiling salted water. Carefully drop in the gnocchi so that they do not break and poach them until they rise and float on the top of the water. Drain gently and serve on a hot dish with melted butter and the remainder of the grated cheese, or, as in Liguria, with a pesto sauce (*see page* 182) to make *gnocchi al pesto*. The *pesto* sauce is thinned down a little with some of the gnocchi liquid.

Left : gnocchi di patate; *right :* gnocchi di Romagna

Gnocchi di semolina

Semolina dumplings

TO SERVE FOUR–SIX

INGREDIENTS
725 ml (1¼ pints) milk
100 g (4 oz) butter
salt, pepper and nutmeg
   to taste
225 g (8 oz) semolina
50 g (2 oz) grated
   Parmesan cheese
100 g (4 oz) hard cheese
175 g (6 oz) rashers fat
   bacon, cut into squares

Almost any kind of strongly flavoured hard cheese such as Parmesan or Cheddar may be used in this recipe, which is a variation of *gnocchi di Romagna* (*see page 52*).

Bring the milk together with a small knob of butter, salt, pepper and nutmeg to the boil, then dribble in the semolina 'like rain', stirring with a wooden spoon all the time to prevent lumps from forming. Continue cooking and stirring for about 5 minutes, or until the mixture is thick enough for the spoon to stand up in it, then add half the Parmesan, mixing it well into the semolina. Turn out on to a flat board or baking sheet and smooth down to a thickness of about 1 cm (¼ in) with a spatula or rolling pin and leave until quite cold: this will take at least 2 hours but it can be kept overnight in the refrigerator if preferred. Preheat the oven to 220°C, 425°F, Gas Mark 7. Cut out 28 discs, either with a pastry cutter or a small glass. Put a layer of these in the bottom of a shallow oven-to-table baking dish. Cut the hard cheese into 4 equal parts, then each part into 7 squares or rounds, one for each round of semolina. Top each round of semolina with a piece of cheese, then with a square of bacon. Cover this layer with another layer of semolina rounds and with cheese and bacon and repeat until all these ingredients are finished. There should be four layers in all. Finally cut the rest of the butter into slivers, sprinkle them over the top of the semolina and then sprinkle with the remainder of the Parmesan cheese. Bake in the oven for about 20 minutes, or until the top has browned. Serve hot.

Left : gnocchi di semolina;
right : gnocchi di spinaci e
ricotta

Gnocchi di spinaci e ricotta
Spinach and cheese gnocchi

TO SERVE FOUR–SIX

INGREDIENTS
450 g (1 lb) spinach
salt, pepper and nutmeg
40 g (1½ oz) butter
225 g (8 oz) Ricotta cheese
75 g (3 oz) flour
1 egg plus 1 extra egg yolk, well beaten
melted butter and grated Parmesan cheese for garnishing

Thoroughly wash the spinach, discarding any coarse leaves or thick stalks. Put into a pan and cook only in the water adhering to the leaves. Add salt, pepper and nutmeg to taste. When the spinach is very tender, drain well and squeeze it absolutely dry. Chop finely and rub through a coarse sieve or mouli-légumes. Add the butter and mix well. Sieve the Ricotta into a large bowl and beat until smooth, add the spinach and mix well, then add the flour, mixing thoroughly before adding the eggs and more salt and pepper, if needed. Prepare a large pan with plenty of boiling salted water. Break off small pieces of the spinach mixture and roll these with well-floured hands into small dumplings, roughly the size of a small walnut (it is important they should not be too large) and put them on to a floured board. When all are ready, drop them a few at a time into the boiling water. As they rise to the surface of the water and float, take them out with a perforated spoon, drain thoroughly in a colander and slide into a hot serving dish. Put into a warm oven to keep hot. When all the gnocchi are in the dish, pour melted butter and grated cheese over them and serve.

The gnocchi can also be put into a hot buttered baking dish and baked in a pre-heated hot oven (220°C, 425°F, Gas Mark 7) for 10 minutes. They are then called *malfatti di spinaci*.

Pizzas

Although the name pizza in its widest sense means 'pie', for many foreigners it simply means the open yeast pastry pie as made in Naples and in southern Italy. Many varieties are produced throughout the country but perhaps the pride of place should be given to the crisp, light pizza of Naples; but even the Neapolitan style of pizza has many variations. In Rome, the pizza is made with the same dough as that used in Naples but with onions and oil, and also with Mozzarella, grated Parmesan, olive oil and chopped basil. In most parts of Liguria an extra-thick pizza is made with tomatoes and black olives. As proof of the diversity, the *pizza di sposa*, or the marriage pizza, made up of layers of spongecake and chocolate cream with alcohol is much more like a *zuppa inglese* than what we think is a pizza.

The best pizzas are made by the expert in the pizzeria in southern Italy and it is a joy to watch the dedicated pizza baker at work. He knows when he is being watched, as does an actor, and like an actor he craves an audience. His stage is the table in front of his oven, his props the faggots with which he heats the oven, his baker's shovel with its long handle, and his piles of risen dough. He works the dough swiftly, shaping it into rounds or oblongs, covering them with his chosen mixture and then loading these on to his shovel he thrusts it far into the oven.

Pizza
Home-made pizza dough

TO SERVE FOUR–SIX

INGREDIENTS
25 g (1 oz) fresh or 15 g
  ($\frac{1}{2}$ oz) dried yeast
150 ml ($\frac{1}{4}$ pint) warm
  water
450 g (1 lb) flour
1 teaspoon salt
olive oil for greasing

Pizza alla napoletana
450 g (1 lb) fresh ripe or
  tinned tomatoes
225 g (8 oz) Mozzarella
  cheese, thinly sliced
12 anchovy fillets
finely chopped oregano
olive oil

Pizza quattro stagioni
50 g (2 oz) mushrooms
  sliced and fried in butter
50 g (2 oz) ham
a few black olives, pitted
3–4 tiny pickled artichokes,
  halved
50 g (2 oz) Mozzarella
  cheese
1 large tomato, peeled and
  sliced
olive oil

Pizza alla siciliana
450 g (1 lb) fresh ripe or
  tinned Italian tomatoes
12 anchovy fillets
a few black olives, pitted
  and coarsely chopped
olive oil

Mix the yeast in the warm water and stir until dissolved. Add enough of the flour to make a soft, pliable dough. Cover and leave in a warm place to rise – about 30 minutes. Sift the rest of the flour with the salt into a bowl, make a well in the middle, add the risen yeast and mix together until the dough is firm enough to be gathered into a ball. Put it on to a floured board and knead it vigorously until smooth and elastic, kneading first in one direction, then in the other. Do this for at least 15 minutes; if preferred, the dough can be mixed and kneaded in an electric mixer. Shape the dough into a ball and put into a bowl, cover with a damp cloth and leave in a warm place until it has doubled its bulk. This quantity of dough will make one large pizza. If smaller pizzas are wanted, break the dough into small lumps, roll into balls and leave to rise separately.

Pizza alla napoletana
Prepare the pizza dough. Spread with tomatoes (peeled and sliced if fresh, crushed if tinned). Spread the Mozzarella cheese over the top, garnish with anchovies and sprinkle with oregano and oil. Bake as indicated.

Pizza Margherita
This pizza is said to have been created in honour of Queen Margherita, the first queen of united Italy. It has the colours of the Italian flag, red with tomatoes, white with Mozzarella, and green with basil.
Prepare in the same way as pizza alla napoletana, substituting chopped fresh basil for the oregano.

Preheat the oven to its hottest (at least 240°C, 475°F, Gas Mark 9). When the dough has risen, flatten it down lightly with a rolling pin and place it on a well-oiled rectangular tin 30 × 35 cm (12 × 14 in), or on small round tins. Stretch and pull the dough with the fingers until it has stretched to the size of the pan. The edges of the dough must be slightly thicker round the sides than in the middle, but at all points it must not be more than 1 cm ($\frac{1}{4}$ in) thick. Make small depressions with your fingers in the dough and brush with oil. Spread with one of the fillings described below.

Bake for 10 minutes, then reduce the heat to moderate (180°C, 350°F, Gas Mark 4) and bake for a further 5–10 minutes, or until brown and crisp. Take from the oven and serve literally at once, as hot as possible. To serve the large pizza, cut into wedges.

Pizza quattro stagioni (Four seasons pizza)
Prepare the pizza dough and place in the tin as indicated above. Divide it mentally into four sections. Fill one section with mushrooms, another with ham and olives, a third with artichokes, the fourth with Mozzarella cheese spread with the tomato. Sprinkle with olive oil before baking.

Pizza alla siciliana
Prepare the pizza dough. Spread with chopped peeled tomatoes, anchovy fillets and the black olives. Sprinkle with olive oil before baking.

Top : pizza alla napoletana;
bottom : pizza quattro stagioni

Pizza al formaggio

Cheese pizza

TO SERVE FOUR–SIX

INGREDIENTS
1 pizza dough (*page* 58)
50 g (2 oz) grated
 Parmesan cheese
25 g (1 oz) grated
 Pecorino cheese
50 g (2 oz) Provolone
 cheese, diced
2 eggs, well beaten
olive oil

This pizza comes from Umbria. If Pecorino cheese is not available use any fairly strong flavoured cheese as a substitute.

Prepare the dough to the point of its first rising. Combine the cheeses and beat into the eggs. Punch down the risen dough, knead it well, adding 2 tablespoons of oil as you knead. Continue kneading until the oil has been absorbed into the dough. Make a well in the centre, pour in the egg and cheese mixture, fold the sides of the dough over the well and carefully knead until the mixture is completely absorbed

into the dough. Roll this into a smooth ball. Preheat the oven to 180 C, 350 F, Gas Mark 4. Brush a large shallow round baking pan generously with oil, add the ball of dough, smooth it down until it fits the inside of the tin, leave it to rise just a little, then bake in the oven until it is a golden brown and has completely risen.

Calzone alla ricotta

Ricotta pasty

TO SERVE FOUR–SIX

INGREDIENTS
pizza dough (*page* 58)
100 g (4 oz) Ricotta
100 g (4 oz) mortadella
 sausage
2–3 leaves fresh basil,
 finely chopped or
 ½ teaspoon dried

The word *calzone* implies a type of pizza that varies from district to district in southern Italy. Some are baked like the ordinary round pizza, others like this Apulian version which is a large crescent-shaped turnover or pasty, while still others are small and deep-fried.

Prepare the pizza dough and continue to the point of spreading and stretching it in the baking tin. Spread one half of the dough with Ricotta, diced mortadella sausage and chopped basil. Fold over the

other half of the dough, press firmly together all round to prevent the filling from oozing out and shape into a half moon. Cover with a damp cloth and leave until the dough rises again. Bake as for pizza (*see page* 58).

Focaccia

A focaccia, also called *schiacciate*, is a pizza-dough, flat pie, usually thicker than the pizza. Sometimes it is quite plain and sprinkled generously with olive oil before baking. It can also be flavoured with sage leaves or onions. In some parts of Liguria, mainly in the Rapallo-Chiavari area, the dough is mixed together with the pulp of pressed olives. When fresh and still hot it is very good and still quite good when cold, spread with plenty of butter. In Rapallo, this type of focaccia is still made in old, almost historic ovens. Focaccia is also eaten a great deal in Tuscany where it is thinner and crisper than that of Liguria. It can be found in all the bars and bakers' shops and today most Italian housewives prefer to obtain it from their local bakers, who still bake their own bread rather than making it themselves.

Focaccia

Pizza with anchovies

TO SERVE FOUR–SIX

INGREDIENTS
pizza dough (*page* 58)
1 small onion
2–3 sprigs fresh oregano and basil
900 g (2 lb) ripe tomatoes
olive oil
100 g (4 oz) salted anchovies
3 cloves garlic, slivered
100 g (4 oz) black olives, pitted and chopped

This focaccia is also called *sardenaira* in the Sanremo dialect and *piscialandrea* in the Diano Marina region. However, in Ventimiglia and Bordighera, further towards the west along the Ligurian coast, it is called *pizza all' Andrea* – perhaps, it is suggested, in honour of Andrea Doria, a great name in those parts. It is not as well known as the Naples pizza but, as the Ligurians proudly say, it is in no way inferior. If you are unable to get salted anchovies, use tinned filleted ones. For absolute accuracy the olives used in this recipe should be small sweet olives from Liguria.

Prepare the pizza dough. Thinly slice the onion, chop the oregano and basil separately, and peel and chop the tomatoes. Heat a little oil, add the onion, and let this brown slightly, then add the basil and the tomatoes and continue cooking until the sauce is thick and begins to look a little dry. Preheat the oven to 220°C, 425°F, Gas Mark 7. In the meantime, wash the salt from the anchovies, fillet them and cut into small pieces. Add to the pan, stir at once, and then take the pan from the heat. Correct the seasoning.

Put the dough into a well oiled baking pan, smooth it down to about 1 cm ($\frac{1}{4}$ in) thick, stick the slivers of garlic into the dough, spread with the olives, then cover with the tomato sauce and sprinkle with the oregano. Some Ligurian cooks also add chopped capers. Bake in the hot oven for 45 minutes and serve hot.

Focaccia dolce

Sweet focaccia

TO SERVE FOUR

INGREDIENTS
175 g (6 oz) butter
3 eggs (size 3)
175 g (6 oz) sugar
175 g (6 oz) flour
1 tablespoon orange-flower
  water (optional)
75 ml (3 fl oz) rum or
  brandy
23-cm (9-in) cake tin

Preheat the oven to 150°C, 300°F, Gas Mark 2. Melt the butter without letting it actually boil, but cool before using. Beat the eggs, add the sugar and beat together thoroughly. Add the flour, whisking lightly all the time, then the butter, orange-flower water and rum. Beat the mixture, then pour into the well-buttered cake tin. Bake in the oven for 45 minutes, raising the heat gently to about 200°C, 400°F, Gas Mark 6.

When ready the cake will be a light brown, the outside crisp and the inside soft, not unlike a Victoria sponge.

It is usual to serve this type of focaccia cold. It is not very sweet and I find it is particularly good when spread with un-salted butter, or served with cheese such as Italian Taleggio or a Bel Paese (see pages 208–9).

Fitascetta

Onion bread ring

TO SERVE FOUR–SIX

INGREDIENTS
350 g (12 oz) bread dough
2 tablespoons olive oil
675 g (1½ lb) onions
75 g (3 oz) butter or
  margarine
salt and pepper
½ teaspoon sugar

In Lombardy large red onions which are mild and very lovely to look at, especially when sliced, are used in this pizza; failing red onions, any mild ones may be substituted. The bread dough can be made from any favourite recipe.

Make the dough and let it rise. Punch it down and work in the oil, kneading the dough thoroughly until it is smooth. Cover and leave again in a warm place to rise until it has doubled its bulk. (The Italians usually have a space underneath their ovens in which to keep plates hot, so they often put their bread dough into this to rise.) In the meantime thinly slice the onions. Heat the butter in a frying pan, add the onions and fry gently until they are soft but not brown. Add salt and pepper to

taste and finally the sugar. When the dough has risen, punch it down again and roll it into a long sausage. Shape it into a ring and place it on an oiled baking sheet, making sure that the two ends are joined together, cover and let it rise again. When it has completely risen, spread the top with the fried onion. Put it into a preheated hot oven (220°C, 425°F, Gas Mark 7), leave for 15 minutes, then lower the heat to 180°C, 350°F, Gas Mark 4 and continue baking for 15–20 minutes, or until the bread is a golden colour.

The onion ring may be served hot or cold, or sliced and spread with butter. Some cooks in Lombardy also add thinly sliced Mozzarella cheese on top of the onions before baking.

Torta tarentina di patate

Potato pizza with
Mozzarella and anchovies

TO SERVE FOUR–SIX

INGREDIENTS
1.5 kg (3 lb) floury
    potatoes
4–5 tablespoons olive oil
salt and black pepper
    to taste
450 g (1 lb) large ripe
    tomatoes
175 g (6 oz) Mozzarella
flour for sprinkling
finely chopped oregano or
    parsley to taste
12 black olives, pitted and
    chopped
6–8 anchovy fillets
50 g (2 oz) grated
    Parmesan cheese

Wash the potatoes and cook them in their skins until soft. Drain, cool, peel and mash thoroughly, making sure that there are no lumps. Add 4–5 tablespoons of oil, beat until the mixture is smooth, and add a pinch of salt and pepper. Preheat the oven to 220°C, 425°F, Gas Mark 7. Peel the tomatoes and thinly slice. Finely slice the Mozzarella and cut each slice into half. Brush the bottom of a flat baking tin with oil and sprinkle lightly with flour. Add the mashed potatoes and spread evenly. Cover with the tomatoes, sprinkle with oregano or parsley, add the Mozzarella, then the olives and anchovies and sprinkle with Parmesan cheese. Trickle 2–3 tablespoons of olive oil over the top and bake in the oven for 15–20 minutes, until a golden brown colour.

Top : torta tarentina di patate;
bottom : fitascetta

Soups

It is by no means simple to classify Italian soups. The word *zuppa* should really indicate a soup prepared with vegetables and invariably served with bread. Having established this we meet the famous *zuppa pavese* which has no vegetables but does have eggs and bread in it. *Zuppa di pesce* is a fish soup and *zuppa di brodo* is a broth or consommé; and very mysteriously there is *zuppa inglese* which is not a soup at all but a type of tipsy cake. In cookery books and on restaurant menus soups are listed under *minestre*, which would appear easy enough except that other first-course dishes appear on this list as well, even risottos. The word *minestra* is derived from the Latin *ministrare*, to serve or put food on the table, therefore it is probably right to list more than soups under the heading *minestre*. In days when inns were scarce, travellers were housed and fed in the monasteries. As weary travellers arrived at all times of day and night, the monks kept a cauldron of meat and vegetables constantly cooking to provide food at a moment's notice, and this became known as *minestra*.

Brodo can be translated as stock, broth or consommé and is served with pasta, tortellini or squares of cheese and other garnishes, such as *crespelle*, strips of pancake, or *crostoncini*, croûtons or tiny gnocchi or ravioli, and strips of lettuce.

Brodetto means a fish soup but in Rome there is a favourite Easter soup, called *brodetto alla romana* or *pasquale*, which is full of meat and vegetables and garnished with Parmesan-spread toast.

In the cooking of the past, *minestra* or *minestrone* was usually sufficient for a main meal, for the stock was always of meat or chicken broth, plus rice or pasta and vegetables, and bits of meat, and often so thick that it was more easily attacked with a fork than a spoon. In fact, the Venetian *risi e bisi* is regarded as a main course, as is the famous *zuppa di fontina*, which consists of layers of bread and sliced Fontina cheese with very little liquid and is baked in the oven. Both of these soups must be eaten with a fork.

But, by whatever name they are called, Italian soups for the most part are excellent, rich and full-bodied, or light and subtly flavoured, and except for clear soups or consommé are seldom served at the same meal as pasta or a risotto.

An engraving taken from Bartolommeo Scappi's *Dell' Arte del cucinare* (1643) showing an Italian kitchen

Brodo di manzo
Beef stock or broth

TO SERVE SIX–EIGHT

INGREDIENTS
900 g (2 lb) lean stewing
  beef or veal
2–3 soup bones
3.5 litres (6 pints) water
1–2 carrots, coarsely
  chopped
1 small turnip, coarsely
  chopped
1–2 leeks, coarsely chopped
1–2 stalks celery with
  leaves, chopped
1 tablespoon tomato
  concentrate
2 sprigs parsley
salt and peppercorns

Put the meat and bones into a large pan, add the water and bring slowly to the boil. Cover the pan and simmer for 1 hour, straining off any foam that may rise to the surface. Add the remaining ingredients and simmer again for a further 2 hours. Strain through a fine sieve. Cool and keep in the refrigerator until required. Skim the layer of fat from the stock before using.

A further amount of broth or stock can be made with the meat and bones, plus fresh vegetables. It will not be quite so concentrated as the first brew but is good nevertheless. Instead of the leeks, a large onion may be used.

Brodo di pollo
Chicken stock or broth

TO SERVE EIGHT–TEN

INGREDIENTS
1 large boiling chicken
1 knuckle of veal or shin
  bone
4 litres (7 pints) water
1 each carrot, onion, leek,
  coarsely chopped
1 good sprig parsley,
  chopped
1–2 stalks celery with
  leaves
salt and peppercorns

Broth is the basis for a great number of Italian soups and can also be made with duck, pigeon, turkey or goose. The chicken can be served separately with a sauce and fresh vegetables, but not those used in the soup.

Place the chicken, veal bone and water into a large, heavy pan and bring gently to the boil. Skim off any foam at the top, then add the remaining ingredients to the pan. Cover, bring to a slow boil, then simmer for about 3 hours. Take the chicken from the pan and strain the broth through a fine sieve. Cool and keep in the refrigerator until required. Before using the broth, remove the layer of fat which forms on the surface with a spoon.

If an extra-clear broth is required, return the strained liquid to the pan and add two crushed egg shells, plus two egg whites, beaten until peaks form. Bring to the boil, stirring all the time, and strain through a cheesecloth.

Acqua cotta

TO SERVE FOUR–SIX

INGREDIENTS
100 g (4 oz) mushrooms
225 g (8 oz) ripe tomatoes,
  peeled
150 ml (¼ pint) olive oil
1–2 cloves garlic, crushed
salt and pepper
2 litres (3½ pints) boiling
  water
25 g (1 oz) grated Parmesan
  cheese
2 eggs, well beaten
4–6 slices oven-toasted
  bread

This is a favourite Tuscan recipe but can vary in the choice of vegetables used.

Wash the mushrooms and slice thinly, stems as well as caps. Chop the tomatoes coarsely, discarding the seeds. Heat the oil in a large pan, add the mushrooms and fry until just soft, then add the garlic, tomatoes, salt and pepper and cook over a gentle heat for 10 minutes. Add the boiling water, stir well, reduce the heat and cook gently for 1 hour, stirring for the first 3–5 minutes. Immediately before serving, beat the cheese into the eggs and pour this mixture into the soup. Stir well. Put a slice of toast into each soup bowl and pour the soup over it. Serve at once.

Top : acqua cotta;
bottom : crema di pomodoro

Crema di pomodoro

Tomato soup

TO SERVE FOUR

INGREDIENTS
50 g (2 oz) butter
2 medium-sized onions,
  finely chopped
1 tablespoon flour
900 g (2 lb) ripe tomatoes,
  peeled and coarsely
  chopped
4 cloves garlic, chopped
salt and pepper
1 heaped teaspoon sugar
1 heaped tablespoon finely
  chopped fresh basil or
  parsley or ½ teaspoon
  dried
750 ml (1½ pints) hot meat
  stock or water
walnut-sized knob of butter
150 ml (¼ pint) single
  cream

Heat the butter in a pan, add the onions and cook gently until soft but not brown. Sprinkle in the flour, stir well and continue cooking for 3 minutes, stirring all the time. Add the tomatoes, garlic, salt, pepper, sugar and basil. Bring to a gentle boil, then lower the heat and simmer until the tomatoes are a pulp. Add the stock and cook for a further 20 minutes. Rub through a coarse sieve, return to the pan, bring once more to a gentle boil, add the knob of butter and cream, stir well and serve.

Serve with toast or croûtons and a bowl of grated cheese.

Minestrone alla genovese con pesto

Vegetable soup with pesto

TO SERVE EIGHT–TEN

INGREDIENTS
225 g (8 oz) dried white
  haricot beans
4 litres (7 pints) water
pinch of salt
1 large onion, coarsely
  chopped
2 stalks celery, sliced
1 large carrot, thinly sliced
6 tablespoons olive oil
2–4 courgettes, sliced
4 medium-ripe tomatoes,
  peeled and coarsely
  chopped
4 large potatoes, peeled and
  chopped
2–3 leaves fresh borage,
  finely chopped or
  $\frac{1}{2}$ teaspoon dried
225 g (8 oz) elbow
  macaroni
2 tablespoons pesto sauce
  (*page* 182)
6 tablespoons grated
  Pecorino cheese

The vegetables used in this soup, as with all minestrone soups, are changed according to season and availability. The distinction *minestrone alla genovese* enjoys is the addition of pesto. When Pecorino is not available, use the most piquant cheese you can find. Elbow macaroni takes its name from its shape but other small macaroni will do.

Soak the haricot beans overnight and partially cook in unsalted water. Drain the beans and put into a large heavy pan with the 4 litres (7 pints) of water, salt, onion, celery, carrot and 4 tablespoons of oil. Bring to a gentle boil, lower the heat and simmer for about 1 hour. Add the courgettes, tomatoes, potatoes and borage and cook for a further 30 minutes. Add the macaroni, cook until *al dente*, for about 15 minutes, stir in the pesto, the rest of the oil and cheese and serve at once.

Minestra di frittata

Pancake soup

TO SERVE FOUR–SIX

INGREDIENTS
4–6 plain pancakes
1.5 litres ($2\frac{3}{4}$ pints) clear
  meat or vegetable stock
1–2 tablespoons finely
  chopped parsley
grated Parmesan cheese

This is an Austrian-influenced soup from the Trentino-Alto Adige region.

Make the pancakes from any favourite recipe. As each one is taken from the pan, roll it up firmly like a Swiss roll. When all the pancakes are finished and rolled, cut them into thinnish strips, like noodles. Bring the stock to a rapid boil, add the strips of pancake and cook for a few minutes, just long enough to reheat. Serve very hot, sprinkled with parsley and cheese. Each bowl of soup should be crammed with strips of pancake.

Minestrone milanese

TO SERVE EIGHT—TEN

INGREDIENTS
225 g (8 oz) dried white
   beans
100 g (4 oz) lean salt pork
   or bacon
2 large onions, finely
   chopped
350 g (12 oz) potatoes,
   peeled and cubed
350 g (12 oz) firm ripe
   tomatoes, peeled and
   chopped
2 carrots, peeled and sliced
   into thin rounds
2 small courgettes, peeled
   and thickly sliced
450 g (1 lb) firm white
   cabbage, shredded
100 g (4 oz) green peas,
   shelled weight
1 clove garlic, finely
   chopped (optional)
225 g (8 oz) short grain
   Italian rice
1–2 leaves fresh basil or
   sage or ½ teaspoon dried
2 sprigs parsley, finely
   chopped
salt and pepper
grated Parmesan cheese

This is Milan's classic winter vegetable soup, thick and sustaining.

The vegetables for this famous soup change not only according to season but also according to taste. Whichever ones are used, it is important to remember to cook them very carefully so that they do not become mushy.

Soak the beans overnight. Next day drain and cook them in fresh unsalted water until almost tender. Drain. Coarsely chop the pork and put into a large pan and cook over a moderate heat until the fat runs freely. Add the onions and cook slowly until soft but not brown. Add the remaining vegetables and garlic, stir gently but

well and cook for 5 minutes. Add about 3.5 litres (6 pints) of water and bring slowly to the boil. Add the beans and continue to cook until they are quite tender. Add the rice, basil, parsley, salt and pepper and cook for 15 minutes, or until the rice is *al dente*. Sprinkle cheese into each bowl of soup immediately before serving.

Minestra di patate

Potato soup

TO SERVE FOUR–SIX

INGREDIENTS

675 g (1½ lb) floury
  potatoes
575 ml (1 pint) water
575 ml (1 pint) milk
salt
2–3 tablespoons oil, or
  melted butter
25 g (1 oz) fat bacon, diced
1 each small onion, carrot,
  stalk celery, finely
  chopped
2 cloves garlic, chopped
2–3 sprigs parsley, finely
  chopped
grated cheese, preferably
  Parmesan
croûtons

Peel and cut the potatoes into halves or quarters, depending on size. Put into a pan with all the water and half the milk. Add salt, but cautiously, as Parmesan cheese is often salty. Cook the potatoes over a moderate heat until very soft. While they are cooking, heat the oil or butter in a pan, add the bacon and, when the fat runs freely, add the vegetables, garlic and parsley and cook until the vegetables are soft but have not changed colour. Mash the potatoes in the pan. Add the rest of the milk and gently cook until this is hot and the potatoes reheated. Add the fried vegetables to the potatoes, stir well and serve the soup with cheese and croûtons.

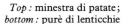

Top : minestra di patate;
bottom : purè di lenticchie

Purè di lenticchie

Purée of lentil soup

TO SERVE FOUR–SIX

INGREDIENTS

225 g (8 oz) lentils
2 litres (3½ pints) water
25 g (1 oz) butter
1 onion, finely chopped
2–3 cloves garlic, chopped
finely chopped mint to
  taste
8 anchovy fillets
salt and pepper
croûtons

Cook the lentils in the water for about 1 hour, or until they are soft. Rub them with their liquid through a sieve. Rinse and dry the pan, heat the butter, add the onion and garlic and fry until the onion is soft and brown. Add the mint and anchovies and continue cooking for a few minutes. Return the lentils, add salt and pepper, stir well and cook until very hot. Serve with croûtons.

Risi e bisi
Rice and peas

TO SERVE FOUR

INGREDIENTS
50 g (2 oz) butter
1 tablespoon olive oil
225 g (8 oz) Italian rice
2 tablespoons finely
   chopped parsley
1 small onion, minced
50 g (2 oz) cooked ham,
   diced
225 g (8 oz) peas, shelled
1 litre (1¾ pints) boiling
   meat stock
salt
butter and grated
   Parmesan cheese for
   garnishing

Although classed as a soup, this dish of rice and peas is so thick that it is eaten with a fork. In the days of the opulent Doges the Venetians considered it to be their soup *par excellence* and served it always at banquets given on the Feast of Saint Mark. Even today it is found on the menus of Venetian restaurants, whether a simple trattoria or a de luxe establishment. A bowl of Parmesan cheese is served separately with it. As with all traditional recipes, it has its variations, but, however, always of paramount importance is the strong green element in the soup – with too much rice it becomes all *risi* and no *bisi* (the local dialect word for peas).

A fastidious Venetian making *risi e bisi* would insist not only on young and tender peas but on those grown in the fields near to the shores of the Venetian lagoons. This limits the season and scope for serving this

soup, but it is a fact that *risi e bisi* is not usually served in Venice if fresh peas are not in season. If using frozen peas, do not choose the so-called *petits pois*.

Heat together the butter and oil, add the rice, parsley, onion and ham and fry until the onion is soft and has begun to change colour. Add the peas and gradually the boiling stock. Cover and cook for 15–18 minutes, or until the rice is tender, has absorbed all the liquid, and is just slightly moist but not mushy. Add salt if required. Serve garnished with slivers of butter and a bowl of grated Parmesan cheese.

Stracciatelle
Egg and cheese soup

TO SERVE FOUR–SIX

INGREDIENTS
3 eggs
1 tablespoon semolina
1 heaped tablespoon grated
   Parmesan cheese
pinch of grated nutmeg
salt and pepper
1.7 litres (3 pints) chicken
   broth

This Roman speciality is one of the classic soups of Italy. The word *stracciatelle* means little rags.

Beat the eggs well, add the semolina, cheese and nutmeg, salt and pepper and dilute with a cup of broth. Bring the remaining broth to a bubbling boil and add the egg mixture, whisking all the time. Reduce the heat and cook gently for 3 minutes, by which time the eggs will have broken up into 'rags'. Serve at once.

A more simple variation is to beat the

eggs with salt and pepper only and, when the stock is boiling, add them, stir well for a minute or so and serve with grated cheese.

Stracciatelle verdi (Green egg and cheese soup)
In this version about 100 g (4 oz) of cooked, drained and finely chopped spinach are added together with the eggs. Proceed as in main recipe.

Zuppa casalinga

Housewife's soup

TO SERVE SIX

INGREDIENTS
450 g (1 lb) dried white
  haricot beans
3 litres (5¼ pints) water
350 g (12 oz) piece of
  bacon
450 g (1 lb) green beans
450 g (1 lb) carrots
450 g (1 lb) turnips
225 g (8 oz) leeks
1 large onion
350 g (12 oz) potatoes
salt and pepper
2–3 sprigs parsley, finely
  chopped

This is certainly more of a stew than a soup and a good example of the old-fashioned soup which is a complete course.

Soak the beans overnight and drain them the next day. Heat the water, add the beans and the bacon and cook over a moderate heat for about 1½ hours. Trim and cut the green beans into short lengths, peel and thickly slice both the carrots and turnips.

Carefully wash the leeks and onion and cut into rings. Add all these ingredients to the pan and continue cooking for 15–20 minutes. Peel and coarsely chop the potatoes, add to the pan with salt and pepper. Take out the bacon and cut into small pieces. Return to the pan and cook for 20–30 minutes until all the ingredients are tender but still firm. Sprinkle with parsley and serve in deep bowls.

Zuppa di castagne

Chestnut soup

TO SERVE FOUR–SIX

INGREDIENTS
675 g (1½ lb) chestnuts
725 ml (1¼ pints) milk
25 g (1 oz) butter
1 small onion, finely
  chopped
flour for dusting
salt, pepper and nutmeg to
  taste
275 ml (½ pint) single
  cream
2–3 sprigs parsley, finely
  chopped
croûtons

Instead of fresh chestnuts, unsweetened, tinned chestnut purée can be used.

Make a slit in each chestnut and boil them in water for 20 minutes. Drain them and pull off the shell and inner skin. Put the chestnuts with the milk into a pan and cook until they are very soft, adding more milk if required. Rub through a sieve. If using tinned chestnut purée, combine this with the milk and continue as follows. Melt the butter in a deep pan and lightly fry the onion until soft but not brown. Sprinkle lightly with a little flour, and add salt, pepper and nutmeg. Mix well, add the chestnut purée and cook for 10 minutes over a low heat. Add the cream, bring gently to boiling point and take from the heat. Garnish with parsley and serve with croûtons. If the soup seems too thick, it can be thinned with milk or cream.

Zuppa di ceci

Chick-pea soup

TO SERVE FOUR

INGREDIENTS
450 g (1 lb) chick-peas
15 g (½ oz) dried
  mushrooms
2 tablespoons olive oil,
  preferably Ligurian
25 g (1 oz) butter
1 large onion, finely
  chopped
1–2 cloves garlic, finely
  chopped
1–2 stalks celery, cut into
  rounds
6 leaves of chard or
  spinach, well washed
  and shredded
3–4 ripe tomatoes, peeled
  and chopped
salt
4–8 pieces oven-baked
  toast

This is a typical peasant soup from Liguria, and is simple rustic cooking but good.

Soak the chick-peas overnight in cold water. Next day drain and cook them, covered, for about 3 hours in plenty of fresh water until soft. Soak the mushrooms in a little warm water for 20–30 minutes. Drain and chop finely. About half an hour before the chick-peas are ready, heat the oil and butter in a large pan, add the onion, garlic, celery, the chard leaves, tomatoes, salt and mushrooms. Mix well and cook to a thick sauce. Drain the chick-peas, add to the sauce and reserve their liquid. Stir and cook for 5 minutes, then add enough of the chick-pea liquid to make a soup as thick or as thin as preferred. Serve with oven-baked toast.

Zuppa di cipolla

Onion soup

TO SERVE FOUR

INGREDIENTS
3 tablespoons olive oil
675 g (1½ lb) onions,
  chopped
2 tablespoons flour
1 litre (1¾ pints) chicken or
  other meat stock
salt and pepper
50 g (2 oz) grated
  Parmesan cheese
50 g (2 oz) Gruyère cheese,
  cubed
small croûtons

Heat the oil in a large pan, add the onions and fry until soft but not brown. Sprinkle in flour, stir well and continue cooking for 3 minutes, stirring all the time. Gradually add the stock, salt and pepper and continue stirring for 5 minutes. Cook gently for 20 minutes, then rub the soup through a coarse sieve or mouli-légumes. Return it to the pan, add the Parmesan and Gruyère cheese. Stir for 2 minutes until the soup is well mixed. Serve very hot with croûtons handed round separately.

Top : zuppa pavese;
centre : zuppa alla romana; zuppa di zucchini;
bottom : zuppa di cipolla

Zuppa pavese

Egg and cheese soup

TO SERVE FOUR

INGREDIENTS
50 g (2 oz) butter
4 thick slices 2-day old
  bread, crusts removed
grated Parmesan cheese
2 litres (3½ pints) clear
  chicken stock
4 eggs
salt and pepper

When correctly made this soup has a subtle flavour, and is also very nourishing. According to legend, it was created by a peasant woman in Pavia. The legend relates that the unfortunate King Francis I of France, beaten in battle by the Spanish and on the way to surrender, was enticed by the aroma of a soup coming from a peasant cottage. He asked the woman if she would feed him. Afraid that her simple broth would not be good enough for a king, she dropped a slice of fried bread into a bowl, added an egg and poured the boiling hot broth over the top, then sprinkled it with Parmesan cheese.

Heat the butter in a frying pan and fry the bread on both sides until a light brown and crisp. Put a slice into each soup bowl and sprinkle it with Parmesan cheese, not less than 1 tablespoon per bowl. Bring the stock to a rapid boil. Carefully break an egg over each slice of bread without breaking the yolk. Sprinkle with salt and pepper. Immediately add 1 ladleful of absolutely boiling stock. This is important, as if the stock is not boiling the egg will not cook. Serve at once.

Zuppa alla romana

Lettuce soup

TO SERVE FOUR–SIX

INGREDIENTS
1 head cos lettuce
1.7 litres (3 pints) meat or
  vegetable stock
salt and pepper
toast and grated Parmesan
  cheese for garnishing

Discard any really wilted leaves of the lettuce and put the rest into a bowl, pour boiling water over it and leave for 5 minutes. Drain, cool, squeeze dry and shred into a large pan. Add 575 ml (1 pint) of the meat or vegetable stock and cook over a moderate heat until soft. Add the remainder of the stock, raise the heat and continue cooking for 15 minutes. Taste for seasoning and add salt and pepper if required. Serve the soup with triangles of toast and Parmesan cheese handed round separately.

Zuppa di zucchini

Courgette soup

TO SERVE FOUR–SIX

INGREDIENTS
6–7 large courgettes
100 g (4 oz) butter
1.7 litres (3 pints) white
  stock, heated
salt and pepper
3 eggs
2 sprigs fresh basil, finely
  chopped or ½ teaspoon
  dried
100 g (4 oz) Parmesan
  cheese, grated
oven-baked toast

Wash, dry and thickly slice the courgettes without peeling them. Heat the butter in a pan, add the courgettes and fry until they just begin to change colour. Add the heated stock, salt and pepper and cook over a gentle heat until the courgettes are soft. Beat the eggs, add the basil and half the cheese, pour this over the courgettes and continue cooking gently without boiling for 3–4 minutes. Serve hot with extra grated cheese and oven-baked toast handed round separately.

If preferred, the courgettes can be rubbed through a sieve and returned to the pan before adding the eggs.

Brodetto dei pescatori dell'Adriatico

Fisherman's soup from the Adriatic

TO SERVE SIX

INGREDIENTS
1.5 kg (3 lb) assorted fish
150 ml ($\frac{1}{4}$ pint) olive oil
3–4 onions, coarsely chopped
5 cloves garlic, chopped
plenty of fresh parsley, coarsely chopped
275 ml ($\frac{1}{2}$ pint) tomato juice
150 ml ($\frac{1}{4}$ pint) dry white wine
275 ml ($\frac{1}{2}$ pint) warm water
salt and pepper
oven-baked toast

All along the Adriatic coast the inhabitants argue passionately on the subject of which town produces the best brodetto. Restaurants never simply advertise they are serving a brodetto, it is always 'the finest brodetto on the coast'. For the layman there seems little difference, and the variations in the local versions are sometimes slight indeed. Sometimes only fish from shallow waters are used, as in Ancona; some cooks dip the fish first in flour, while others cook it straight; some use only wine, others a little vinegar. This recipe originally called only for a very strong vinegar but in recent years a dry white wine has been a happier substitute for palates other than a hardy fisherman's. The fish recommended for this dish are eel, grey mullet, squid, cuttlefish, red mullet, inkfish, sea scorpion and flounder. Much of this fish should not be too difficult to find in Britain, and where the original cannot be found, then use a passable substitute; this must be left to the imagination of the reader and, no doubt, to the ingenuity of the fishmonger. The fish should be thoroughly cleaned by the fishmonger and left whole. Brodetto is a complete course, and almost a meal in itself. It is usual nowadays for the fish and its liquid to be served in the same serving dish, although formerly they were separated and you had a fish soup followed by a

dish of fish, taking your own choice. And, if you cannot get all the ingredients mentioned, take heart; in Cattolica they do not use parsley, nor all the same fish; in Riccione (another town in the same region) they scorn garlic, onion and parsley and prefer a red wine to white. And finally, in Cesentino they leave out the onion and use neither wine nor vinegar, making a really dry type of brodetto. The preparation of a brodetto, therefore, in Britain is something of a challenge and no one can say your version is not quite right because no one knows what is 'right' since every sea port in Italy has its own version.

Put the oil into a large pan, add the onions, garlic and parsley and cook over a moderate heat until the onion begins to soften. Add the tomato juice, wine, warm water, salt and pepper. Stir these ingredients well and cook over a moderate heat for 15 minutes. Add the fish, the large ones first and, as they start to cook, the smaller ones. Remember that squid and the inkfish family all take quite a time to cook. When all the fish are in the pan, cover and cook over a low heat for about 30 minutes. While the brodetto is cooking, prepare some oven-baked toast. Turn the brodetto into a large, deep serving dish. Serve in deep earthenware soup bowls, with the bread separately.

Zuppa di arselle or **vongole**

Clam soup

TO SERVE FOUR

INGREDIENTS
900 g (2 lb) small clams
150 ml ($\frac{1}{4}$ pint) olive oil
the white part of 1 small
    leek, chopped (optional)
1 small onion, finely
    chopped
275 ml ($\frac{1}{2}$ pint) dry white
    wine or dry cider
225 g (8 oz) tin Italian
    peeled tomatoes, crushed
2–3 cloves garlic, crushed
2–3 sprigs fresh oregano or
    marjoram, finely chopped
    or $\frac{1}{2}$ teaspoon dried
2–3 sprigs parsley, finely
    chopped or $\frac{1}{4}$ teaspoon
    dried
oven-baked toast, spread
    with garlic

Wash the clams thoroughly in cold running water or, better still, in seawater. Leave in fresh cold salted water (or seawater) for 1 hour to make sure they are completely free from sand. Heat the oil in a large shallow pan, add the leek and onion and fry until just brown. Add the clams, drained but not dried, cover the pan and cook for 5 minutes over a brisk heat. Add the wine, tomatoes, garlic, oregano and parsley and cook again for 5 minutes, or until all the clams are fully open, discarding any that are closed. Turn into a hot serving dish.

Serve with oven-baked toast, spread with crushed garlic. Another variation is to put a piece of toast into the soup bowls, add the clams and cover with the liquid.

Top: zuppa di arselle; *bottom*: zuppa di cozze

Zuppa di cozze

Mussel soup

TO SERVE FOUR

INGREDIENTS
2 kg (4$\frac{1}{2}$ lb) mussels
150 ml ($\frac{1}{4}$ pint) olive oil
1–2 cloves garlic, peeled
2 large tomatoes, peeled
    and seeded
$\frac{1}{4}$ teaspoon chilli pepper
salt and pepper
plenty of finely chopped
    parsley and marjoram
oven-baked toast

Wash the mussels in several changes of water until all the grit has been removed. Pull off their beards. Put the oil into a pan with the garlic and cook over a moderate heat until the garlic changes colour. Remove the garlic and discard. Add the tomatoes, stir well and cook over a brisk heat for 10 minutes. Add the mussels and chilli pepper and stir again. Cover the pan, cook for 8–10 minutes, shaking the pan every couple of minutes or until the mussels are fully opened. Discard any mussels that have not opened. Add a little salt, plenty of pepper, parsley and marjoram and cook for a minute or two longer. Turn out to serve in a large hot bowl, with the oven-baked bread spread with crushed garlic served separately.

The mussels can be taken out of their shells and returned quickly to the pan to reheat and the bread placed in the bottom of each soup bowl and topped with mussel soup.

In Taranto, the great southern mussel centre in Italy, an almost identical soup is made with about 275 ml ($\frac{1}{2}$ pint) of dry white wine added to it just before the mussels are served. A dry cider also could be used in this soup with good effect.

In the Tuscan hills

Eggs

Eggs have formed part of the diet of mankind since the dawn of time. These were not the eggs of domesticated birds but what one might call wild eggs, those of wild birds from forests and the sea, even those of insects and tortoises (ants' eggs are still a delicacy in South-East Asia). Eggs to the superstitious Ancients meant birth, rebirth, fertility, magic, and fortune, both good and bad. The traditional Easter egg was emblematical of the resurrection of man, as by incubation a living creature is born from a dormant state resembling death. Indeed, eggs were credited with such magical powers that they were widely used by witches (they are still used in parts of the West Indies and elsewhere in magic rituals, especially when casting an evil spell on someone). The Romans felt so strongly the evil influence of egg shells that they always completely crushed them to prevent their further use in magic potions.

However, superstitions apart, eggs are one of our most complete foods. The Romans would often start a meal with a light dish of eggs, and even today in Italy eggs are not just part of the Italian breakfast but, instead, form part of a main course or are a main course in themselves.

Eggs should be taken from the refrigerator at least 20 minutes before they are to be used so that they reach room temperature. This is particularly important when boiling eggs, as the shells of cold eggs will crack more easily on contact with boiling water than those at room temperature. If there is not enough time before cooking to let the eggs gain room temperature naturally, hold them for a couple of minutes under running hot water, prick them with a pin or needle (there are gadgets which do this easily), or put a little vinegar into the water with the eggs.

Shelling hard-boiled eggs, especially when very fresh, can be tiresome if the shell sticks to the white and takes off some of the white with it. Equally difficult is keeping the yolks in the middle of the egg. Here are two hints from Tuscany. When you put the eggs into the water, turn them round and round frequently so that the yolks do not become lodged on one side. When they have been cooked, take them from the pan as quickly as possible, crack the shells all over until they look lacy, then drop into cold water and leave for a few minutes. To shell, take a large fork and slip one prong under the egg shell and draw it up through the 'lace' to the top of the egg, thus splitting the 'lace' or shell into halves. It will then be easy to remove the shell without breaking off bits of the white.

An engraving taken from Bartolommeo Scappi's *Dell' Arte del cucinare* (1643) showing the traditional cooking methods

Uova strapazzate con fegatini di pollo

Scrambled eggs with chicken livers

INGREDIENTS
100 g (4 oz) chicken livers
100 g (4 oz) butter
4–5 tablespoons dry
  Marsala or sherry
8 eggs
salt and pepper

Serve this either as a light luncheon course or as a starter.

Trim the livers and chop each into 2–3 pieces. Heat half the butter over a moderate heat and quickly fry the livers for 2 minutes. Take from the pan with a perforated spoon, put them aside and keep warm. Add the dry Marsala to the pan, cook until it is reduced by half. Add the livers and leave the pan over the lowest possible heat. Lightly beat the eggs and add the seasoning. Heat the remaining butter until it just melts in a second pan, add the eggs but at this point do not stir; instead let the underneath portion of the eggs set, then carefully lift it up with a spatula and let some of the uncooked egg from the top run underneath. When this has set, repeat the performance until all the egg is cooked, but fairly moist. Take the eggs from the pan, turn at once on to a hot serving dish, garnish with the chicken livers in their sauce and serve at once.

Top : uova strapazzate con fegatini di pollo;
bottom : uova alla castagne

Uova alla castagne

Scrambled eggs with chestnuts

INGREDIENTS
6 eggs
50 g (2 oz) butter
24 chestnuts, roasted and
  peeled
salt and pepper
good pinch of paprika
  pepper

This is a dish of excellent flavour. When peeling the chestnuts, try to keep the flesh in as large pieces as possible.

Lightly beat the eggs. Heat the butter in a heavy frying pan and add the eggs but at this point do not stir them; instead let the underneath portion of the eggs set, then carefully lift it up with a spatula and let some of the uncooked egg from the top run underneath. When this has set, repeat the performance until all the egg is cooked, but fairly moist. When they are almost ready, add the chestnuts, mix well but gently, sprinkle with salt and pepper and paprika. Serve at once.

Uova alla cacciatora

Poached eggs hunter style

TO SERVE FOUR

INGREDIENTS
25 g (1 oz) butter
1 small onion, finely
    chopped
4 chicken livers, trimmed
    and chopped
flour for dusting
275 ml ($\frac{1}{2}$ pint) tomato
    juice
275 ml ($\frac{1}{2}$ pint) dry white
    wine
2–3 leaves each fresh
    rosemary, basil and
    thyme or $\frac{1}{2}$ teaspoon
    dried
8 black or green olives,
    pitted and chopped
salt and pepper
4 eggs
4 slices hot toast
chicken liver pâté

This can be served as a starter or light luncheon course, and is rather rich but very good.

Heat the butter, add the onion and fry until it is soft but do not let it become too brown; add the livers and when they change colour sprinkle them lightly with flour and cook gently for 5 minutes. Add the tomato juice and stir well, then add the wine, herbs, olives, salt and pepper and gently mix. When the mixture is bubbling gently, add the eggs, one by one, and continue to cook over a moderate heat until they are set. Spread the toast with pâté, place an egg on top of each piece, then cover each one with the hot sauce and serve at once.

Uova affogate con salsa di funghi

Poached eggs in a
mushroom sauce

TO SERVE FOUR

INGREDIENTS
450 g (1 lb) button
    mushrooms
50 g (2 oz) butter
1–2 cloves garlic, finely
    chopped
450 g (1 lb) tinned peeled
    tomatoes
1 bayleaf
salt and pepper
1 teaspoon sugar
4 eggs
4 slices crisp toast

Wash the mushrooms well and slice both the caps and stems in medium-thick slices. Heat the butter, add the garlic and as this begins to change colour add the mushrooms and cook lightly for about 5 minutes. Add the tomatoes, crush down with a fork in the pan, add the bayleaf, salt and pepper to taste, and the sugar, and cook gently for about 30 minutes; if necessary add a little hot water as the sauce should be thick but loose. Discard the bayleaf. When the sauce is almost ready, add the eggs one by one. Make the toast. Place the toast on a long, flat serving dish, put one egg on each piece of toast and surround with the sauce.

Left : uova in trippa alla romana; *right :* uova nella neve

Uova in trippa alla romana

Eggs disguised as tripe

TO SERVE FOUR

INGREDIENTS
275 ml (½ pint) tomato
  sauce (*page* 184)
6–8 eggs
50 g (2 oz) grated
  Parmesan cheese
salt and pepper
olive oil
1 tablespoon finely
  chopped mint or parsley

This dish can be served either as a starter or a light main luncheon course.

First prepare the tomato sauce and keep hot. Lightly beat the eggs, adding half the cheese and salt and pepper to taste. Preheat the oven to 180°C, 350°F, Gas Mark 4. Heat a little oil in a frying pan and pour in about a quarter of the egg mixture to make a thin French-style omelette. Cook over a moderate heat until the omelette begins to set, then prick it with a fork and run a spatula round the edges to let the loose, unset egg on the top run down the sides. When the egg is set, turn the omelette over

and let it brown on the other side. Take from the pan and while still hot roll up like a Swiss roll. Repeat this with the remaining beaten egg, making four omelettes in all. Cut the rolls into strips to resemble tripe. Open up the strips after cutting. Rub the bottom of a casserole with oil and arrange a layer of the strips of omelette on the bottom. Sprinkle lightly with some of the remaining cheese and spread with the hot tomato sauce and chopped mint. Continue in this manner until all the ingredients are used up, finishing with a layer of cheese. Bake for about 15 minutes in the oven and serve at once.

Uova nella neve

Eggs in snow

TO SERVE FOUR

INGREDIENTS
450 g (1 lb) floury potatoes
25 g (1 oz) butter
milk, warmed
extra butter
1 Mozzarella cheese, about
  100 g (4 oz), sliced
4 eggs
salt and pepper
grated Parmesan cheese

Instead of Mozzarella, other soft cheeses such as Bel Paese or Fontina may be used.

Peel and boil the potatoes until soft – if they are very large, they should be halved or quartered before boiling. Drain and mash until smooth, then beat in the measured quantity of butter and enough warmed milk to make them creamy. Preheat the oven to 200°C, 400°F, Gas Mark 6. Rub a baking dish generously with butter and lightly fill with the mashed potatoes – they should not come to the top or be pressed down. Cover with the sliced Mozzarella and, using the back of a wooden

spoon, make four wells and into each break one whole egg. Sprinkle with salt and pepper, Parmesan cheese and slivers of butter. Bake in the oven for 10–15 minutes until the eggs are set and the cheese melted.

Uova sode con salsa al Marsala

Hard-boiled eggs in Marsala sauce

TO SERVE FOUR

INGREDIENTS
15 g (½ oz) dried
  mushrooms
25 g (1 oz) butter
1 small onion, finely
  chopped
1 tablespoon flour
150 ml (¼ pint) dry Marsala
  or sherry
275 ml (½ pint) meat or
  vegetable stock
salt and pepper
1 tablespoon finely
  chopped parsley
juice of 1 lemon
150 ml (¼ pint) single
  cream
4 eggs, hard-boiled

Soak the mushrooms for about 20 minutes in warm water. Drain well and chop. Heat the butter in a small pan, add the onion and fry gently until soft. Sprinkle in the flour, stirring all the time, then add the Marsala, still stirring. Slowly add the stock and continue cooking until you have a thick sauce. Add salt and pepper and finally the mushrooms. Stir well, then continue cooking for 5 minutes. Add the parsley, lemon juice and cream. Preheat the oven to 180°C, 350°F, Gas Mark 4. Peel the eggs, slice lengthwise and place in a shallow oven-to-table baking dish. Pour the sauce over the eggs. Put into the oven and bake for 10 minutes. Serve hot.

Top: uova sode con salsa al Marsala;
bottom: uova alla sarda

Uova alla sarda

Hard-boiled eggs in a garlic and parsley sauce

TO SERVE FOUR

INGREDIENTS
4 eggs, hard-boiled
3 tablespoons olive oil
1 tablespoon wine vinegar
salt and pepper
1 clove garlic, crushed
2–3 sprigs parsley, finely
  chopped
2–3 tablespoons soft
  breadcrumbs

This dish can be served hot, cold or even warm, either as a starter or a light luncheon course.

Peel the eggs and slice them in halves lengthwise. Put the oil, vinegar, salt and pepper into a frying pan, add the eggs and cook gently, turning them from time to time until the vinegar has evaporated. Take from the pan with a perforated spoon and place them in a hot serving dish, cut side uppermost, and keep warm in the oven. Mix the garlic and parsley together and add to the oil still in the pan. Cook over a low heat for 2–3 minutes, then add the breadcrumbs, stirring them into the garlic–parsley mixture and cook for a minute or so until the crumbs are just brown. Spread the mixture over the eggs and serve.

Tortino tirolese

Italian Tyrolean eggs

TO SERVE FOUR

INGREDIENTS
3 hard-boiled eggs, shelled
50 g (2 oz) butter
225 g (8 oz) tin peeled
  tomatoes
anchovy paste
finely chopped parsley
fine breadcrumbs
3 eggs
275 ml (½ pint) single
  cream

This is not a pie or tart in the real sense of the word but is an extremely easy dish to prepare. I have called it Italian Tyrolean to distinguish this area from the Austrian Tyrol. The Italians buy anchovy paste in tubes which is of a softer consistency than paste sold in jars. If cream is not available, use a fairly thin béchamel sauce.

Preheat the oven to 190°C, 375°F, Gas Mark 5. Cut the hard-boiled eggs into quarters. Heat the butter in a round, moderately shallow casserole. Add the tomatoes in a layer and lightly crush them so that the bottom of the dish is completely covered. Sprinkle with blobs or rings of anchovy paste, then fairly generously with parsley. Add the hard-boiled eggs, arranging them neatly round the sides of the dish. Sprinkle lightly with breadcrumbs. Beat the remaining eggs and then whisk into the cream. Pour this mixture over the top of the hard-boiled eggs and bake in the oven for about 30 minutes, or until the mixture has completely set. Serve hot.

Frittata

A frittata is a sort of omelette, but there is no true translation of this rather thick cross between an omelette and a pancake. Not difficult to make, frittate of all kinds are very good. They can be served as a light luncheon or supper dish. When finished, a frittata should be 1–2 cm ($\frac{1}{4}$–$\frac{1}{2}$ in) thick. The frittata can be eaten hot or cold, and even taken on a picnic.

The fillings for a frittata are many and varied and depend simply upon the contents of the larder or refrigerator. Cold diced meats, or plenty of chopped cooked bacon; grated cheese, chopped tomatoes,

Frittata con il salame

Salami omelette

TO SERVE THREE–FOUR

INGREDIENTS
6 eggs (size 2)
15 g ($\frac{1}{2}$ oz) butter
1 tablespoon olive oil
salt and pepper
diced salami

This is a country recipe and the type of salami which should be used is the fat but not too salty one. Failing salami, diced ham or cooked sausage could be used.

Beat the eggs thoroughly. Heat the butter and oil together in a large frying pan. Add the beaten eggs, salt and pepper and when they are half cooked and set underneath but the top is still runny, add the salami and continue cooking until the eggs are completely set and brown underneath. Hold a large, preferably rather flat plate over the top of the frying pan, turn the pan right over and gently ease the frittata on to the plate. Add a little more oil to the pan, heat this and then slide the frittata back into the pan and continue cooking until the other side is brown.

Frittata ai peperoni

Sweet pepper omelette

TO SERVE FOUR

INGREDIENTS
225 g (8 oz) spinach
1–2 sweet red peppers, according to size
6 eggs (size 2)
2–3 tablespoons grated Parmesan cheese
2–3 tablespoons fine breadcrumbs
salt
olive oil

For this recipe the horn-shaped sweet peppers are preferable.

Clean the spinach, wash it thoroughly and cook it only in the water adhering to its leaves until it is soft. Drain well, squeeze dry, then chop. Slice off the top of the peppers cut into halves, remove the cores and seeds and dice the flesh. Put aside. Break the eggs into a bowl, add the cheese, breadcrumbs and salt. Beat well, then add the diced peppers and the chopped spinach. Heat a little oil in a frying pan, just enough to cover the bottom. Add the egg mixture, stir lightly for a moment or so with a fork and let it begin to set but from time to time levelling it down with the fork. When the eggs are set underneath, hold a large, preferably rather flat plate over the top of the frying pan, turn the pan right over and gently ease the frittata on to the plate. Add a little more olive oil to the pan, heat this and then slide the frittata back into the pan and continue cooking until the other side is brown.

Top: frittata con il salame;
bottom: frittata ai peperoni

86

any chopped leftover cooked vegetables, cooked carrots cut into rounds make an excellent frittata, so do leeks, thickly cut fried onions, and of course cooked and diced potatoes. To serve, the frittata should be put on to a hot or cold plate, depending on how it is to be served, and cut into wedges like a cake.

Frittata con spaghetti

Spaghetti omelette

TO SERVE FOUR

INGREDIENTS
6 eggs (size 2)
salt and pepper
1 cup of cooked spaghetti, chopped
40 g (1½ oz) butter
1 tablespoon finely chopped parsley
50 g (2 oz) grated sharp-flavoured cheese

Frittata con le vongole

Clam omelette

TO SERVE FOUR

INGREDIENTS
675 g (1½ lb) clams
4–5 tablespoons olive oil
6 eggs (size 2)
salt and pepper
2–3 sprigs parsley, finely chopped

Frittata di zucchini

Courgette omelette

TO SERVE FOUR

INGREDIENTS
225 g (8 oz) courgettes
3–4 ripe tomatoes
50 g (2 oz) butter
1 tablespoon olive oil
1 small onion, finely chopped
salt and pepper
6 eggs (size 2)

Leftover cooked noodles cut into short lengths, macaroni and other pasta shapes can all be made into a frittata and served with any of the pasta sauces.

Whisk the eggs lightly with salt and pepper. Cut the spaghetti into short lengths. Heat the butter in a pan, add the parsley, cheese and spaghetti, mix well, then add the eggs. Mix gently and cook until the underneath is brown and set. Hold a large, flat plate over the top of the frying pan, turn the pan right over and gently ease the frittata on to the plate. Add a little more oil to the pan, heat this and then slide the frittata back into the pan and cook until the other side is brown.

Wash the clams in several changes of water, wipe dry and put them into a pan with half the oil. Cover and cook over a moderate heat for 5–8 minutes until the shells open, discarding any that remain closed. Take from the pan and pick out the clams from their shells. Put aside in a bowl. Beat the eggs lightly, add a pinch of salt and pepper, the parsley and the clams. Mix gently but well. Heat the rest of the oil in a frying pan, add the egg and clam mixture and cook until set and brown underneath. Hold a large, flat plate over the top of the frying pan, turn the pan right over and gently ease the frittata on to the plate. Add a little more oil to the pan, heat this and then slide the frittata back into the pan and cook until the other side is brown.

Wash the courgettes and slice fairly thinly. Blanch and peel the tomatoes, discard their pips and chop coarsely. Heat the butter and oil together, add the onion and when it begins to change colour, add the courgettes, salt and pepper and continue cooking until the courgettes are just soft. Add the tomatoes and stir well but gently and the mixture must not become a mush. If the mixture should seem too dry, add a few drops of stock or water but no more than a few drops. When the tomatoes are soft, beat the eggs well and pour them over the mixture in the pan. Stir gently to ensure that the eggs are evenly distributed. Cook until the eggs are set and brown underneath. Hold a large, preferably rather flat plate over the top of the frying pan, turn the pan right over and gently ease the frittata on to the plate. Add a little more oil to the pan, heat this and then slide the frittata back into the pan and cook until the other side is brown.

Fish

With the exception of the mountainous regions in the north, Piedmont together with the Valle d'Aosta, Lombardy, Trentino, and Umbria in central Italy, all the regions of Italy have access to the sea. The Italians over the centuries have learned to have a hearty respect for seafood and to treat it with love and discretion.

Apart from the bounty of the sea, the abundance of fish from the great freshwater lakes of the country should not be ignored. The lakes of Lombardy and Veneto are filled with salmon trout, small golden carp, trout, roach, and grey mullet. Lake Como has a somewhat rare small fish, called *agono* or *missoltino*, which is protected by a clearly defined season. This small fish, a species of shad, is cooked fresh in various ways but is also dried and exported in boxes packed between layers of bayleaves. In Lake Trasimeno in Umbria there are roach, trout, mullet, perch and eels.

I have the impression that no other people are as fond of eels as the Italians. Although their collective name is *anguille*, the various types have quite different names. For example, *capitoni* – the fat, succulent eels found around Grosseto – are not only appreciated locally but exported in large quantities both to Rome and Naples to become part of the Christmas meal. Rome also has its own eels, the small *ciriole*, found in the Tiber, delicate in flavour and easy to digest. Pisa, of leaning tower fame, also has a gastronomic curiosity in its blind baby eels or elvers, locally called *cieche*, meaning the blind, or in dialect *le cèe*. These are caught in shoals at the mouth of the Arno, cooked in oil and flavoured with sage. Comacchio, in Emilia-Romagna, which lies amidst the miles of lagoons just north of Ravenna, produces some of the fattest eels in Italy and there are many recipes for cooking them. Eels are spit-roasted, baked, poached, made into stews using plenty of wine, or cooked in rich sauces flavoured with lemon and orange juice, pine-nuts, raisins and even chopped candied peel.

Tuscany also has plenty of fish, but when speaking of fish the Tuscans think only of one dish, their *cacciucco alla livornese*. And if when in this region you want fish fresher than fresh, go across to tiny Elba, the island to which Napoleon was once exiled, where the locals only buy fish when it is still writhing.

When in Venice I go as though on a pilgrimage to the fish market, to gaze at the sheer beauty of the fish, trays and trays of strange shapes in all the colours of a watery rainbow, delicate pinks, lilac and silver, gold and brittle lead blues; or I slip over to nearby Chioggia not only for a meal of fish in peace but also to watch the fishing fleet bring in the day's catch. And yet, with all this miracle catch of fresh fish on their doorstep, the Venetians are the largest consumers of salt fish, *baccalà*, prepared from cod, hake, whiting and other large white fish, all imported from Norway, to which the Venetian cooks give lavish attention, creating dishes which have become internationally famous.

In the realm of fish cooking, the Venetians observe several rules which to a great extent apply throughout the country. They do not often either bake or boil fish but when they do they serve it either cold or tepid. Mullet, angler-fish, mackerel, tuna and similar so-called blue fish usually are grilled and served hot simply with wedges of lemon. Sole, small fish and cutlets of fish such as John Dory are fried and served hot, also with lemon.

In my own region of Liguria the locals claim to cook fish with love and imagination. Here too you find fish galore, fascinating fish markets and small fishing ports where you can watch the tiny fishing fleets come in. A local speciality is the *bianchetti* or *gianchetti*, sardine fish fry, transparent and about 2 cm ($\frac{1}{2}$ in) long, which are usually fried in deep olive oil and served with lemon, or made into a *frittata*, or omelette. Genoa, the capital of the region, is particularly proud of its *buridda*, yet another version of the fish stew. Camogli, a small fishing port and on the tourist itinerary, holds a *sagra*, or festival, of fried fish in May; you can also attend a *sagra* of eels in Comacchio in April, and one of *baccalà* or *stoccafisso* in Alessandria in the same month. These are but three of dozens of similar food festivals all worth looking out for when on an Italian holiday.

Well down south in Apulia there is considerable fish and most methods of cooking it are an inheritance from the Greeks, early settlers in the region. Fish is prepared in hot, rich and thick sauces. Taranto has been famous for its oysters since the days of the Romans, as well as for its mussels – its great mussel beds are worth a visit. It is an immensely large fish port and boasts one of the finest and largest fish markets in the country, the variety making it a fish museum of living species. The coast of Sicily offers swordfish, tuna and a wealth of other fish, including mussels. Fish meals eaten anywhere in this region, often on quaysides in the open, are to be savoured and remembered.

Sardines actually do come from Sardinia and are fished in vast quantities to be piled in great silvery mounds in the local markets at the height of the season. Curiously, the Sardinians have quite a different approach to fish from their compatriots on the mainland. They scarcely consider mullet or whiting as worth eating, but their treatment of the sparlot, a member of the sea-bream family, shows nothing less than the tenderest gastronomic care. They too have their fish stew and here it is called either *buridda* or *cassòla* and is not to be confused with the Milanese dish of pork of the same name. The variety and freshness of the fish chosen for this dish make it quite impossible to reproduce outside of the island. Sardinians also produce *bottargo*, locally called *butteriga*, which is either tuna or grey mullet roe pounded in salted water, pressed and dried and served in slivers with lemon juice. Finally, the Sardinians have really tender lobsters, full of good flavour. These are grilled and served with an oil and lemon dressing, as indeed is so much of the fish eaten in Sardinia.

This second-century B.C. mosaic from the House of the Faun in Pompeii and now in the Museo Nazionale, Naples shows many varieties of Mediterranean fish and molluscs still common today in Italian cooking. The centre of the mosaic shows an octopus attacking a lobster.

1. Carp	6. Whiting	11. Dublin Bay prawns	16. Dover sole
2. Anchovies	7. Red mullet	12. Grey mullet	17. Sardines
3. Freshwater bream	8. Tuna fish steak	13. Octopus	18. King prawns
4. Mackerel	9. Wings of skate	14. Prawns	19. Giant squid and baby squid
5. Eel	10. Rainbow trout	15. Cuttlefish	20. Salt fish

Acciughe or Alici (Anchovies)

The anchovy is a small, bluish-silver fish found throughout the Mediterranean. Although it can and does attain 20 cm (8 in) in length it can be as small as 8 cm (3 in). The flesh of these little fish is excellent, white in colour and possessing a good flavour, quite different from that of the fillets preserved in oil. They are much used in Mediterranean cooking with literally dozens of fascinating recipes. Tobias Smollett wrote of them in 1764 in his *Travels through France and Italy*: 'Nothing can be more delicious than fresh anchovies fried in oil: I prefer them to the smelts of the Thames.'

In the following anchovy recipes other small fish, such as smelts or sprats, can be substituted. Consult your fishmonger.

Acciughe in padella

Fried fresh anchovies

TO SERVE FOUR

INGREDIENTS
Method 1
900 g (2 lb) fresh anchovies
flour for coating
275 ml ($\frac{1}{2}$ pint) olive oil
Method 2
900 g (2 lb) fresh anchovies
flour for coating
275 ml ($\frac{1}{2}$ pint) olive oil
1 clove garlic, crushed
1 tablespoon chopped
     parsley
salt and pepper to taste
150 ml ($\frac{1}{4}$ pint) dry white
     wine
1 tablespoon wine vinegar

Method 1

Remove the heads and gut the anchovies. Open them along the belly to the tail and carefully but firmly pull out the centre bone without breaking the fish into halves; this is not as difficult as it sounds as the bone does not appear to stick too tightly to the flesh. Wash and pat dry and dip in flour. Heat the oil in a fish frying pan, add the anchovies a few at a time and fry first on one side until brown, then turn and fry on the other side. Take out with a perforated spatula and drain on kitchen paper. Serve with lemon.

Method 2

Clean and prepare the anchovies as in Method 1. Heat the oil, add the crushed garlic, parsley, salt, pepper, wine and vinegar. Add the anchovies a few at a time and brown on each side as above. Take out with a perforated spatula and drain on kitchen paper. Serve hot – the anchovies need no further accompaniment.

Left : acciughe in padella;
right : acciughe in saôr

Acciughe in saôr

Marinated anchovies

TO SERVE FOUR

INGREDIENTS
900 g (2 lb) fried fresh
     anchovies
4 tablespoons olive oil
2 large onions, thinly sliced
275 ml ($\frac{1}{2}$ pint) white wine
     vinegar
25 g (1 oz) pine-nuts
     (optional)
50 g (2 oz) sultanas

A recipe from Venice where the expression *saôr*, a dialect word, indicates flavour or, in Italian, *sapore*. At one time the Venetians, who had more fish then they could contend with, preserved a great deal of their fish in *saôr*, but with the introduction of modern refrigeration this method nowadays seems only to be used with fresh anchovies and sardines, and sometimes with sole.

Prepare and fry the fish as in previous recipe (Method 1). Put the oil into a pan, add the onions and very lightly cook them until they become a golden brown. Add the vinegar and cook for 3 minutes. If the sultanas are dry, they must be steeped for a while in hot vinegar. Arrange the anchovies on the bottom of an earthenware serving dish, add the pine-nuts and sultanas and cover with the marinade. Leave in a cool place for 2 days before using. The marinated anchovies can be served as they are or, as in Venice, with polenta (*see page 50*).

Baccalà in bianco con patate

Salt fish in white sauce with potatoes

TO SERVE FOUR–SIX

INGREDIENTS
450 g (1 lb) salt fish
50 g (2 oz) butter
450 g (1 lb) potatoes,
    peeled and thinly sliced
salt and pepper
1 litre (1¾ pints) milk
275 ml (½ pint) single
    cream
parsley for garnishing

There is a difference between *baccalà* and stockfish which is not always realized. In Italy the names are used indiscriminately – *baccalà* is salt fish and includes cod, hake, coalfish and large haddock and is salted before it is dried. Stockfish also is made from the same types of fish but is dried in the sun and wind without being previously salted and is popular in African countries. It is not the salt fish used in Italy and in the south Mediterranean; so when Italians talk of *stoccafisso*, they mean *baccalà*. Salt fish in Italy is usually sold in one of three ways.
1. Dried, which then must be soaked for 48 hours with at least three or four changes of water;
2. Half-soaked, which means home-soaking for 12–24 hours, depending on how long

the vendor says he has soaked the fish;
3. *Baccalà*, which has been completely soaked, is sold still in the water.
In the following recipe stage 1 has been assumed.

Soak the salt fish in water for 48 hours, changing the water at least three or four times. Then pull off the skin and remove all the bones. Cut into stew-sized pieces. Heat the butter in a large pan, add the fish and the potatoes, very little salt but plenty of freshly ground pepper, stir gently, then add the milk and cream. Cover and cook over a moderate heat for 30–40 minutes. Serve on a hot serving dish, add a little of the sauce and garnish with small sprigs of parsley. Serve the rest of the sauce separately.

Stoccafisso alla siciliana

Salt fish Sicilian style

TO SERVE SIX

INGREDIENTS
675 g (1½ lb) salt fish
200 ml (scant ½ pint) olive
    oil
1 large onion, coarsely
    chopped
2–3 cloves garlic, crushed
275 ml (½ pint) dry white
    wine
675 g (1½ lb) ripe tomatoes
salt and pepper
4 good-sized potatoes,
    peeled and chopped
25 g (1 oz) capers
15 g (½ oz) pine-nuts
1 tablespoon sultanas
225 g (8 oz) large black
    olives, pitted

Prepare the salt fish (*see above*). Preheat the oven to 180°C, 350°F, Gas Mark 4. Heat the oil in a casserole, add the onion and garlic and stir well. Add the fish and wine and cook over a moderate heat until the wine is almost evaporated. While it is cooking, blanch, peel and chop the tomatoes to a pulp. Add to the pan with enough water to cover the fish generously. Sprinkle

lightly with salt and with plenty of freshly ground pepper and bring to the boil. Take the casserole from the heat and put into the oven. After the fish has been cooking for 1 hour, add the remaining ingredients, cover and continue cooking until the potatoes are soft and the sauce reduced. Serve in the casserole in which the fish was cooked.

Top: baccalà in bianco;
bottom: stoccafisso alla siciliana

Bisato sull'ara
Baked eel

TO SERVE FOUR

INGREDIENTS
675 g (1½ lb) skinned eel
plenty of bayleaves
salt and pepper

The literal translation of the title of this recipe is 'eels on the altar' and it comes from Murano near Venice where the famous glass is made. The *ara* or altar is the enclosed space above the wood-fired kilns used by the glass makers, where the red-hot glass was put to cool slowly. Someone discovered that the local fat eels could also be baked in the *ara* and although the old-fashioned kilns are being replaced by other kilns, local restaurants still make a speciality of cooking eels in these *are*. The *ara* does not give any special flavour to the eels, so they can be cooked in any type of available oven. It is important that a good fat eel is chosen for this dish.

Preheat the oven to 160°C, 325°F, Gas Mark 3. Cut the eel into 5–6 cm (2–2¼ in) lengths. Spread a good layer of fresh bay-leaves on the bottom of a baking dish (the Muranese prefer to use a copper pan), cover with the eel pieces, keeping them slightly apart. Sprinkle lightly with salt and pepper, add a little water (the eels should cook in their own fat as far as possible) and bake in the oven until very tender, for about 45 minutes.

Bisato in tecia
Stewed eels

TO SERVE FOUR–SIX

INGREDIENTS
675 g (1½ lb) skinned eel
4–5 tablespoons olive oil
50 g (2 oz) butter
2–3 sprigs parsley, chopped
1 clove garlic, chopped
3–4 sage leaves, chopped
150 ml (¼ pint) dry Marsala or sherry
225 g (8 oz) tomatoes, peeled, seeded and chopped
salt and pepper

For this Venetian recipe a good old, dry Marsala is recommended. The eels are served in their sauce with thick polenta (*see page* 50).

Cut the eels into pieces 5–6 cm (2–2¼ in) long. Heat the oil and butter together in a pan, add the eel pieces and cook over a good heat until they take on a strong golden brown colour. Add the parsley, garlic, sage leaves and the Marsala. Simmer this mixture for 5 minutes, then add the tomatoes, salt and pepper. Continue cooking over a good heat for another 20 minutes, by which time the sauce will be a rich brown colour and the eel tender.

Top : bisato sull'ara;
bottom : bisato in tecia

Top : orata al cartoccio; *bottom :* carpione al vino

Orata al cartoccio

Orata cooked in parcels

TO SERVE FOUR

INGREDIENTS
900 g (2 lb) orata or bream
1 onion
2 sprigs parsley
1 clove garlic
2–3 bayleaves
3–4 tablespoons olive oil
a little diced ham or bacon
lemon juice
salt and pepper

The orata, a gilt-head and a member of the bream family, is an excellent fish.

Scale, gut, wash and pat dry the fish but keep whole. Preheat the oven to 180°C, 350°F, Gas Mark 4. Finely chop the onion, parsley, garlic and bayleaves. Heat the oil, add the chopped ingredients and the ham and cook until the onion is soft. Rub a good-sized sheet of greaseproof paper or foil with oil, put the fried ingredients down the centre, add the fish, sprinkle well with lemon juice and lightly with oil, salt and pepper and fold over the foil, making

sure the contents are completely sealed. Bake in an oiled shallow baking pan in the oven for about 40 minutes. Serve in the foil.

Other smaller fish can be cooked *al cartoccio*, particularly small red mullet, trout and mackerel. The fish are prepared in the same manner but each fish, however small, is put into a separate packet. The smaller packets take 15–20 minutes to bake. Sliced dried mushrooms (previously soaked in warm water) can also be added to the mixture in the frying pan and also 2–3 tablespoons of tomato juice.

Carpione al vino

Carp in red wine

TO SERVE FOUR

INGREDIENTS
1.5 kg (3 lb) carp
1 each carrot, potato,
    stalk of celery
mixed chopped fresh
    herbs – bayleaves, thyme,
    parsley
pinch of salt
275 ml (½ pint) red wine

Carp is a fish of excellent flavour but must be carefully cleaned and washed in several changes of water and finally rinsed in lemon water. Some carp have scales, others none and some a few. This recipe calls for scaled carp.

Scale the carp. Remove the gall sac which lies behind the head, otherwise the fish will be bitter. Preheat the oven to 180°C, 350°F, Gas Mark 4. Wash and coarsely chop the vegetables, place in the bottom of a deep baking pan and sprinkle with the

herbs. Put the prepared fish on top, add the salt and wine and bake in the oven until it is tender, for about 30 minutes, basting frequently. When it flakes easily when tested with a fork, it is ready.

Take the fish from the pan with a perforated spatula and place it on a serving dish. Put into a warm oven to keep hot. Rub the vegetables and the fish liquid through a sieve and pour this sauce over the fish immediately before serving. Serve with plain boiled potatoes.

Merlano in salsa d'aceto

Whiting in a vinegar sauce

TO SERVE FOUR

INGREDIENTS
4 small whiting, about
    350 g (12 oz) each
pinch of salt
25 g (1 oz) butter
150 ml (¼ pint) wine
    vinegar
1 sprig rosemary
1 clove garlic, finely
    chopped
pepper

The *merlano*, a variety of small cod, is the Italian equivalent of the whiting, to which it is related.

Preheat the oven to 180°C, 350°F, Gas Mark 4. Scale and gut the fish, slit their bellies open from head to tail and remove the head and backbone. Wash the fish in slightly salted water and put them in a

buttered shallow baking dish. Sprinkle lightly with salt and slivers of butter. Bake in the oven for 25 minutes, or until the fish is tender and lightly browned. Just before the fish is ready, heat the vinegar in a small pan, add the rosemary, garlic and pepper. Bring gently to the boil and strain it over the fish just before serving.

Pesci all'agliata

Fish with a garlic sauce

TO SERVE FOUR

INGREDIENTS
675 g (1½ lb) fish
   steaks or small whole fish
oil for frying
3 cloves garlic, crushed
3 tablespoons vinegar
3–4 tablespoons soft
   breadcrumbs

The Genoese recommend mullet or *boghe*, a silvery fish with yellow tints, or fresh sardines with this sauce. Failing these, the recipe can also be made with any white fish steaks.

Fry the fish in oil and put on to a hot plate. Mix the garlic with the vinegar and then add enough breadcrumbs to make a thick spreading sauce. Smear this over the hot fish and leave for 15 minutes before serving.

Pesce spada alla griglia

Grilled swordfish

TO SERVE FOUR

INGREDIENTS
4 swordfish steaks
3–4 tablespoons olive oil
juice of 1 large lemon
salt and pepper
fresh herbs, finely chopped

Swordfish is a good eating fish with the palest of rose-pink meat. Although a member of the mackerel family, it can reach a weight of anything from 27–135 kg (60–300 lb). The town of Messina in Sicily is famed for its swordfish and in season it is fascinating to watch the fishing fleets lined up ready to sail, or having just returned from a successful encounter. The boats are specially designed, long and narrow, with a high steel mast, at the top of which the look-out man sits in the crow's nest. From this vantage point he can spot the fish in the clear waters and direct the helmsman, while the harpoonist, perched at the end of a long horizontal mast, takes his aim. Modern boats have made this operation less hazardous than of old when many fishermen lost a hand or fingers when landing the fish. Swordfish men are superstitious, and women are not allowed on board for they would bring ill fortune. The men always sing as they pass

the famous rock of Scylla and the whirlpool, Charybdis, no doubt to fool the monster of the seas, for the entrance to the Messina Straits, where the fish swarm in the mating season, is narrow and the fishermen remember the legend of the monster who snatched sailors from the seas.

All parts of the swordfish are eaten, including its liver, heart and roe (the latter is considered a delicacy). In Britain swordfish is not obtainable in all fish shops but if one tries hard it can be found from time to time. Other firm white fish steaks can be cooked in the same way as swordfish, particularly halibut, used opposite.

Skin the steaks. Mix the oil, lemon juice, salt, pepper and herbs in a bowl, add the steaks and leave them for 1 hour, turning from time to time. Heat the grill and cook the steaks for 4 minutes on either side. Serve at once with lemon.

San Pietro alla griglia

Grilled John Dory

TO SERVE FOUR–SIX

INGREDIENTS
1.5 kg (3 lb) John Dory, filleted
olive oil
lemon juice
salt and pepper
2–3 tablespoons grated breadcrumbs

The John Dory would never win a beauty prize, although it is not as ugly as the *rospo* or toadfish, but its flesh is good and is highly rated in Venice. Ask your fishmonger to fillet the fish, as only the fillets are eaten in this dish, but it would be sensible to ask him for the remains from the filleting and use them as a basis for a fish soup.

This method of cooking *pesce San Pietro* is traditional along the Adriatic coast. Other firm white fillets, particularly hake, cod and haddock, can be cooked in the same manner.

Put the fillets into a deep dish. Mix enough oil with lemon juice (two parts oil to one part lemon juice), salt, pepper and 2–3 tablespoons of fine breadcrumbs together to make a paste and spread this over the fillets. Leave for 1 hour. Heat the grill medium high, rub the fish lightly with oil and slowly grill for 15 minutes on either side, 30 minutes' cooking in all.

Serve with boiled potatoes.

Sarda a beccafico alla siciliana

Sicilian style fresh sardines

TO SERVE FOUR

INGREDIENTS
675 g (1½ lb) fresh sardines
1–2 cloves garlic, finely chopped
3–4 sprigs parsley, finely chopped
2 tablespoons fine breadcrumbs
50 g (2 oz) grated sharp-flavoured cheese
1 tablespoon capers, chopped
olive oil
1 egg, well beaten
275 ml (½ pint) tomato sauce (*page* 184)
salt and pepper

This is a popular Sicilian dish. *Beccafichi* are tiny birds much sought after in Sicily and in this dish the sardines are arranged to look like them. The same treatment can be applied to anchovies and other small fish. This is a fussy dish to prepare but well worth the trouble.

Preheat the oven to 220°C, 425°F, Gas Mark 7. Prepare the tomato sauce and keep hot in a *bain-marie*. Remove the heads and gut the sardines. Split them open down the belly almost to the tail (1). Carefully pull out the backbone (2). Mix together the garlic, parsley, breadcrumbs, cheese and capers and add just enough oil to make a fairly stiff stuffing. Paint the inside of each sardine with beaten egg (3), then fill each with a little of the stuffing and close them up firmly (4). Rub a shallow, oblong baking dish generously with oil and cover the bottom with a layer of the hot tomato sauce. Arrange the sardines in one layer in the dish, packing them close together with

their tails sticking up. Quite often bay-leaves are placed between the sardines. Pour the rest of the tomato sauce over the top, sprinkle with salt and pepper and bake in the oven for 20–25 minutes.

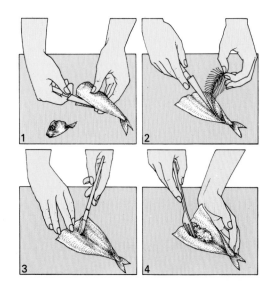

Sarde al forno al vino bianco

Sardines baked in white wine

TO SERVE FOUR

INGREDIENTS
675 g (1½ lb) fresh sardines
3 salted anchovies, filleted
100 g (4 oz) butter
salt and pepper
275 ml (½ pint) dry white wine

Sardines get their name from the island of Sardinia where the true variety abounds.

Preheat the oven to 180°C, 350°F, Gas Mark 4. Remove the heads and gut the sardines, split them open down the belly and pull out the backbones without splitting the fish. Wash in cold water and pat dry. Wash the anchovies thoroughly to remove any excess salt and pound them to a paste with half the butter. Spread a little of this mixture over the open side of each sardine. Take two sardines and sandwich them together. Repeat this procedure with the rest. Generously rub a round baking dish with butter and arrange the sardines on the bottom in one layer. Dot with slivers of butter, add a little salt and plenty of pepper, then the wine. Cover the pan and bake in the oven for 20–30 minutes, or until the sardines are cooked. Serve in the dish in which they were baked.

Top: sarde al forno al vino bianco; *bottom:* sarde a beccafico alla siciliana

Scapece alla vastese

Marinated skate

TO SERVE FOUR

INGREDIENTS
generous pinch saffron
1 litre (1¾ pints) white
    wine vinegar
4 tablespoons of olive oil
900 g (2 lb) skate, cut into
    pieces
flour for coating
pinch of salt

Dissolve the saffron in 3 tablespoons of the vinegar, leave for a few minutes, then stir into the remaining vinegar. Heat the oil in a large fish frying pan. Lightly coat each piece of skate with flour and fry in the hot oil until lightly browned on both sides. Take from the pan with a perforated spatula, drain on kitchen paper, sprinkle lightly with salt and place in a shallow

dish. Bring the vinegar to the boil, pour this over the fish and leave for 24 hours in a cool place to marinate. Drain and serve the fish cold.

Sgombri alla sarda

Sardinian style mackerel

TO SERVE FOUR

INGREDIENTS
4 mackerel
salt and pepper
flour for coating
2 large onions, thinly sliced
575 ml (1 pint) dry white
    wine
3 bayleaves
4 tablespoons olive oil
lemon slices for garnishing

The mackerel is a fish with an ancient history; it was well known to the Egyptians and to the Romans, who were so fond of it that they used to salt it for despatch to their legions abroad.

Gut the mackerel, remove the heads and tails, slit down the stomach, take out the backbone but do not divide the two halves. Wash well, pat dry, lay flat and lightly sprinkle with salt and dip into flour. Put a layer of onions into a casserole, add a layer of mackerel, skin side down, and continue in this way until all the ingredients are used up. Mix the wine with the bayleaves, add plenty of freshly ground

pepper and pour this over the fish, add the oil and cook gently, tightly covered, for 20–25 minutes, or until the fish is very tender.

Serve the mackerel with the onions in their sauce, garnished with lemon and with plain boiled potatoes.

102

Sgombri con marinata

Marinated mackerel

INGREDIENTS
4 mackerel
425 ml (¾ pint) white wine
salt and pepper
2–3 cloves
small stick of cinnamon
2–3 sprigs parsley
4 small onions
3 tablespoons olive oil
flour for coating
rosemary for garnishing

Remove the head and gut the mackerel; wash under running water. Put into a shallow dish, adding the wine, salt, pepper, cloves, cinnamon and parsley. Peel two of the onions and add to the marinade. Cover and leave for 5–6 hours, or overnight in the refrigerator.

Slice the remaining onions. Heat the oil in a shallow pan and fry the sliced onions gently. Take the fish from its marinade, pat dry and roll in flour. Add to the pan on top of the fried onions. Strain the marinade and add this, plus enough water to cover the fish completely. Bring to a gentle boil and cook over a moderate heat for about 30 minutes.

Serve the mackerel hot in its sauce and garnished with rosemary.

Top: sgombri con marinata;
bottom: sgombri alla sarda

Sogliole al Marsala

Sole with Marsala

TO SERVE FOUR

INGREDIENTS
8 sole fillets or other
   flat fish
1 egg, well beaten
fine semolina
butter
salt and pepper
1–2 tablespoons dry
   Marsala or sherry

Wash the fillets and gently pat them dry. Dip first into the beaten egg, then in the semolina. Heat enough butter in a large shallow pan to just cover the bottom. Add the fillets; they should all be cooking in the pan at one time, so if your pan is not large enough, use two pans. Fry the fillets until they are cooked through but not brown. Sprinkle lightly with salt and pepper and then with the Marsala. Continue cooking for a moment or so, then serve the fish in the sauce.

Sogliole al vino bianco

Sole cooked in white wine

TO SERVE TWO

INGREDIENTS
2 filleted sole, about 450 g
   (1 lb) each
75 g (3 oz) butter
1 spring onion, finely
   chopped
salt and freshly ground
   pepper, to taste
275 ml ($\frac{1}{2}$ pint) white wine,
   dry cider or beer
225 g ($\frac{1}{2}$ lb) small white
   grapes
2–3 tablespoons single
   cream

Preheat the oven to 180°C, 350°F, Gas Mark 4. Skin the soles, wash in running water, dry carefully, place in a large oval baking pan and sprinkle with slivers of butter, the scallion, salt, pepper and wine. Rub a piece of foil with butter and cover the fish. Cook in the oven for 20 minutes. Wash the grapes and remove the pips if necessary. After about 10 minutes remove the fish from the oven and pour about one-third of its liquid into a small casserole. Add the grapes to the fish and return to the oven to continue cooking.

Cook the fish liquid over a good heat, add the cream, whisking it all the time. Let this boil for 2–3 minutes. Take the pan from the heat and add the remaining butter, cut into slivers. Serve the sole on a hot serving plate, garnished with grapes and the sauce. Serve hot.

Tonno fresco in gratella

Grilled fresh tuna fish

TO SERVE FOUR

INGREDIENTS
4 tuna steaks
150 ml ($\frac{1}{4}$ pint) white wine
   vinegar
150 ml ($\frac{1}{4}$ pint) olive oil
salt and pepper
juice of 1 lemon

The steaks should be fairly thin and weigh between 100–175 g (4–6 oz) each and preferably cut from the belly.

Spread the steaks out on a large plate, sprinkle with vinegar and leave in a cool place for 30 minutes. Wipe dry. Rub the vinegar off the plate, replace the fish and cover with oil; sprinkle with salt and pepper. Leave in a cool place again, this time for 2 hours, turning the fish every 20 minutes. Drain well. Heat the grill and grill the steaks for 5 minutes on both sides. Serve at once with lemon juice and a little olive oil.

Other meaty, firm fish steaks can be prepared and grilled in the same manner.

Tonno fresco alla sarda

Tuna steaks Sardinian style

TO SERVE FOUR

INGREDIENTS
4 tuna steaks
4 cloves garlic, peeled
4 leaves each fresh basil
  and mint or ½ teaspoon
  dried
flour for coating
150 ml (¼ pint) oil,
  preferably olive
salt and pepper
1 tiny chilli pepper,
  chopped and with pips
  removed if preferred
275 ml (½ pint) red wine
1–2 sprigs parsley, chopped
100 g (4 oz) black olives,
  pitted and coarsely
  chopped
2 tablespoons fine
  breadcrumbs

Tuna is a saltwater fish which can grow to an enormous size. It is usually sold in slices or steaks. Its flesh is firm and compact and lends itself to a variety of methods of cooking. Fresh tuna fish is extremely popular in Italy. The preferred part of the fish generally is the belly, *ventresca*. Most tuna caught in Italian waters is found around the coasts of Sicily and Sardinia.

Wash the fish under cold running water and dry thoroughly. With a toothpick fix a clove of garlic and one leaf each of basil and mint on to each steak. Sprinkle each steak lightly with flour. Heat the oil in a shallow pan, add the fish and fry lightly on both sides until brown. Sprinkle with salt and pepper, preferably freshly ground black pepper, and the chopped chilli pepper. Add the wine, cover the pan and continue cooking over a very low heat until all the wine has evaporated. Add the parsley and olives, sprinkle with breadcrumbs, cover the pan again and continue cooking for a further 5 minutes. When the fish is very tender, add 2–3 tablespoons of warm water, stir gently and serve the steaks hot in their sauce.

Tranci di pesce alla livornese

White fish steaks in tomato sauce

TO SERVE FOUR

INGREDIENTS
4 fairly thick white fish
  steaks
4 tablespoons olive oil
3–4 sprigs parsley, chopped
4–5 tomatoes, peeled and
  chopped
150 ml (¼ pint) dry white
  wine
salt and pepper

Preheat the oven to 220°C, 425°F, Gas Mark 7. Heat the oil in a pan, add the parsley, tomatoes, wine, salt and pepper and cook over a moderate heat until it is a thick sauce. Pour half the sauce into a shallow casserole, add the fish and cover with the rest of the sauce. Bake in the oven for about 15 minutes, or until tender.

Triglie alla ligure

Red mullet poached in a wine and tomato sauce

TO SERVE FOUR

INGREDIENTS
4 red mullet, about 225 g
  (8 oz) each
olive oil for frying
1 clove garlic, chopped
2–3 sprigs parsley, finely
  chopped
150 ml (¼ pint) dry white
  wine
4 ripe tomatoes, peeled and
  chopped
2–3 anchovy fillets, finely
  chopped
pinch of salt
12 black olives, pitted
1 tablespoon capers
lemon juice

Mullet are a delicate fish and need careful handling.

Scale the fish, wash and wipe dry. It is not usual to gut them as the fish gains in flavour if cooked with the gut. Heat the oil, add the garlic and parsley and fry for 2–3 minutes. Add the wine, cook this for a few minutes, then add the tomatoes and anchovies. Stir well and continue cooking until the tomatoes are a pulp, about 15 minutes. Add the fish, sprinkle lightly with salt and continue cooking until they are tender, about 15 minutes. Immediately before taking the fish from the pan, add the olives, capers and a good squeeze of lemon juice. Serve the sauce with the fish.

Triglie alla pescatori

Red mullet with white wine

TO SERVE FOUR

INGREDIENTS
12 small red mullet
flour for coating
olive oil
1 onion, finely chopped
1–2 cloves garlic, finely
  chopped
450 g (1 lb) tinned tomatoes
2–3 sprigs parsley, finely
  chopped
mixed fresh herbs – thyme,
  bay, rosemary or basil
pinch of salt
275 ml (½ pint) dry white
  wine

Lightly scale the fish, wash and wipe dry. Roll in flour. Heat plenty of oil and fry the fish until brown all over, turning them carefully from time to time. Take from the pan with a perforated spatula and drain on kitchen paper. Pour a little of the oil into another pan, add the onion and garlic, and fry until the onion softens, then add the tomatoes, stir well and mash to a pulp. Cook the sauce for about 10 minutes, then add the parsley and herbs, a little salt and the wine. Cook over a low heat until the sauce is thick and much reduced. Add the mullet, cook them for a moment or so until reheated, then serve very hot. Serve in a large shallow serving dish.

Top to bottom : tranci di pesce alla livornese; triglie alla ligure; triglie alla pescatori

Cefalo ripieno
Stuffed grey mullet

TO SERVE FOUR

INGREDIENTS
4 small grey mullet –
    about 350 g (12 oz) each
    or 2 larger ones
100 g (4 oz) black olives,
    pitted and chopped
2–3 sprigs parsley, finely
    chopped
3 cloves garlic, finely
    chopped
salt and pepper
olive oil
275 ml (½ pint) dry white
    wine
lemon wedges for
    garnishing

The grey or striped mullet is not related to the red mullet and is caught on both sides of the North Atlantic and along the coasts of the North Pacific. It is a fish with a coarse but firm white flesh. Instead of grey mullet, small whiting could be used in the same manner.

Scale, thoroughly wash and clean the fish. Mix the chopped ingredients, add salt and pepper and enough oil to bind them. Push a little of this stuffing into each mullet. Put a little oil, about 4 tablespoons, into a shallow pan, add the fish and gently fry them until they begin to change colour. Sprinkle with salt and pepper, add the wine and either continue cooking on top of the stove or bake in a hot oven for 15 minutes. Serve with wedges of lemon.

Trote in mattone
Trout in a fish brick

TO SERVE FOUR

INGREDIENTS
4 small trout
a little olive oil

In Tuscany fish bricks, *mattoni*, are produced on the same lines as the well-known chicken brick but shaped to take fish. They come in various sizes and make fish cooking very simple; they also reduce fishy smells in the kitchen.

Soak the brick in cold water for 10 minutes. Rub the fish lightly with oil, put into the brick, cover and place in a cold oven. Heat the oven to moderate (180°C, 350°F, Gas Mark 4) and keep it at that temperature until the trout are tender, 20–30 minutes. Serve with plain boiled potatoes.

Trote lessa all'aglio
Trout with garlic sauce

TO SERVE FOUR

INGREDIENTS
4 small trout
450 g (1 lb) potatoes
1 small bread roll
white wine vinegar
salt and pepper
8–10 cloves garlic
olive oil
1 lemon, sliced

Clean the trout and poach in lemon-flavoured boiling water until tender, for about 15 minutes. Leave them in their liquid to cool. Peel the potatoes, cut into halves or quarters and boil in salted water. While these are cooking, prepare the sauce. Pull off the soft inside from the roll, crumble it and soak in vinegar. Squeeze dry and sprinkle with salt and pepper. Crush the garlic and mix into the bread. Gradually add enough oil to make a sauce of mayonnaise consistency. Drain the potatoes. To serve, take the trout from its liquid and place on a serving dish. Arrange the hot potatoes on one side and the slices of lemon on the other. Serve the sauce separately.

Top left to right : cefalo ripieno; trote in mattone; *bottom :* trote lessa all'aglio (only three shown)

108

Molluscs

Quite extraordinary quantities of molluscs are consumed in Italy, some of which look very pretty but which on the whole look more interesting than they are. However, they can vary tremendously in shape, size, colour and most particularly both in flavour and tenderness. Some are both tough and rubbery, and sometimes no amount of careful cooking overcomes this state. However, against this, many of the smaller varieties, which one finds in particular along the Ligurian and Adriatic coasts, can be very tender, with a good flavour, and can usually find a place in the *fritto misto al mare*, or fish salad. The *calamari* and the *totani* are closely related, with eight long tentacles and two short ones and roundish bodies, while the *seppia* or inkfish is somewhat longer but with the

same number of tentacles, long and short. Recipes for both can be interchanged.

When most Britons think of octopus, they think of monsters of the deep, in tropical seas, but the varieties eaten in Italy and other Mediterranean waters are far from monsters; in fact, like the tiny Ligurian octopus, locally called *moscardini*, they are anything but monsters and when properly cooked can be well flavoured and tender. Again these are usually sold cleaned but if you come across those which are not, they must be skinned, their insides and eyes removed, as well as the mouth and beak, and thoroughly washed.

In Naples, where they consider themselves to be connoisseurs of octopus, they simply boil and serve them with olive oil, lemon juice and freshly ground black pepper.

Calamari farciti

Stuffed squid

TO SERVE FOUR

INGREDIENTS
8 large squid
3 cloves garlic, finely chopped
50 g (2 oz) soft breadcrumbs
1 tablespoon grated cheese
2–3 sprigs parsley, finely chopped
1–2 anchovy fillets, finely chopped
salt and pepper
1 egg
4 tablespoons olive oil
275 ml (½ pint) dry white wine
1 lemon

Today it is usual for a fishmonger to clean squid and other molluscs; but if you do it yourself, wash the squid well and remove the eyes, ink sac and tentacles (1). Discard the eyes and ink sac and then finely chop the tentacles and mix with the garlic, breadcrumbs, cheese, parsley, anchovy fillets, salt and pepper. Mix well, then add

the egg and again mix thoroughly. Push this stuffing into the squid and sew up the open end (2). Heat the oil in a large pan, add the squid and cook gently until they begin to change colour. Add the wine, cover the pan and cook over a low heat for 30–40 minutes, depending on their size. Serve hot, garnished with slices of lemon.

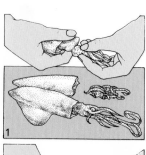
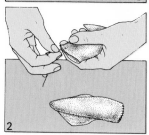

Seppioline in padella

Cuttlefish cooked in a frying pan

TO SERVE FOUR

INGREDIENTS
900 g (2 lb) cuttlefish,
  cleaned and prepared by
  the fishmonger
flour for coating
150 ml (¼ pint) olive oil
3–4 cloves garlic, finely
  chopped
3–4 tablespoons finely
  chopped parsley
salt and pepper
2 lemons, thickly sliced

Thoroughly wash t___ ___ ___ ___
cold running water, ___ ___ ___ ___
with a cloth. Coat w___ ___ ___ ___
a sieve and shake o___ ___ ___ ___
oil in a large fryin___ ___ ___ ___
and cook over a f___ ___ ___ ___
begin to change ___ ___ ___ ___
with a woode___ ___ ___ ___
tender, after 2___ ___ ___ ___
the garlic an___ ___ ___ ___
salt and pepp___ ___ ___ ___
pan once m___ ___ ___ ___
serve the c___ ___ ___ ___
fresh lemo___

Polpi al vino bianco

Octopus baked in white wine

TO SERVE FOUR–SIX

INGREDIENTS
1.6 kg (3 lb) octopus,
  cleaned and prepared by
  the fishmonger
3 tablespoons olive oil
575 ml (1 pint) white wine
2–3 sprigs parsley, finely
  chopped
salt and pepper

Preheat the oven to 180°C, 350°F, Gas Mark 4. Place the prepared octopus in a casserole, add the rest of the ingredients, cover tightly and bake in the oven for about 2½ hours. Remove the dish from the oven, take out the octopus, cut it into large pieces, arrange in a hot serving dish and keep warm. Pour the sauce into a pan, cook it until it is reduced by half and pour over the octopus.

111

Scampi and prawns

The name scampi in some parts of Italy is applied indiscriminately to both the giant or Adriatic prawn, as well as other large prawns (called in Liguria *gamberoni*) but also more disastrously to the Dublin Bay prawn, which is not a prawn at all but what the French call a *langoustine*.

The confusion in the name has arisen because the giant Adriatic prawns originally were, and still are, called scampi in Venice. They are really large, from 9–15 cm (3½–6 in) long, pale amber in colour with a thick shell and no claws. Their flesh, which fills the body from head to tail, is delicious, tender and bringing with it the true flavour and aroma of the sea. Similar prawns, called *mazzacuagne*, are found also in the Bay of Gaeta. These giant prawns are very much larger than prawns of British waters.

The Dublin Bay prawn is not a prawn at all. Its official name is *Nephrops norvegicus* and it belongs properly to Norwegian waters where it grows to some 26 cm (10 in) in length. It is also found in large numbers in Welsh and Irish waters, where it is much smaller. Its flesh, while extremely good, is less flavoursome than the Adriatic prawns but it has a good consistency. Only the flesh from its tail is eaten. Another difference between the Dublin Bay prawn and the true prawn is that the former does not turn red when cooked, whereas the true prawn does.

The story of the present-day fame of the Dublin Bay prawn is somewhat ironic. Around 1914 Dublin Bay prawns migrated from their cold northern waters far south to the Adriatic. Once they arrived off Venice and were joyfully discovered, they were dubbed scampi and the name has remained with them ever since, even spreading to other countries. Today the name is fashionable and sadly most people do not know what they should really be eating when they order scampi. The Dublin Bay prawn used to be thrown out of the nets of North Sea fishermen before the First World War until an Italian restaurateur discovered them in Venice and had them flown to Britain where he served them with great aplomb in his establishment. Suddenly there was a universal demand for these succulent shellfish. Today the Dublin Bay prawn has come into his own, albeit more often under a false or wrong name.

Top left : scampi all'olio e limone;
right : gamberi alla panna;
centre : scampi alla griglia;
bottom : scampi fritti con pastella

Scampi all'olio e limone

Prawns with lemon and oil dressing

TO SERVE FOUR

INGREDIENTS
450 g (1 lb) fresh prawns
3–4 tablespoons olive oil
juice of ½ a lemon
salt and pepper
lemon for garnishing

This recipe is only suitable for really large fresh prawns.

Cook the prawns in lightly salted boiling water for 10 minutes. While they are cooking, whisk the oil, lemon, salt and pepper together. Take the cooked prawns from the pan, shell them as quickly as possible and drop them, still warm, into the dressing. Garnish with slices of lemon.

Gamberi alla panna

Prawns in cream sauce

TO SERVE THREE–FOUR

INGREDIENTS
24 large uncooked prawns
1 tablespoon Continental
   mustard
50 g (2 oz) butter
150 ml (¼ pint) single
   cream
2 tablespoons brandy
1–2 sprigs parsley
   (optional)

Although this recipe is meant for uncooked prawns, cooked and peeled large prawns can be used instead. If using uncooked prawns, take off their shells and remove the thin black thread.

Rub the prawns with mustard. Heat the butter in a pan large enough to take all the prawns at once. Add the prawns and cook quickly for a few minutes. Add the cream and cook over a very low heat for 5 minutes, add the brandy and continue cooking for another 15 minutes. Just before serving, add the sprigs of parsley, if using. Serve on a hot plate.

Scampi alla griglia

Grilled giant prawns

TO SERVE FOUR

INGREDIENTS
12 giant prawns
salt and pepper
5 tablespoons olive oil
finely chopped parsley
lemon juice

Cut the shell of each prawn lengthwise along the back. Pull off the black thread and sprinkle each prawn lightly with salt and pepper. Rub well with oil. Grill the prawns under a moderate heat for about 10 minutes. Serve hot sprinkled with parsley, oil and lemon juice.

Scampi fritti con pastella

Fried scampi in batter

TO SERVE FOUR

INGREDIENTS
24 scampi tails
100 g (4 oz) flour
½ teaspoon salt
2 eggs, well beaten
150 ml (¼ pint) milk or
   water
olive oil
lemon wedges for
   garnishing

Peel the tails. Mix the flour with the salt, add the eggs, mix well then add the milk or water (you can use beer if preferred, it makes a lighter batter). Mix to a smooth, loose batter. Prepare a pan of boiling hot oil for deep frying. Dip the scampi tails into the batter, a few at a time, and fry them at once in the hot oil for a few minutes. Drain well and serve with thick wedges of fresh lemon.

Instead of making a batter, the scampi tails can be simply coated in flour, dipped in milk or egg and breadcrumbs and then deep fried.

Meat

An attempt to describe the various cuts of meat in Italy can only prove abortive, for not only do they differ completely from British and American cuts but also from province to province in Italy. Equally they are not easy to recognize laid out on the butchers' marble slabs, for meat is usually sold deboned, and if for roasting neatly rolled and tied. And if this is not enough to confuse both Italians and foreigners, each region has a different name for the same cut of meat. Take, as one typical example, the eight main names for a piece of rump roast. Milan calls it *scamone*; Rome *pezza*; Turin *sotto filetto*; Bologna *fetta*; Naples *colarda*; Foggia and Calabria *a codata*; Palermo *sotto codata*; while Catania, just round the corner, prefers *osso piatto*. The name of only one cut remains the same throughout the country, the *filetto*.

Twenty or so years ago it was estimated that half of all Italian families ate meat only on Sundays, if then. Today things have changed and the Italians have become heavy meat eaters, with steaks and roast beef something of a status symbol.

One of the results of that earlier lack of meat was that the average Italian house-wife learnt to make good use of all cuts and turn them into appetizing dishes that over the years have become traditional. Offal, in all its forms, the heart, liver, brain, and spleen, were and are still today cooked together with assorted herbs, tomatoes, onions and garlic, sweet peppers and usually wine. Also considerable use is made of boiled and stewed meats, often from overworked beasts and therefore rather tough. Boiled meats, for example, provide not only a main dish of meat but also stock for soups or sauces. Leftover meat is turned into a *ragù* for pasta or a stuffing for vegetables. Fresh minced meat is used for meat loaves and meat balls.

When roasting or grilling meats, the Italian taste is for rare to almost raw or, as they say in Italian, *blu* or *quasi cruda*. In Tuscany, where the people have always been meat eaters (as they have also in Piedmont), grilling is preferably done over a charcoal fire and meat cooked in the oven is regarded, correctly, as baked rather than roasted.

An endearing characteristic of the Italians is their extreme chauvinism. There-fore, it comes as no surprise to find Italians convinced that their meat is the best in the world, a claim which many would dispute. After this flamboyant claim, the cattle-producing provinces all claim 'the finest meat in Italy'. The butchers and cattle breeders of Piedmont are in no doubt that they are selling Italy's finest beef, an opinion not shared by the man from Padua, who knows he is doing this, as well as living in a town 'with the largest meat market in the world'. The Tuscans have no shadow of doubt that there is nothing to equal the meat coming from their special breed of cattle, the *chianina*, reared solely for eating and naturally 'the oldest, tallest and heaviest breed of cattle in the world' which produces a 'young beef' neither true beef nor true veal, but certainly tender. It is sold as *vitellone*.

Veal generally is called *vitello*, but the Tuscans confuse the issue. They also use the word *vitella* which means heifer, a word current south of Florence, while north of the city we find *vitello*, which should be meat from a calf which has lived for two or three months. There is also *vitello al latte* which is milk-fed and almost white in colour.

Veal is such a favourite meat in Italy it has been suggested that the very name Italy is derived from the word *vitello* or *vitella*, because the people – Ostrogoths, Lombards, Byzantines – who inhabited the region before it became known as Italy were immense consumers of veal.

Lamb and kid are also great Italian favourites, but the Italians are not great eaters of mutton (although some of their so-called lamb looks oddly large), and goat, although eaten, does not have many recipes for its cooking. The Italians consider the goat rather too odorous, whereas the kid is eaten with considerable enthusiasm, and there are many recipes for it.

Pork is perhaps not one of the favourite fresh meats, and is one of the cheaper ones. Pigs are bred to a monstrous size, mainly to be turned into hams, bacon, sausages and salami. However, today there is a new, smaller and leaner pig being bred to provide a pork for the table for roasting. In Umbria, however, considerable quantities of spit-roasted pig are eaten and sold still on the spit in the market and in the piazza, as well as in many delicatessen stores. They are beautifully roasted and stuffed with rosemary. In Sardinia sucking pigs are spit-roasted in front of wood fires or wrapped in myrtle leaves and baked in a trench, heated with red-hot embers which have been allowed to die down. The trench is covered with earth, a second fire is built on top and the pig cooks slowly below.

A glance into the window of the average butcher's shop in the main Sardinian towns reveals some meat oddities. Offal from lambs, pigs and kid – and their heads. Well displayed are horses' heads from which the brains have been removed – not to be discarded but made into a favourite Sardinian dish. Another Sardinian recipe, *cordula* or *corda*, dates back to Homer who noted in his *Odyssey* that this was a dish of plaited lamb or kid intestines, herb-flavoured and grilled over charcoal. There is a similar dish in the south of Italy called *gnemmarielli*. But all is not pork and offal in Sardinia, and escalopes of veal cooked in the local wine, Vernaccia, are much appreciated.

Sicily cannot boast of her meat dishes, although one local butcher told me, while admitting this, that he personally had over a thousand recipes for turning poor quality meat into dishes of the utmost delicacy. There is no doubt that the Sicilians have learned to make the most of their cuts of meat with complicated but aromatic sauces and in stuffings.

Horse meat has many passionate adherents, even today, not because it is cheaper, which it is not, but because it is claimed that the meat has more flavour (I think it is rather sweet) and also is more nourishing. It is certainly rich and red looking against the usually more pallid veal. Donkey and mule meat at one time were considered superior to horse meat, and there is still a considerable taste for both. In the township of San Agata in Sicily a mortadella is made from donkey meat.

Apart from fresh meats the list of Italian smoked and cured meats is imposing, with a variety which beggars description. Generally these meats are served as antipasto, not as main-course meats. Many of them, together with sausages and salami, are made in the mountain villages by peasants, using recipes unchanged from those advocated by the Roman Apicius centuries ago. Those connoisseurs who can, go to the villages at the time of curing to buy up a store of hams, bacons, etc., or go to make an order at the time of slaughtering, staying on long enough to join in the communal supper of pigs' offal made by the village women, a dish cooked in wine flavoured with local herbs, hot peppers and tomatoes, served naturally with a glass of red wine, as strong and as rugged as the people and the food itself.

Ancient Roman carved relief drawn by Pietro Santi Bartoli in 1697

Bollito or bollito misto
Boiled meats

Do not be misled by the name as boiled meats may sound dull to some ears but this is one of the great dishes of northern Italy. It is a dish which is usually prepared for at least 12 people and even then there will be much left over. Served correctly, with the right meats and vegetables, it is a fine convivial dish or, as they say in Liguria, a table dish, always served with good local table wines.

Probably the best known of the several Italian *bollito* dishes is that from Piedmont and, if travelling near Cuneo in the early morning on the day of the local cattle market, do not hesitate to throw caution to the winds and stop and make a breakfast of a portion of *bollito misto*. From very early in the morning until midday the restaurants are busily serving *bollito*. Some of these 'restaurants' are little more than stands and operate only on cattle-market day. Apart from the fun of the fair or market, one has a splendid opportunity to see the local farmers as well as join in their meal.

For those who know the French pot-au-feu it could be said that, for example, the Piedmontese version is the same but far more lavish in its presentation and number of ingredients. But it is served rather differently, far more dry than the pot-au-feu, and the stock which results from the cooking is not offered as a soup but is put aside to be later included in a sauce for a risotto or a pasta dish.

According to the Piedmontese, the meat for boiling must not only be of the finest quality but rich in variety, young veal from the Langhe (the Barolo country), somewhat more elderly veal from Carrù and Monferrato, beef from anywhere in the province, a calf's head, pig's feet, a chicken or so, and often a turkey. Add to all this carrots, celery and onions stuck with cloves, and you can see it is not just an ordinary 'boiled beef and carrots' sort of meal. In Moncalvo, also in Piedmont, is found what is considered to be the finest *bollito* of all; there is talk of a secret formula consisting of seven types of meat, seven of vegetable, three sauces and a variety of herbs. One can imagine the size of pot required for this lot and the cooking time involved. When the dish is served in a family, the head of the house must carve the meat, and in particular the huge piece of beef, without crumbling it – no easy feat since the meat is cooked until very tender indeed. All *bollito* dishes have one thing in common – the piece of beef takes pride of place. All are served dry, but with a sauce; in Piedmont with a green, red or anchovy sauce and in Emilia-Romagna with *mostardo di Cremona*, which is a sweet concoction of candied fruits in a mustard-based sauce which, although like a sweet chutney, goes well with all these mouth-watering meats.

A genuine *bollito* is expensive and I would not suggest trying to compromise, since for some dishes there can be no compromise, so wait until you visit Piedmont to taste one.

Piatto elefante
Elephant platter

A delightful misnomer, for at first glance you might well think this is a dish of elephant steaks. It is a vast meal or mixture of local foods, the main course being served on an enormous platter. The meal is served in three courses, the first a mammoth dish of antipasto with smoked and boiled hams, salami and assorted local sausages, a selection of salads and often, depending on the company, hard-boiled eggs in a mayonnaise sauce, sardines and tuna fish. Enough for most of us as a main course. But no, it goes on to a tremendous second course served on a three-foot-long dish piled high with mixed meats and vegetables. These may and indeed do vary from time to time, but there is an invariable rule that there must be at least six different kinds of meat and 12 different sorts of vegetables, preferably cooked in varying ways. If all the meats are local, so are all the methods of cooking. The meats will include those grilled, fried and boiled; the vegetables, sauerkraut, potatoes, carrots, salsify, peas, beans, courgettes, tomatoes; also pasta and rice to help fill up empty corners. Finally, if you are still able to face it, comes a platter of local cheeses, stewed and fresh fruits and cakes. A black coffee and a liqueur or *digestivo* is a good way of rounding off the meal.

However, it is no good trying to order such a gargantuan meal unless you are a party of at least four, preferably far more, for it is not a dish that is actually on tap all the time. But, if you are in the town of Bressanone in the province of Bolzano with a party, try it in the spirit of 'once in a lifetime'.

Fritto misto
Mixed fry

A *fritto misto* has no set rules or set servings. It may consist of three ingredients or a dozen, or even more on very special occasions. All the ingredients must be very fresh and cut in small pieces but all more or less the same size, not like a British mixed grill in which you may have a largish chop alongside a small kidney. Another important point is that the *misto* must be served as soon as it comes from the pan.

Such dishes differ from region to region or, if you like, from town to town and even restaurant to restaurant. In Liguria, for example, the local *fritto misto* is more likely to be a mixture of fish than meats, while Emilia-Romagna proudly calls its *misto, grande fritto misto,* and grand it is, with 15 or more different ingredients. Let me list them, for it does give an idea of what can be found in an Italian *fritto misto,* although admittedly seldom as many all at one time: fried sweet custard; veal or pork cutlets, or both; apple fritters; savoury beignets; baby lamb cutlets; Bologna-style skewered meats, including brains, bone marrow, mortadella and Gruyère cheese. Then come rice croquettes, and several varieties of vegetable fritters. There are also small fried artichokes, sliced courgettes and aubergines or sweetbreads. Some of these ingredients are cooked plainly in butter, others are dipped in egg and breadcrumbs or a batter and fried in deep oil, usually olive oil. All are served as soon as they are taken from the pan.

Some *fritto misto* combinations have become better known than others. For example, a *fritto misto milanese* should consist of fried liver, heart, brains, sweetbreads, potato croquettes, bone marrow gently simmered in butter, thin slices of fried veal, fried courgettes, tiny artichokes and cauliflower flowers. A *fritto misto fiorentino* is less varied, with fried chicken breasts, artichoke hearts, brains and sweetbreads and fried Mozzarella cheese. Therefore, one realizes that a *fritto misto* is simply a question of preparing any of the above-mentioned ingredients in the usual manner of frying, remembering to keep the items a uniform size and deciding whether a batter or a coating of eggs and breadcrumbs, or *au naturel,* is the best suited. Generally a *fritto misto* is considered as an antipasto, but there is nothing to prevent one from serving one as a main luncheon dish followed by a salad and some cheese.

Detail from an Etruscan urn showing the preparations for a feast

Brasato al Barolo
Beef in red wine

TO SERVE FOUR

INGREDIENTS
900 g (2 lb) boned rib lean
  beef
1 bottle Barolo or other red
  wine
1 each onion, carrot, stalk
  of celery, all coarsely
  chopped
1–2 bayleaves
salt and pepper
50 g (2 oz) butter or other
  cooking fat

Barolo is a fine red wine from Piedmont. Lamb, kid and game meat is also cooked in a similar fashion in the Barolo region.

Put the meat into a bowl with the wine, vegetables, bayleaves and freshly ground black pepper. Cover and leave for 24 hours. Take the meat from the marinade, wipe it dry, then roll up and tie it neatly with string. Heat the fat in a casserole, add the meat and brown it all over. Strain the marinade over the meat and cook fairly rapidly until the liquid has been reduced by half. Add salt to taste, lower the heat, cover the pan and cook the meat slowly for about 2 hours, or until it is very tender. Take the meat from the pan, slice rather thickly, discard the string, arrange on a hot serving dish and pour the gravy over it.

Manzo alla certosina
Beef cooked Carthusian style

TO SERVE FOUR

INGREDIENTS
900 g (2 lb) sirloin beef,
  boned
2–3 tablespoons olive oil
25 g (1 oz) butter
50 g (2 oz) speck or fat
  bacon, chopped
salt, pepper and freshly
  grated nutmeg
4 anchovy fillets
1–2 sprigs parsley, finely
  chopped
stock or water

Speck is very, very fat pork and available in some supermarkets (see page 213).

Roll up the meat and tie with string. Heat the oil in a large pan together with the butter and speck and cook gently until the fat has run from the speck. Add the meat and a pinch of salt, pepper and nutmeg and cook until the meat is brown, turning it from time to time. Add the anchovies, parsley and stock to almost cover, then cook gently for 2 hours. From time to time add more liquid, if needed. The sauce should be thick and plentiful. When the meat is quite tender (in Italy this means 'it can be cut with a spoon'), take it from the pan, discard the string, slice thickly and arrange on a large hot serving plate. Pour the sauce through a sieve over the meat and serve at once.

Carbonata
Beef stew with red wine

TO SERVE FOUR

INGREDIENTS
900 g (2 lb) sirloin beef
flour for coating
100 g (4 oz) butter
1 medium-sized onion,
  coarsely chopped
575 ml (1 pint) red wine
garlic to taste
8–10 juniper berries, well
  crushed
salt and pepper

This is a typical 'antique' Piedmontese dish of good quality beef cooked in red wine. The recipe varies in different parts of the province. For example, in San Vincent, a pleasant alpine town at the foot of Monte Rosso, the meat is cut into strips, whereas in the Matterhorn area the meat is sliced and, instead of wine, a rather bitter beer is used, as in France and in Belgium for a dish of the same name. In Piedmont *carbonata* is usually served with polenta or with large stuffed onions. This recipe originated in the last century and calls for preserved meat, but today fresh meat is preferred.

The *carbonata* can be prepared the day before it is required and then gently reheated; it will also keep for several days in the refrigerator.

Cut the meat into slices or stew-sized pieces and lightly coat with flour. Heat the butter in a large pan, add the meat and cook until it has changed colour but is not brown. Take from the pan but keep hot. Add the onion to the pan and fry until very brown, return the meat and cook over a simmering heat for about 15 minutes, adding about one-quarter of the wine, the garlic and juniper berries. Continue to cook, uncovered, until the wine has completely evaporated, then add the rest of the wine and continue cooking, covered, until the meat is very tender for 1½–2 hours. Just before serving, add salt and freshly ground black pepper and serve with hot, stiff polenta (see page 50) or stuffed onions (see page 169).

Top : brasato al Barolo; *bottom left to right :* manzo alla certosina; carbonata

Bistecca alla pizzaiola

Steaks in Neapolitan
tomato sauce

TO SERVE FOUR

INGREDIENTS
salsa alla pizzaiola
  (*page* 184)
4 beef steaks
olive oil for frying

This recipe is the answer to meat which is
not as tender as it should be. Instead of
steaks, thickish slices from a round of beef
may be used but they will require longer
time to cook.

First make the sauce. Beat the steaks until
fairly thin, taking care not to break them.
Cut away any skin or sinews. Heat the oil
in a shallow pan, add the steaks and cook
until brown on both sides. Spread the
tomato sauce over the steaks, cover the pan
and continue cooking over a low heat for
at least another 10 minutes, longer if the
meat is still not sufficiently tender. Serve
without any additional vegetable, except
perhaps a green salad.

Capretto all'ascolana

Kid Ascolana style

TO SERVE FOUR–SIX

INGREDIENTS
900 g (2 lb) leg or loin of kid
12 thin small rashers bacon
50 g (2 oz) butter, slivered
salt and pepper
275 ml (½ pint) meat stock
275 ml (½ pint) Verdicchio or other dry white wine
2–3 sprigs parsley
2–3 cloves garlic
175 g (6 oz) soft breadcrumbs
150 ml (¼ pint) dry Marsala or sherry

Young goat or kid is often preferred to lamb and considered a delicacy in most parts of Italy. It is at its best around Easter. Kid is available in Britain, in areas where there are Italians and other Mediterranean people living. Verdicchio is a sound white wine from the Marches made from grapes of the same name. Lamb can also be cooked in the same manner.

Cut the kid into 12 equal-sized pieces or ask your butcher to do this for you. Preheat the oven to 160°C, 325°F, Gas Mark 3. Wrap each piece of kid neatly in bacon. Put them side by side in a baking tin. Add the butter and sprinkle with salt and pepper. Put into the oven and roast for 30 minutes. Heat the stock in a saucepan. Add the Verdicchio to the meat, raise the heat to moderate (180°C, 350°F, Gas Mark 4) and continue cooking for a further 40 minutes, basting from time to time with a little hot stock. In the meantime, finely chop the parsley and garlic and mix with the breadcrumbs. When the meat is tender, take the pan from the oven, sprinkle the meat with the flavoured breadcrumbs and return to the oven to cook long enough to brown the breadcrumbs. Take the meat from the pan, put on to a hot serving dish and keep hot. Put the baking tin on top of the stove and stir the gravy over a moderate heat until it is hot, then add the Marsala. Continue cooking until this has almost evaporated, add the rest of the heated stock, stir well and strain. Serve separately with the meat.

Agnello al forno con patate

Roast or baked leg of lamb

TO SERVE FOUR–SIX

INGREDIENTS
900 g (2 lb) leg or loin of
    lamb
1 clove garlic
50 g (2 oz) lard or other
    cooking fat
1–2 sprigs rosemary
4 large potatoes
salt and pepper

This is a typical spring dish from Lazio and also popular in other parts of Italy.

Preheat the oven to 220°C, 425°F, Gas Mark 7. Wipe the meat with a damp cloth. Coarsely chop the garlic and insert the pieces under the skin of the meat. Rub the lard round the sides and bottom of a baking tin. Add the meat and top with rosemary. Peel and cube the potatoes and pack them round the sides of the pan. Sprinkle with salt and pepper and put into the hot oven.

Baste the meat with its own juices from time to time. When the meat is cooked (time depends much on its age but the Italian recommended time is 1 hour, remembering that they eat their lamb somewhat rare), take it from the pan and place on a hot serving dish surrounded by the potatoes.

A similar dish from Campania uses new potatoes and small onions which are added to the pan after the meat has been cooking for about 20 minutes.

Left : capretto all' ascolana;
right : agnello al forno con patate

Agnello in fricassea

Fricassee of lamb

TO SERVE FOUR–SIX

INGREDIENTS
900 g (2 lb) leg or loin of lamb
salt and pepper
50 g (2 oz) butter
3 tablespoons olive oil
1 small onion, finely chopped
275 ml (½ pint) boiling stock
juice of 1 lemon
1 tablespoon flour
2 sprigs parsley, finely chopped
2 egg yolks or 1 whole egg

In Abruzzo-Molise a recipe of the same name is lamb roasted in one piece in the oven in a covered casserole with garlic and finely chopped parsley. Another similar recipe is *pollo in fricassea*, or chicken jointed into very small pieces and cooked in the same manner.

Wipe the meat with a damp cloth and cut into equal-sized pieces. Sprinkle with salt and pepper. Heat the butter and oil together in a pan, add the onion and meat and cook gently until the meat is brown, turning it from time to time. Add the boiling stock and continue cooking for about 30 minutes. Mix the lemon juice and the flour to a paste, add the parsley; beat the egg yolks and whisk into the lemon and flour mixture, add to the pan, stir vigorously and continue cooking over a low heat for 5–10 minutes without letting the sauce come to the boil. Serve with potatoes and a salad.

Abbacchio alla romana
Roman lamb chops

TO SERVE FOUR–SIX

INGREDIENTS
900 g (2 lb) baby lamb
  chops
5–6 tablespoons olive oil
2 cloves garlic, crushed
salt and pepper
1 sprig fresh rosemary or
  ½ teaspoon dried
2–3 anchovy fillets, finely
  chopped
3 tablespoons white wine
  vinegar

In Rome, baby lamb chops are bite size.

Wipe the chops with a damp cloth. Heat the oil in a deep, heavy frying pan, stir half the garlic into the oil, then add the chops, turning them often to brown all over. Sprinkle with salt and freshly ground black pepper and cook over a low heat for 20 minutes.

Meanwhile make the sauce. Rub the leaves off the rosemary and put them together with the rest of the crushed garlic and the anchovies into a mortar and pound to a paste, adding the vinegar as you pound. Instead of being crushed in a mortar the rosemary, garlic and anchovies can be finely chopped and then mixed with the vinegar.

As soon as the chops are brown and tender, add the sauce and stir it well into the juices in the pan. Continue cooking for 2–4 minutes. Serve the chops at once on a hot plate, sprinkled with the juices taken from the pan.

Agnello con olive nere
Lamb with black olives

TO SERVE FOUR–SIX

INGREDIENTS
900 g (2 lb) lamb – neck or
  other less expensive cuts
2–3 tablespoons olive oil
4–6 garlic cloves, peeled
275 ml (½ pint) dry white
  wine
12 black olives, pitted
salt and pepper
1–2 sprigs fresh rosemary
  or ½ teaspoon dried
1 tablespoon tomato
  concentrate

This is a Tuscan recipe of peasant origin with no exact quantities. For example, my handwritten recipe calls for a handful of black olives and plenty of garlic.

Wipe the meat with a damp cloth and cut it into pieces, the size is not important. Heat the oil in a heavy pan, add the garlic and, when this has browned, add the meat. Turn the pieces over several times to brown them evenly, add the wine, olives, salt, pepper, rosemary and the tomato concentrate, diluted with a little wine or water. Stir it all well and cook gently for 40 minutes until the lamb is tender and the sauce thick. Serve on a hot plate with polenta (*see page* 50).

Cervella alla napoletana
Neapolitan lambs' brains

TO SERVE FOUR

INGREDIENTS
450 g (1 lb) lambs' brains
1 tablespoon vinegar or
  lemon juice
olive oil or melted butter
1 teaspoon capers, chopped
50 g (2 oz) black olives,
  pitted and chopped
fine breadcrumbs
salt and pepper

In Naples the large black olives from the Gaeta area are used for this dish.

Soak the brains for 30 minutes in cold water. Put them into a pan with fresh cold vinegar or lemon water, bring to the boil, drain and drop again in cold water. Drain and pat dry. Preheat the oven to 230°C, 450°F, Gas Mark 8. Put a little oil or melted butter into the bottom of a baking dish, add the brains, capers and olives, sprinkle with breadcrumbs, salt, pepper and oil. Bake in the oven for 10–15 minutes, or until the top is brown. Serve in the same dish.

A few tablespoons of dry white wine are often added after the olives.

Top to bottom: abbacchio alla romana; agnello con olive nere; cervella alla napoletana

Lombo di maiale con castagne

Roast loin of pork with chestnuts

TO SERVE SIX

INGREDIENTS
1.6 kg (3 lb) loin of pork
3 cloves garlic, peeled and halved
salt and pepper
4–5 cloves
good pinch of dried rosemary or oregano
450 g (1 lb) large chestnuts

Preheat the oven to 180°C, 350°F, Gas Mark 4. Wipe the meat with a damp cloth and insert the garlic here and there under the skin. Score the fat diagonally with a sharp knife and lightly rub with salt and pepper. Stick the cloves into the fat, sprinkle the whole lightly with dried herbs and put into a baking tin, adding a little water. Roast, fat side up, in the oven for 30–40 minutes per 450 g (1 lb) of meat. While the meat is roasting, prepare the chestnuts. Cut a gash in the roundish side of the shells and cook the chestnuts in boiling water until the skins start peeling, or, if preferred, grill or bake them in a hot oven until the skins burst – either way

takes 10–20 minutes. Shell and skin the chestnuts as soon as possible while they are still hot and put them round the sides of the pork after 1 hour of cooking time.

Serve the meat on a hot dish surrounded by the chestnuts.

Arrosto di maiale al latte
Roast fillet of pork in milk

TO SERVE SIX

INGREDIENTS
1.6 kg (3 lb) fillet of pork
24–30 cloves garlic
725 ml (1¼ pints) full cream milk
salt, pepper and freshly grated nutmeg

Cooking meat in milk is a method used by the Italians when the meat is not sufficiently tender for plain roasting. Do not be afraid of the garlic, it is not too much; on the contrary, at the end of cooking the milk will have taken on a delicate perfume without an acute flavour of garlic.

Preheat the oven to 200°C, 400°F, Gas Mark 6. Roll up the pork and tie it neatly with string to preserve its shape while cooking. Place it in a flameproof pan and arrange the garlic along either side. Add the milk; it should come three-quarters up the side of the pork. Add salt, pepper and freshly grated nutmeg. Put the pan on top of the stove and cook over a moderate heat

until the milk has formed a thickish skin and is trembling or bubbling underneath. Do not disturb this skin; but put the pan into the oven and continue cooking until the meat is very tender and the milk thick. Baste from time to time with the milk in the pan and scrape away at the sides of the pan, putting the scrapings back into the milk. By the time the pork is ready the milk sauce should be thick.

To serve, take the pork from the pan, discard the strings and slice the meat fairly thickly. Arrange on a hot serving plate. The milk sauce can either be rubbed with the garlic through a sieve, or simply left as it is, with the whole pieces of garlic garnishing the meat, and served separately.

Costolette di maiale alla toscana
Tuscan pork chops

TO SERVE FOUR

INGREDIENTS
4 spare-rib or loin chops
fennel seeds
salt and pepper
2–3 tablespoons olive oil
1 clove garlic, sliced
1 cup water, dry white wine or beer

With a sharp knife score the chops in 2–3 places on each side. Sprinkle with fennel seeds, salt and pepper and leave for about an hour in the refrigerator or a cold larder. Heat the oil in a shallow pan, add the garlic, fry for a minute, then add the chops and

cook these over a moderate heat until they are brown on both sides. Add the hot water (or white wine or beer), cover the pan and continue cooking for about 25 minutes until the chops are tender.

Salsicce con l'uva fresco

Pork sausages with white grapes

TO SERVE FOUR–SIX

INGREDIENTS
675 g (1½ lb) pork sausages, preferably Italian
450 g (1 lb) large white grapes
2 tablespoons olive oil
2 tablespoons white wine or water

Perhaps it would be better to say 1½ metres of this type of Italian sausage since they come in one long 'rope'. This is cut into serving lengths and each length is coiled like a Catherine wheel and fixed with a toothpick to prevent it unwinding. They look most effective when served. This is an unusual dish but extremely good.

Prick the sausages lightly with a fork. Peel and pip the grapes. Heat the oil in a heavy shallow pan, add the wine, let this cook until it has evaporated (this applies also to water), then add the sausages and fry over a moderate heat, turning them from time to time, until they are brown all over. Add the prepared grapes, cover the pan and continue to cook gently for 20 minutes. Serve the sausages and grapes hot in their sauce, arranged on a flat dish.

128

Pasticcio di patate con le salsicce

Pork sausage and potato pie

TO SERVE FOUR–SIX

INGREDIENTS
900 g (2 lb) floury potatoes
450 g (1 lb) pork sausages, preferably Italian
2 tablespoons finely chopped parsley
50 g (2 oz) butter
275 ml ($\frac{1}{2}$ pint) lukewarm milk
freshly grated nutmeg to taste
50 g (2 oz) grated Parmesan cheese
2 egg yolks, well beaten
salt and pepper
butter for greasing

A peasant recipe from the Abruzzo-Molise region and not unlike the British cottage pie. Sausagemeat may be used instead of pork sausages.

Wash but do not peel the potatoes and cook in boiling salted water until soft. While the potatoes are cooking, skin the sausages and crumble the meat with a fork. Fry them in their own fat until the meat is brown. Preheat the oven to 180°C, 350°F, Gas Mark 4. Cool the potatoes, peel and rub through a ricer or mash and, while still hot, add the parsley and butter and beat well. Add enough milk to cover the potatoes, a good sprinkling of nutmeg, the cheese, egg yolks, sausagemeat, salt and pepper, beating well. Pour this mixture into a buttered baking dish and bake in the oven for 20–30 minutes, or until the top is crisp and brown.

Scaloppine (Veal escalopes)

For veal escalopes only the finest veal should be used. It should be almost white, hardly pink at all, finely textured and come from calves, fed entirely on milk, who have been cosseted and kept quiet all their short lives.

Escalopes must be cooked quickly, 3–4 minutes on either side, and they will hardly change colour but will be tender. If they are to be served with a sauce, unless the sauce is being made in another pan, take the escalopes from the pan, put aside and keep hot. If the meat comes into contact with boiling or very hot liquid, once it has been cooked, it will toughen.

Usually veal escalopes are about 1 cm ($\frac{1}{4}$ in) thick before they are pounded, and most butchers are willing to do this pounding for you – certainly they do so automatically in Italy. However, if you prefer to pound the escalopes yourself until wafer-thin, it is not difficult to wield a kitchen mallet on them until they reach this condition.

Saltimbocca alla romana

Veal escalopes with ham

TO SERVE SIX

INGREDIENTS
6 wafer-thin slices Parma ham
12 8-cm (3-in) slices veal, well pounded
salt and pepper
12 sage leaves
50 g (2 oz) butter
4 tablespoons olive oil

The word *saltimbocca* literally means 'to jump in the mouth'. This recipe originated from Brescia in Lombardy but was 'conquered' and naturalized by the Romans. Now it is found in almost every Roman restaurant. Italian smoked ham, *prosciutto*, is sliced in such paper-thin slices that 100 g (4 oz) will serve 6 escalopes. If Italian *prosciutto* is not available, use any smoked ham sliced as thinly as possible.

Cut each slice of ham in two. Sprinkle the veal slices lightly with salt and pepper and put a sage leaf on to each one. Cover each slice with a slice of ham, roll up and secure with a toothpick. Heat the butter with the oil in a pan large enough to take all the veal rolls at once and fry them briskly for about 5 minutes over a good heat. Serve straight away.

Often a little dry white wine is stirred into the juices in the pan and poured over the *saltimbocca* before serving. Usual accompaniments with this dish are sautéed potatoes, French beans (*see page* 170), or green salad.

Scaloppine di vitello al Marsala

Veal escalopes in Marsala

TO SERVE FOUR–SIX

INGREDIENTS
4–6 veal escalopes, well
   pounded
salt and pepper
flour for coating
50 g (2 oz) butter
4 tablespoons olive oil
150 ml (¼ pint) dry
   Marsala or sherry
2 tablespoons hot stock or
   water

This recipe is also called *piccata al Marsala*. Chicken and turkey breasts can be cooked in exactly the same manner.

Lightly sprinkle the veal with salt and pepper. Dip in flour but shake off any that is surplus. Heat the butter and oil together in a frying pan, add the pieces of veal (or as many as will go into the pan) and cook for 3–4 minutes on either side.

Add the Marsala, cook for 1 minute (no longer), take the meat from the pan, put on to a hot serving dish and keep hot. Quickly stir the stock into the juices in the pan, scrape the pan, pour the sauce over the escalopes and serve at once.

Serve with French beans or a mixed green salad.

Top: scaloppine di vitello al Marsala;
bottom: scaloppine alla perugina

Scaloppine alla perugina

Perugian escalopes of veal

TO SERVE FOUR

INGREDIENTS
1–2 chicken livers
1 tablespoon capers
1–2 cloves garlic
50 g (2 oz) fat bacon
3 tablespoons olive oil
1 tablespoon lemon juice
1 teaspoon grated lemon
   rind
salt and pepper
2–3 sage leaves
450 g (1 lb) veal escalopes
4 anchovy fillets

The anchovies should be in brine, but anchovies in oil make a good substitute. However, if you use brined anchovies, they must be washed well to remove the salt and filleted.

Finely chop the chicken livers, capers, garlic and bacon. Heat the oil in a frying pan, add the lemon juice and rind, then the

chopped ingredients, salt, pepper and the whole sage leaves. Stir well, then add the escalopes and cook first on one side, then on the other until they are quite tender, 6–8 minutes in all. Discard the sage leaves.

Serve on a hot plate garnished with the anchovies, with a green salad and sautéed potatoes.

131

Ossobuco milanese
Braised veal shin bones

TO SERVE THREE–SIX

INGREDIENTS
6 veal shin bones
salt and pepper
flour for coating
75 g (3 oz) butter
olive oil
1 small onion, finely
   chopped
150 ml (¼ pint) dry white
   wine
2 tomatoes, peeled and
   chopped
a little hot stock
risotto alla milanese
   (*page* 46)
1 clove garlic, finely
   chopped
2 sprigs parsley, very
   finely chopped
1–2 teaspoons grated
   lemon rind

This is justifiably one of the great dishes of Milan and is always served with yellow or saffron-coloured rice. The main ingredients of this dish are the veal shin bones with marrow and plenty of meat attached, sawn, preferably crosswise, into pieces 6–8 cm (2½–3 in) thick, and the so-called *gremolata*, or flavouring of garlic, parsley and grated lemon rind which is added to the dish just before serving. In Milan restaurants a small marrow spoon is supplied to assist in the digging out of the marrow from the bones, which is then either spread on bread, or eaten as it is. In Lombardy veal shin bones are cut thicker for this dish than elsewhere in the country. Also important when preparing *ossobuco* is the pan. It should be comparatively shallow and of a size that all the bones can be placed upright and close together to prevent the marrow from falling out.

Nick the meat around the bones with kitchen scissors to prevent the meat from curling up. Sprinkle lightly with salt and pepper and dip into flour. Heat the butter and a little oil in a shallow pan, add the onion and cook this for 2–3 minutes, then add the shin bones. First brown the undersides, then carefully turn over and brown the top sides. Add the wine, cook over a fairly good heat until it has almost evaporated, add the tomatoes, lower the heat, cover the pan and cook gently for 1–1½ hours, it depends on the thickness of the shin bones but certainly until the meat is so tender it literally falls from the bones. From time to time baste with hot stock. After about 1 hour of cooking, prepare the risotto. Finally mix the remaining ingredients to make the *gremolata* and sprinkle it over the top of the bones immediately before serving. Turn the risotto out on to a large, hot serving plate and either garnish with the *ossobuco* or serve the *ossobuco* and rice separately, which is rather more usual.

Costolette alla valdostana

Veal chops Valdostana fashion

TO SERVE FOUR–SIX

INGREDIENTS
4–6 veal chops
salt and pepper
flour for coating
1 egg, well beaten
fine breadcrumbs
100 g (4 oz) butter
4–6 thin slices ham
4–6 fairly thick slices
    Fontina or Bel Paese
    cheese
2 tablespoons hot meat
    gravy

For this recipe the chops must be tender. In the Valdostana smoked mountain ham is used but cooked ham may be substituted.

Trim the chops and lightly pound the meat. Sprinkle with salt and pepper, coat with flour and brush off the excess. Then dip into beaten egg and finally coat generously with breadcrumbs. Preheat the oven to 230°C, 450°F, Gas Mark 8. Heat the butter in a large fireproof shallow pan, add the chops and cook them on both sides until a golden brown. On each chop place a slice of ham and cover it with a slice of Fontina. Put the pan into the oven. As soon as the Fontina begins to melt, take the pan from the oven and serve the chops immediately on hot plates sprinkled with the pan juices and the gravy.

Spezzatino di vitello

Veal stew

TO SERVE FOUR

INGREDIENTS
900 g (2 lb) veal – breast or
    leg
2–3 tablespoons olive oil
50 g (2 oz) butter
1 onion, chopped
1–2 sprigs parsley, chopped
salt and pepper
225 g (8 oz) new potatoes,
    scrubbed
275 ml ($\frac{1}{2}$ pint) clear meat
    stock
225 g (8 oz) peas, shelled
2 eggs, well-beaten
juice of $\frac{1}{2}$ a lemon

This recipe comes from Liguria. In the artichoke season small sliced artichokes are added. In Umbria a similar *spezzatino* is made, adding their so-called white olives which are, in fact, sweet black ones. Some regions do not use peas or potatoes but peeled tomatoes and garlic instead, also white wine instead of stock. If using tinned or frozen peas, add these towards the end of cooking.

Instead of veal, shoulder of lamb may be used, or chicken jointed into very small pieces and boned.

Cut the meat into stew-size pieces. Heat the oil and butter together in a casserole, add the meat and fry until brown, turning it from time to time. Add the onion, parsley, salt, pepper and potatoes. When the onion

is brown, add the stock, then the peas and cook over a moderate heat until the meat is tender, 1–1$\frac{1}{2}$ hours. About 5 minutes before serving, beat the eggs into the lemon juice and add about 1 tablespoon of hot stock from the pan, pour this mixture over the meat, stir it well and at once take from the heat.

Vitello tonnato

Veal with tuna fish sauce

TO SERVE SIX

INGREDIENTS
900 g (2 lb) boned leg of
    veal
1 each carrot, stalk of
    celery, and onion
275 ml ($\frac{1}{2}$ pint) dry white
    wine
juice of 2 large lemons
2 bayleaves
2 cloves
salt and pepper
175 g (7 oz) tinned tuna
    fish
3 anchovy fillets
2 eggs
4 tablespoons olive oil
1 tablespoon capers

This is an excellent cold meat dish and a favourite in Lombardy. Similar dishes also are made with boiled pork, chicken or turkey.

Soak the veal for 30 minutes in cold water. Meanwhile chop the carrot, stalk of celery and onion. Dry the veal well, then put into a casserole together with the chopped vegetables, wine, 2 tablespoons lemon juice, bayleaves, cloves, salt and pepper. Cover and bring gently to the boil, lower the heat and continue cooking until the veal is tender, about 1$\frac{1}{2}$ hours depending on the quality of the veal. When it is tender, take the meat from the pan, pat it dry and leave uncovered until it is cold. Finely chop the tuna, or purée in a liquidizer, together with the anchovies. Beat the eggs with the remaining lemon juice, then add enough

oil, drop by drop, to make a fluid dressing. Add the tuna paste and whisk the dressing until it is creamy. Chop the capers and add to the dressing. Finally thinly slice the veal and lightly spread a little of the dressing on each slice. Arrange the slices on a long narrow serving plate and spread with the remaining dressing. Cover and leave in a cool place for several hours, or overnight in the refrigerator before serving. The veal may be left up to 3 days in the sauce if kept in the refrigerator.

Top: spezzatino di vitello;
bottom: vitello tonnato

Fegato alla veneziana or alla 'Sbrodega'
Venetian-style liver and onion

TO SERVE FOUR

INGREDIENTS
25 g (1 oz) butter
2–3 tablespoons olive oil
675 g (1½ lb) onions, sliced
2–3 sprigs parsley, finely
 chopped
675 g (1½ lb) calves' liver,
 finely sliced
a little hot stock or meat
 gravy
salt and pepper

This dish is generally served on its own as an antipasto but can also be served as a light luncheon dish.

Heat the butter and oil together in a frying pan, add the onions and parsley and cook slowly over a low heat until the onions are soft but not brown (my original recipe suggests cooking for 1 hour which gives an idea of how slow the cooking should be). When the onions are soft, raise the heat, add the liver and no more than 3 tablespoons of stock and cook over a brisk heat for 5 minutes. Take from the heat, add salt and pepper and serve on a hot plate surrounded by triangles of fried bread.

Fegato in dolcegarbo
Liver in a sweet-sour sauce

TO SERVE FOUR

INGREDIENTS
450 g (1 lb) calves' liver
flour for dusting
1 egg, well-beaten
fine breadcrumbs
100 g (4 oz) butter
75 ml (3 fl oz) red wine
 vinegar
1 teaspoon sugar
salt to taste

Preheat the oven to 160°C, 325°F, Gas Mark 3. Thinly slice the liver. Lightly coat with flour, then dip into beaten egg and finally into breadcrumbs. Heat the butter and quickly fry the liver over a good heat until brown on both sides. Drain on kitchen paper and put on a hot serving plate. Combine the vinegar, sugar and salt and sprinkle this over the top of the liver. Put into the oven and leave for 10 minutes. Serve with risotto (*see pages* 44–47).

Polpette al forno
Baked meat croquettes

TO SERVE SIX

INGREDIENTS
25 g (1 oz) butter
50 g (2 oz) flour
150 ml (¼ pint) warm
 water
3 eggs
3–4 tablespoons grated
 cheese
salt and pepper
450 g (1 lb) cooked meat,
 minced
2–3 fresh basil leaves,
 finely chopped or
 ½ teaspoon dried
fine breadcrumbs
50 g (2 oz) butter
pine-nuts (optional)
2–3 whole basil or mint
 leaves or sprigs of
 parsley for garnishing

Melt 25 g (1 oz) of butter, add the flour and stir well to make a roux. Gradually add the water, stirring all the time. The paste must be very thick so do not add any more liquid. Stir and cook for 5 minutes then leave until cool. Preheat the oven to 180°C, 350°F, Gas Mark 4. Break the eggs into a bowl and beat well, add the cheese, salt and pepper. When the paste is cool, combine it with the eggs and cheese to make a smooth sauce, then add the meat and basil. Mix well and knead the mixture thoroughly. Break off pieces of the mixture, making about 8–12 croquettes, and mould them into any preferred shapes. Roll lightly in breadcrumbs and arrange in a well-buttered pan, using some of the second quantity of butter. Melt the remaining butter and sprinkle this over the top of the croquettes, and garnish with pine-nuts (if using them). Bake in the oven for about 30 minutes, basting from time to time with the butter in the pan.

Serve hot with boiled potatoes and garnish with the whole basil or mint leaves or the sprigs of chopped parsley.

Rognone alla bolognese

Bologna-style kidneys

TO SERVE FOUR–SIX

INGREDIENTS
4–6 calves' kidneys
2–3 tablespoons olive oil
150 ml (¼ pint) red wine
    vinegar
50 g (2 oz) butter
1 small onion, finely
    chopped
1 clove garlic, peeled but
    whole
2–3 sprigs parsley, finely
    chopped
freshly ground black
    pepper
150 ml (¼ pint) stock

In this recipe calves' kidneys, which are small and many lobed, are recommended, but lambs' or sheep kidneys may be cooked in the same manner.

Remove the fat surrounding each kidney, cut away the hard core and membrane and slice thinly. Put 2–3 tablespoons of oil into a pan and, when this is hot, add the kidneys and fry for not more than 5 minutes, stirring frequently. Sprinkle with half the vinegar and continue cooking for 2–3 minutes. Take from the pan and drain. In the same pan heat the butter, add the onion, garlic and parsley and cook until the garlic changes colour. Discard the garlic, add the kidneys, raise the heat, stir well, continue to cook until the pan looks dry, and add the rest of the vinegar, pepper and stock. Cook for a further 10 minutes, no longer, and serve immediately. This is important if the kidneys are to retain their fragrance.

Top left : fegato alla veneziana;
top right : risotto milanese;
bottom left : fegato in
dolcegarbo; *bottom right :*
rognone alla bolognese

Rane in guazzetto

Frogs' legs stew

TO SERVE FOUR–SIX

INGREDIENTS
900 g (2 lb) prepared frogs'
    legs
pinch of salt
275 ml (½ pint) dry white
    wine
75 g (3 oz) butter
1 tablespoon flour
1 ladleful hot water or
    stock
1 tablespoon finely
    chopped parsley
juice of ½ a lemon

Put the frogs' legs into a casserole, add salt, wine and 50 g (2 oz) of the butter and cook over a moderate heat until most of the wine has evaporated. At this point sprinkle in the flour, stir well, then add the hot water or, better still, stock. Add the parsley, stir and cook for 12–15 minutes. Just before serving, add the lemon juice and the rest of the butter cut into slivers.

An alternative method is to fry 1 large sliced onion together with a stalk of finely chopped celery and one or two chopped cloves of garlic. When these are a golden brown the frogs' legs are added, fried until brown, then the wine is poured over them and cooked until it has evaporated. Finally 3–4 peeled and chopped tomatoes and chopped parsley are added and cooking continued for a further 15–20 minutes.

This second method produces a richer dish than the first.

Left : polpette al forno;
right : rane in guazzetto

Poultry
and game

In general poultry in Italy is of a high quality and many of the country's finest and best-known traditional dishes have been based on chicken. In most Italian towns there is not one but several excellent poultry shops selling unfrozen chickens as well as free-range birds. The Italian classification of poultry is fairly international. Under the term *pollo*, we find birds of a general category which can be roasted or boiled. For grilling, the *pollastro* or *pollastra* (a young bird between 7 and 8 months) is preferred. Also for grilling is the *galletto di prima canta*, or a young pullet which has only just learned to crow. For soup, the *gallina* is used – *vecchia gallina fa un buon brodo*, in other words, soup is all an old hen is fit for.

Apart from buying whole chickens, there are chicken breasts, wings, legs and of course carcasses for soup or stock-making. Chicken livers are sold together with the kidneys and stomachs, and these are made into delicious dishes. The wise housewife when her poulterer cleans and prepares her bird for the pan, asks him for the head, legs, feet, etc., all for the stock pot. In recent years spit-roasted chickens have become one of the 'national' dishes of Italy and no self-respecting poulterer is without his ever-turning spit. Mostly the birds are stuffed only with rosemary or other locally preferred herbs.

Another bird well worth going for in Italy is the guinea fowl, a farmyard bird but with plenty of flavour and, curiously, somewhat cheaper than rabbit. Goose is available usually only in October and November. But large turkeys are available throughout the year. Their great legs are like legs of mutton and indeed they can be roasted in the same way, provided you can pull out their thick and tough tendons. The flesh cut from the huge breasts looks like chunks of veal and is sold in slices or steaks, again like veal, or cut into small pieces to make stews.

Rabbit is also a general favourite, especially in Liguria, but is expensive. Its flesh is creamy coloured and has a good flavour. Most Italians treat rabbit with respect and give it quality treatment, which pricewise it deserves.

There are good quantities of game in the hills and forests of Italy but altogether far too many trigger-happy so-called hunters. Anything that flies is considered by the Italians as game and sadly too many small birds fall prey to the guns. The general quality of game is not as good as in Britain which no doubt is why even pheasant is given long, slowish cooking and often cooked in a sauce that many would find too rich in Britain. Quail, as in Britain today, is a farmyard bird; there are also plenty of partridge, hare and wild rabbit. Large game is plentiful – in Liguria not far from the coast the wild boar is hunted for its excellent meat. Generally venison, wild boar and hares are cooked and served with a rather rich sweet-sour sauce which in fact is extremely good.

This seventeenth-century painting by the Neapolitan Luca Giordano shows the plentiful supply of poultry and game at that time and its already important role in Italian cooking.

Pollo alla diavola

Chicken diavolo

TO SERVE TWO–FOUR

INGREDIENTS
2–4 spring chickens
lemon juice
salt and freshly ground
  black pepper
olive oil

There are several versions of this recipe; this one comes from a Tuscan grandmother who cooks the chicken in a deep, solid frying pan weighed down with a heavy *mattone*, or brick; this also can be achieved by using a plate or flat lid with a heavy weight on top.

Cut the chickens down through the breast but do not cut them into halves. Rub with lemon juice, salt, a great deal of freshly ground black pepper and oil. Rub a large flat plate with oil and lemon juice, put the prepared chickens on to this, rub another plate with oil and lemon juice and with this cover the chickens. Leave for an hour or

so, although if in a hurry this procedure is not absolutely essential. Put the chickens into the pan, cover with the weighted lid and cook gently until the underneath is brown and crisp, for 20–30 minutes. Then turn the chickens and cook the top sides until crisp and brown.

Serve with lettuce or fried potatoes, and carrots cooked in butter. Instead of cooking the chickens in a frying pan, they are often grilled, preferably over charcoal. You can also smear the chickens liberally with crushed garlic before cooking; not orthodox but good and to be recommended for garlic lovers.

Pollo al succo d'uva

Chicken cooked in fresh grape juice

TO SERVE FOUR

INGREDIENTS
2 spring chickens or 1 large
  but tender bird
4–6 tablespoons olive oil
2 cloves garlic, chopped
handful parsley, finely
  chopped
salt and pepper
450 g (1 lb) green grapes
2–3 tablespoons brandy
extra grapes for garnishing

This is an extremely simple but good dish and light on the digestion.

If using spring chickens, cut into halves; if the larger bird, cut into quarters. Heat the oil in a casserole, add the chicken pieces and cook until they begin to brown. Add the garlic, parsley, salt and pepper. Whirl the grapes in a liquidizer or crush them to

obtain the juice. Strain. Add the juice to the chicken pieces and continue cooking until tender, turning them from time to time. For spring chickens, 25 minutes' cooking will be enough; for the quartered pieces somewhat longer is necessary. Just before serving, add the brandy and a few whole, pitted grapes to serve as a garnish. Serve with boiled rice or potatoes.

Top : pollo alla diavola
bottom : pollo al succo d'uva

Pollo allo spumante

Chicken cooked in sparkling wine

TO SERVE FOUR

INGREDIENTS
1 900-g (2-lb) chicken
50 g (2 oz) butter
275 ml (½ pint) dry
  Spumante or sparkling
  wine
salt and pepper
225 g (8 oz) tomatoes,
  peeled and chopped
warm stock

Spumante is the Italian equivalent of Champagne; it varies in quality and price but for this dish it is not necessary to buy the most expensive provided it is dry.

Joint the chicken into 4 pieces. Heat the butter in a pan, add the chicken pieces and brown. Add the Spumante, salt and pepper, then the peeled and chopped tomatoes and cook gently until the chicken is tender, about 1 hour, adding stock only if required. Serve the chicken in its sauce with boiled potatoes or rice, and French beans, or a mixed green salad.

Pollo ripieno arrosto
Stuffed roast chicken

TO SERVE FOUR–SIX

INGREDIENTS
1.8-kg (4-lb) chicken, trussed, plus liver and heart
2 tablespoons olive oil
50 g (2 oz) butter
1 medium-sized onion, finely chopped
50 g (2 oz) ham, minced
100 g (4 oz) coarse breadcrumbs
salt and pepper
25 g (1 oz) grated Parmesan cheese
3 tablespoons hot stock or water

Chop the liver and heart of the chicken. Heat the oil and butter in a small pan, add the onion and cook until a golden brown. Add the chicken liver, heart, ham and breadcrumbs, mix well and cook over a moderate heat until the crumbs are lightly browned. Add salt, pepper, cheese and stock, stir again and take from the heat. Cool the stuffing before putting it into the chicken. Preheat the oven to 180°C, 350°F, Gas Mark 4. Place the chicken on its side on the rack of a roasting pan and place in the oven and roast for 20 minutes. Turn the bird so that it roasts on the other side, then turn the bird again so that it roasts breast uppermost, basting frequently until tender. Allow 20 minutes per 450 g (1 lb).

Petti di pollo trifolati

Chicken breasts in a tomato sauce

TO SERVE FOUR

INGREDIENTS
4 chicken breasts or small
  legs
350 g (12 oz) ripe tomatoes
1 each onion, carrot and
  celery stalk
100 g (4 oz) ham
50 g (2 oz) butter
2 tablespoons olive oil
salt and pepper
150 ml (¼ pint) dry white
  wine
4 good sprigs parsley,
  finely chopped

Very lightly pound the chicken breasts with a kitchen mallet. Blanch, peel and chop the tomatoes. Chop the onion, carrot and celery into small pieces. Cut the ham into thin strips. Heat the butter and oil together in a shallow pan, add the onion, carrot and celery and cook until they begin to change colour. Add the chicken breasts and cook these for 3–4 minutes, turning from time to time. Sprinkle lightly with salt and pepper, then add the wine and cook until this has evaporated. Add the tomatoes, parsley and ham. Stir well and continue cooking until the tomatoes are pulpy, pressing them down from time to time to make a thick tomato sauce. This should not take more than 10–15 minutes – longer cooking will ruin the chicken breasts. However, cook chicken legs for slightly longer. Serve with rice.

Petti di pollo alla Duca d'Alba

Chicken breasts à la Duke of Alba

TO SERVE FOUR

INGREDIENTS
4 chicken breasts
flour for coating
25 g (1 oz) butter
salt and pepper
4 thin slices Gruyère
  cheese
slivers of butter
150 ml (¼ pint) dry white
  wine
white truffles (optional)

Preheat the oven to 220°C, 425°F, Gas Mark 7. Gently flatten the chicken breasts with a kitchen mallet and snip around the edges with kitchen scissors to prevent curling while cooking. Sprinkle with flour. Heat the butter in a flameproof casserole. Add the chicken breasts, salt and pepper and cook for 5–6 minutes on both sides. Cover each breast with a slice of cheese, add a sliver of butter and sprinkle with dry white wine. Take the pan from the top of the stove and put into the oven and leave for 7–8 minutes. When the cheese has melted, take the casserole from the oven and sprinkle slivers of truffle over the top. Serve at once with a mixed green salad.

Filetti di tacchino al Marsala

Turkey breast cooked in Marsala

TO SERVE FOUR

INGREDIENTS
75 g (3 oz) butter
4 fillets turkey breast
flour for coating
salt and white pepper
150 ml (¼ pint) dry
  Marsala
wafer-thin slivers white
  truffle (optional)

In Italy turkeys are grown to an enormous size and the breast meat is cut off in large chunks, like a slab of veal. This is then sliced into fillets and flattened slightly with a meat mallet. They are very good. If fillets are not available, use chicken breasts or veal fillets. In Piedmont white truffle is usual but, alas, an optional ingredient outside the region.

Heat the butter, add the turkey fillets, sprinkle with flour, salt and pepper and cook them first on one side for 5 minutes, or until lightly browned, then turn and cook on the other side for the same time. Take from the pan, place on a hot serving dish and keep hot in the oven while you make the sauce. Add the Marsala to the pan, raise the heat and cook, stirring all the time, until the butter and Marsala are well mixed. Pour this hot sauce over the fillets and sprinkle with truffle, if used.

Top to bottom : petti di pollo trifolati; petti di pollo alla Duca d'Alba; filetti di tacchino al Marsala

Ali di tacchino in fricassea

Fricassée of turkey wings

TO SERVE FOUR

INGREDIENTS
900 kg (2 lb) turkey wings
225 g (8 oz) carrots
150 g (6 oz) small onions
2 stalks of celery
salt and pepper
parsley, thyme and
    bayleaves
40 g (1½ oz) butter
1 tablespoon flour
2 eggs
juice of 1 lemon
275 ml (½ pint) single
    cream or milk

Put the wings into a large pan with enough cold water to cover. Cook over a good heat until the water boils. While this is cooking, prepare the vegetables. Trim the carrots, peel or scrape them and put them whole into the pan with the wings. Add the onions, peeled but whole, and the celery stalks cut into halves. Add salt, pepper and the herbs and, once the water has come to the boil, lower the heat and let the wings cook slowly for about 45 minutes, or until tender. Strain the wings and vegetables in a colander over a bowl. Dry the pan in which the wings were cooked and add the butter. Heat this, add the flour, stirring all the time to avoid lumps. Pour in about a cupful of the hot turkey stock, stirring all the time until the sauce is smooth and thick. Cook this gently for 10 minutes, then add the turkey wings. Cut the carrots into thick slices, the celery into short lengths, the onions, if small, are left whole, if large, divided into sections. Add these all to the pan. Stir gently and cook for a few minutes. While this is simmering, beat the eggs with the lemon juice, add the cream, stir well and add 3 tablespoons of the hot stock. Stir well, then pour this sauce into the pan, stirring all the time but not letting the sauce boil. Arrange the wings and vegetables in a hot deep serving dish, add the sauce and serve hot.

This dish can be served with boiled potatoes or with a plain or herb-flavoured risotto; if the latter, choose the same type of herbs as used in cooking the wings.

145

Tacchino ripieno arrosto

Stuffed roast turkey

TO SERVE EIGHT–TEN

INGREDIENTS

1 3.6–4.5 kg (8–10 lb)
  turkey
butter
salt and pepper
fresh rosemary
150 ml ($\frac{1}{4}$ pint) dry white
  wine

Stuffing

25 g (1 oz) butter
1 medium-sized onion,
  chopped
liver and giblets of turkey
225 g (8 oz) veal or beef,
  chopped
225 g (8 oz) Italian sausage,
  skinned and crumbled
1 firm sharp-flavoured
  apple, peeled and
  chopped
3 slices fat bacon, diced
225 g (8 oz) peeled, cooked
  and crumbled chestnuts
salt, pepper and a pinch of
  freshly grated nutmeg
50 g (2 oz) grated
  Parmesan cheese
pinch of dried sage and
  thyme
2 eggs

Preheat the oven to 180°C, 350°F, Gas Mark 4. First of all make the stuffing. Heat the butter and gently fry the onion until soft but not brown. Cook the liver and giblets in water until tender, drain and chop. Mix these ingredients with the chopped veal or beef, sausage, apples and bacon, then add the remaining stuffing ingredients. When thoroughly mixed, stuff loosely into the turkey cavity and sew up the opening. Rub the turkey with butter, salt, pepper and fresh rosemary and place on the rack of a large roasting tin. Roast in the oven for $3\frac{1}{2}$ hours, or until tender,

basting often with the juices. During the last hour of cooking baste with the dry white wine, a little at a time. Serve the pan juices separately as a sauce.

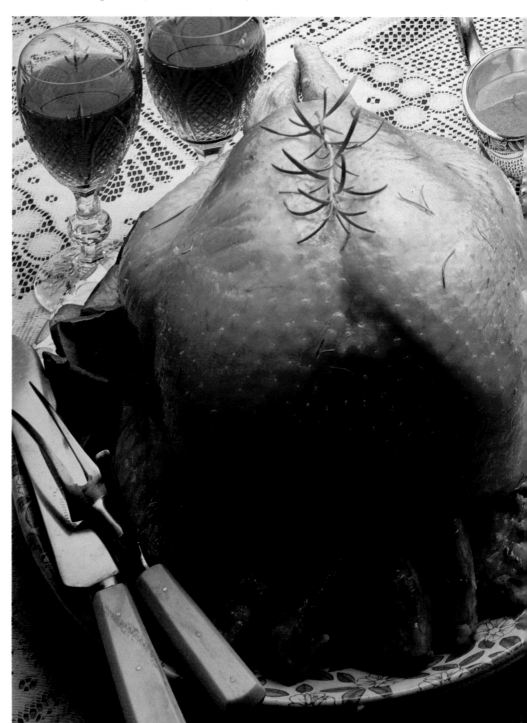

Left : tacchino ripieno arrosto;
right : anitra all'olivo

Anitra all'olivo
Duck with olives

TO SERVE FOUR

INGREDIENTS
1 2.3–2.7 kg (5–6 lb) duck
  plus liver and heart
  (optional)
salt and pepper
2–3 leaves sage or basil or
  ½ teaspoon dried
1 onion, chopped
275 ml (½ pint) beef stock
100 g (4 oz) green or black
  olives, pitted

This is a typical recipe from Liguria.

Preheat the oven to 260°C, 500°F, Gas Mark 9. Take out the heart and liver of the duck and rub the bird inside and out with salt and pepper. Put the sage inside the cavity. Prick the skin all over. Put the duck into a baking pan and bake in the oven for 15 minutes. Take from the oven and pour away the fat which has been rendered from the duck. Lower the heat to 230°C, 450°F, Gas Mark 8, chop the duck heart and add with the onion, stock and the olives to the pan. Continue roasting the duck, basting frequently and allowing 15–18 minutes per 450 g (1 lb) roasting time. While the duck is cooking, finely chop its liver and add this to the pan about 30 minutes before the duck is ready. Add more stock if required in order to have a generous sauce. Take the duck from the pan and serve on a hot platter. Skim off the fat from the duck gravy and serve the gravy separately without straining.

Faraona in casseruola

Casserole of guinea fowl

TO SERVE TWO—THREE

INGREDIENTS

1 900-g (2-lb) guinea fowl
salt and pepper
8 juniper berries
50 g (2 oz) butter
2–3 tablespoons stock or
  water
2–3 tablespoons brandy
225 g (8 oz) seedless grapes
150 ml ($\frac{1}{4}$ pint) white wine
1–2 tablespoons dry
  Marsala or sherry

Guinea fowl are related to the pheasant family and indigenous to Africa. The Greeks first brought them to Europe, later they came with the Romans, then disappeared and finally reappeared with the return of Portuguese colonists from the West African coast. They are now reared domestically and much appreciated for their tender and delicately flavoured flesh, with just a hint of gaminess. Recipes for guinea fowl and pheasant are usually interchangeable.

Preheat the oven to 150°C, 300°F, Gas Mark 2. Wipe the bird inside and rub it well with salt and pepper. Crush the juniper berries and put into the cavity. Heat two-thirds of the butter in a heavy casserole, add the guinea fowl and brown it evenly all round. Add the stock and about 1 tablespoon of brandy, cover the casserole and finish cooking the bird in a cool oven. Add a little stock if required but this is not necessary if the bird is well covered and cooked slowly, in all between 45–60 minutes until tender. While the bird is cooking, steep the grapes in the white wine. After the bird has been cooking for 30 minutes, take it from the oven and put it on a dish. Keep hot. Add the rest of the butter to the sauce in the casserole, then the grapes and white wine, replace the bird and baste it well with this sauce. Pour the remaining brandy over it, add the Marsala, return the casserole to the oven, uncovered, and continue cooking until the bird is completely cooked, basting 2–3 times with its juices. Serve with unsweetened chestnut purée and red cabbage.

Faraona al mattone

Guinea fowl in a chicken brick

TO SERVE FOUR

INGREDIENTS

1 large sprig of rosemary
2–3 leaves fresh sage or
  $\frac{1}{2}$ teaspoon dried
50 g (2 oz) butter
small pinch of salt
black pepper, freshly
  ground
6–8 juniper berries,
  crushed
1 900-g (2-lb) guinea fowl
75 g (3 oz) rashers of bacon

Chicken can also be cooked in this way.

Soak the brick in cold water for 10 minutes. Finely chop the herbs. Mix with the butter, salt, pepper and juniper berries. Push half this mixture into the guinea fowl and rub the rest over the breast and round the legs. Cover with the bacon. Drain the brick from the water, but do not dry it; put the guinea fowl into it, cover and put into a cold oven, set to moderate (180°C, 350°F, Gas Mark 4) and leave for $1\frac{1}{2}$–2 hours. Remove from the oven and put the brick on to a wooden board; be careful not to put it on anything cold, like marble or tiles, otherwise the brick will crack. Uncover, take the bird from the brick and serve garnished with the bacon.
  The juice from the guinea fowl can be made into a gravy.

Top : faraona in casseruola;
bottom : faraona al mattone

Pernici in salsa d'aceto

Partridges in a vinegar sauce

TO SERVE FOUR

INGREDIENTS
4 partridges
pinch of salt
1 medium-sized onion,
  chopped
2 stalks of celery, chopped
1 large carrot, cut into
  rounds
4 tablespoons olive oil
2 tablespoons white wine
  vinegar
1 tablespoon small capers
1 tablespoon finely
  chopped parsley

This rather robust recipe for partridges comes from Sardinia. Pigeons, particularly wood pigeons, can be cooked in the same manner.

Rub the partridges inside with salt and put into a pan with the vegetables and just enough water to cover. Cook gently for about 30 minutes, or until the birds are tender. Take from the pan and cut each one into two. Place on a serving dish with the vegetables and juices around the birds. Keep hot in a warm oven. Mix the olive oil, vinegar, capers and chopped parsley, add salt if liked, and pour this over the partridges immediately before serving.

Pernici alla panna
Partridges cooked in cream

INGREDIENTS
4 partridges
juice of 2 large lemons
salt and pepper
4 thin strips streaky bacon
40 g (1½ oz) butter
2–3 leaves fresh sage and
   rosemary or ½ teaspoon
   dried
275 ml (½ pint) single
   cream

This is a pleasant recipe from Venice. Pigeons can be cooked in the same way.

Rub the birds inside and out with lemon juice and lightly sprinkle with salt and pepper. Tie a strip of bacon over each bird. Heat the butter in a large casserole, add the partridges and brown them all over. Add the herbs, the rest of the lemon juice and only just enough hot water to prevent burning. Cover the casserole and cook gently until the partridges are tender, 25–30 minutes. Add the cream, simmer until this is hot but do not let it boil or it might curdle. Serve the partridges on a hot dish with the sauce poured over them and preferably with game chips.

Fagiano in casseruola

Casserole of pheasant

INGREDIENTS
1 good-sized pheasant
salt
olive oil
8 juniper berries, crushed
100 g (4 oz) butter
150 ml ($\frac{1}{4}$ pint) brandy or
    rum
50 g (2 oz) raisins,
    preferably Muscat
275 ml ($\frac{1}{2}$ pint) dry white
    wine
150 ml ($\frac{1}{4}$ pint) dry
    Marsala or sherry
pinch of ground clove

Instead of pheasant, guinea fowl may also be used.

Preheat the oven to 180°C, 350°F, Gas Mark 4. Rub the bird inside and out lightly with salt, brush with oil and put the juniper berries into the cavity. Melt two-thirds of the butter in a casserole (one that can be used on top of the stove and in the oven), add the pheasant and lightly brown it all over. Add the brandy, cover the pan and put it into the oven. Bake for 45–60 minutes, basting from time to time. While the pheasant is cooking, make a basting sauce. Stem and stone the raisins (if using muscat on the stem) and cook gently in a little water until they plump out. Drain well and put into a small pan with the rest of the butter and simmer until the butter is melted. Add the white wine, Marsala and the clove. Cook gently for 5 minutes. After the pheasant has been cooking for 30 minutes, baste it with this sauce, using all of it, then continue cooking and basting the bird for 20–30 minutes until tender.

Serve the pheasant in its sauce with a chestnut purée, creamed potatoes or polenta (*see page 50*).

Quaglie con olive verdi e vino bianco

Quail with olives and white wine

TO SERVE FOUR

INGREDIENTS

8 quail
salt and pepper to taste
2 tablespoons olive oil
2–3 rashers streaky bacon, chopped
1 each small onion and carrot, minced
150 ml ($\frac{1}{4}$ pint) white wine
2–3 fresh sage leaves or $\frac{1}{2}$ teaspoon dried
12 green olives, pitted and chopped
25 g (1 oz) butter
150 ml ($\frac{1}{4}$ pint) stock
225 g (8 oz) long grain rice
2 tablespoons brandy

Quail are farm bred in Italy and are generally small and rotund. Two are usually considered to be a fair portion for one person. This recipe comes from Lazio.

Rub the quail with salt and pepper. Heat the oil in a large casserole dish, add the quail and quickly brown. Add the bacon, onion and carrot and cook over a good heat for 5 minutes. Add the wine, sage, salt and a little pepper and cook for a further 5 minutes. Add the olives, butter and stock. Lower the heat and cover. Simmer for about another 20 minutes. Cook the rice in lightly salted boiling water until tender, about 15 minutes. The quail should be tender by this time and their liquid reduced by half. Warm the brandy, pour this over the quail and ignite it. This is for flavour not glamour. Replace the lid and keep hot while you prepare the rice. Drain the rice and arrange in a ring on a hot round serving dish. Put the quail in the centre. Scrape off every bit of sauce in the pan, stir well and pour it over the top of the quail.

Serve with a green salad.

Piccioni in salmi

Pigeons cooked in a
wine sauce

TO SERVE FOUR

INGREDIENTS
4 pigeons
2–3 fresh sage leaves or
  ½ teaspoon dried
2–3 sprigs parsley
4 anchovy fillets
1–2 cloves garlic
1 tablespoon capers
150 ml (¼ pint) olive oil
grated rind of 1 lemon
275 ml (½ pint) red wine
salt and pepper

In Italy hares, rabbits and pigeons are
frequently cooked *in salmi*, that is in a
rich red wine sauce. It is generally considered better to cook them the day before
serving, and then to reheat them, for the
flavour of the sauce is then absorbed into
the flesh. For this recipe it is essential that
fat young pigeons or squabs are used.

Cut all the flesh from the bones, keeping
the breast meat as intact as possible. The
rest of the flesh should be cut into small
even-sized pieces. Mix the giblets with the
sage, parsley, anchovy fillets, garlic and
capers and chop all together finely. Heat
the oil in a pan, add the pigeon breasts and
the grated lemon rind. Cook over a
moderate heat until the meat is lightly
browned, turning it from time to time.
Add the wine, then the rest of the meat and
seasonings. Cover the pan tightly, placing
a piece of foil or cloth under the lid and
continue to cook slowly for about 1 hour
without uncovering. The dish is then
ready to serve but, as I have already mentioned, it can be left until the next day, in
which case do not uncover the pan until
the contents have been reheated and are
ready to be served.

   The *salmi* can be served with polenta
(*see page* 50), mashed potatoes, fried bread
or on toast.

Il coniglio (Rabbit)

Although fairly expensive, rabbits both tame and wild are a common food in Italy, both in town and country. They are usually sold whole, often still with their furry skins, but the poulterer will prepare them for the pot. Many people in Britain dislike what they describe as the rabbit's strong flavour. This can be eliminated by soaking the rabbit for an hour or so in cold water and then scalding it in boiling water for 1–2 minutes before dealing with it as directed in a recipe.

Coniglio in umido con olive e pinoli

Rabbit stewed with olives and pine-nuts

TO SERVE FOUR–SIX

INGREDIENTS
2–3 tablespoons olive oil
25 g (1 oz) butter
1 900-g (2-lb) rabbit, jointed
1 medium-sized onion, chopped
150 ml ($\frac{1}{4}$ pint) dry white wine
salt and pepper
20 black olives
1 sprig rosemary or $\frac{1}{4}$ teaspoon dried
1 clove garlic, chopped
pine-nuts to taste

This recipe comes from Liguria where both black olives and pine-nuts are greatly in demand in the kitchen. The local black olives are small but sweet and are not usually pitted. But, if using larger olives which can be easily pitted, this can be done. Unfortunately pine-nuts are expensive anywhere; my original recipe says 'a handful of pine-nuts'.

Put the oil and butter in a casserole, add the rabbit pieces and cook until they are brown all over. Add the onion, let this brown a little, then add the wine, salt and pepper and cook over a low heat. After 30 minutes add the remaining ingredients. Cover the pan and continue cooking for a further 45 minutes, or until the rabbit is tender. If the rabbit seems dry, add either a little hot water or stock. Serve the rabbit in its sauce, either with polenta, spaghetti or noodles (*see* Chapter 2).

Coniglio con funghi e pancetta

Rabbit cooked with bacon and mushrooms

TO SERVE FOUR

INGREDIENTS
4 tablespoons olive oil
1 rabbit, jointed
1 onion, coarsely chopped
flour for coating
1 teaspoon tomato concentrate
salt and pepper
stock (meat or game)
rosemary and thyme to taste
2 bayleaves
450 g (1 lb) mushrooms
4 slices fat bacon, chopped

Top : coniglio in umido con olive e pinoli; *bottom :* coniglio con funghi e pancetta

Heat the oil in a heavy, deep frying pan, fry the rabbit pieces and the onion until a golden brown. Sprinkle the rabbit with flour, add the tomato concentrate, salt, pepper and enough stock to cover. Bring gently to the boil, add the herbs, cover the pan and cook slowly for 30 minutes. Wash the mushrooms, remove the stems (these can be used in a soup) and thickly slice the caps. Preheat the oven to 230°C, 450°F, Gas Mark 8. Transfer the rabbit to an oven casserole and strain the sauce. Spread the mushrooms over the top of the rabbit, sprinkle with bacon and spread with the sauce. Cover and bake in the oven until the rabbit is completely tender, for about 1 hour (baking time will slightly depend on the size and age of the rabbit).

Lepre alla Marengo

Hare Marengo

INGREDIENTS
1 saddle of hare
3 tablespoons olive oil
25 g (1 oz) dried
  mushrooms
25 g (1 oz) butter
1 tablespoon tomato
  concentrate
salt and pepper
150 ml ($\frac{1}{4}$ pint) dry white
  wine

Marinade
4 tablespoons olive oil
1 each small onion, carrot,
  celery stalk, chopped
1–2 cloves
1 clove garlic, finely
  chopped
2–3 sage leaves or
  $\frac{1}{2}$ teaspoon dried
1 small sprig rosemary or
  $\frac{1}{4}$ teaspoon dried
pinch of salt
6 peppercorns
425 ml ($\frac{3}{4}$ pint) red wine
150 ml ($\frac{1}{4}$ pint) red wine
  vinegar

Wipe the hare with kitchen paper, cut into four and put into a large earthenware dish. Cook the marinade ingredients: heat the oil, add the vegetables and simmer until the vegetables are soft but not brown. Add the cloves, garlic, herbs, salt and peppercorns. Cook for 2 minutes, then add the red wine and vinegar. Bring gently to the boil, take from the heat and let the marinade cool. Pour this over the hare. If the hare is young, leave for only 12 hours; if elderly, up to 24 hours, or even to 48 hours.

Drain the hare pieces from the marinade. Reserve the marinade. Heat 2 tablespoons of oil in a casserole, add the hare pieces and brown them all over. Add the marinade, pouring it slowly through a strainer over the hare. Cover the pan and cook slowly until tender, $1\frac{1}{2}$–2 hours according to the age of the hare. While it is cooking, soak the mushrooms in warm water for 20 minutes. Drain and dry on kitchen paper. Heat the butter with the rest of the oil, add the mushrooms and fry for 5 minutes. Dilute the tomato concentrate with a little hot water and add to the mushrooms. Add salt and pepper and pour this mixture over the hare, add the white wine and continue cooking for another 15 minutes.

The hare can be served in the casserole in which it was cooked. Serve with noodles, rice, polenta (see page 50), or creamed potatoes.

Left : lepre alla Marengo;
right : camoscio in civet

Camoscio in civet
Civet of venison

INGREDIENTS
900 g (2 lb) venison
1 each large carrot, onion
  and stalk celery
1 bottle red wine
1–2 cloves garlic, chopped
3–4 sage leaves or
  $\frac{1}{2}$ teaspoon dried
1 large sprig each
  rosemary and thyme or
  $\frac{1}{4}$ teaspoon dried
3 tablespoons olive oil
25 g (1 oz) butter
flour for dusting

This dish should be prepared 3–4 days in advance. The original recipe came from the country around Valdostano (Aosta) and called for chamois or *camoscio*. Wild chamois is strictly protected but today there are so-called farm-bred, free-range chamois with more tender but less flavoured flesh than the wild chamois but cooked in the same manner. Venison can also be used.

Sponge the meat, wipe dry and cut into stew-size pieces. Slice or chop the vegetables. Put these ingredients together in a bowl with the wine, garlic and herbs. Leave for 3–4 days. Take the meat from the marinade and wipe it dry. Heat the oil and butter together in a large pan, add the meat and cook until it is browned all over. Sprinkle lightly with flour and stir the meat until it is well coated. Add the marinade with vegetables and herbs and cook for about $1\frac{1}{2}$ hours. Take out the meat and rub the vegetables through a sieve. Return the meat to the pan and cover with the sieved vegetables. Continue cooking until the meat is really tender. Sprinkle with freshly chopped parsley.

In the Valdostano region this dish is served with hot polenta (*see page* 50) but it goes equally well with creamed potatoes or chestnuts, creamed or whole.

Cinghiale in agrodolce

Wild boar in a sweet-sour sauce

TO SERVE SIX–EIGHT

INGREDIENTS
boned leg of boar,
  1.8 kg (4 lb)
150 g (5 oz) butter
100 g (4 oz) fat bacon,
  chopped
1 stalk celery, coarsely
  chopped
2 carrots, coarsely chopped
1 large onion, thickly sliced
3 cloves garlic, chopped
4 cloves
2 bayleaves and a little
  fresh sage or $\frac{1}{2}$ teaspoon
  dried
8 peppercorns, crushed
$\frac{1}{2}$ bottle red wine
2 teaspoons salt
4 tablespoons red wine
  vinegar
50 g (2 oz) bitter cooking
  chocolate, grated
3–4 tablespoons single
  cream
1 tablespoon pine-nuts
1 tablespoon sultanas
1 tablespoon sugar,
  preferably brown
a little lemon and orange
  candied peel, chopped
5–6 dried prunes, soaked
  until soft and pitted
Marinade
275 ml ($\frac{1}{2}$ pint) olive oil
a little chopped onion,
  carrot and celery
2–3 cloves garlic, chopped
2–3 bayleaves
plenty of sage leaves
6 peppercorns
1 teaspoon salt
$\frac{1}{2}$ bottle red wine

This recipe should be prepared 1–2 days in advance. A joint of pork (*see facing page*) or boiling ham can also be cooked in the same way if boar meat is not readily available.

First prepare the marinade. Heat the oil, add the vegetables and cook them gently for 5 minutes. Add the remaining ingredients and simmer for 10 minutes. Cool and pour over the meat. Leave for 1–2 days, turning the meat from time to time. Before using, take the meat from the marinade and wipe it dry. Strain the marinade and put aside. Heat the butter in a large pan, add the bacon and fry this until the fat begins to run, then add the boar meat. Brown this all over and add the celery stalk, carrots, onion, garlic, cloves, bayleaves, sage and peppercorns. Cook for a few minutes, add the wine and the wine marinade, bring to a quick boil, cover and cook until the wine has evaporated by about half. Add salt and cook over a moderate heat until the meat is tender, about 3 hours. Take the meat from the pan, put aside but keep hot. Rub the gravy through a sieve, return it to the pan, add the vinegar and the remaining ingredients, stir well and cook for 10 minutes, or until the sauce has thickened slightly. Pour some of the sauce over the meat and serve the rest in a sauceboat.

You can either serve the meat in one piece and carve at table, or cut into slices in the kitchen, put into an appropriate hot serving dish and serve in its sauce, garnished with the prunes. Serve it with creamed potatoes, polenta (*see page* 50) or rice and, if liked, shelled and peeled roasted chestnuts.

Another pleasant flavouring added to the dish in Rome is that of wild cherries. If the sultanas are dry, they should be steeped in water or wine until they are plumped out. Instead of candied peel, I prefer to use dried orange and lemon peel which I dry in the winter on central-heating radiators and keep tightly sealed for even a year or more. Also, for an extra flavour, soak the prunes in wine, brandy or gin instead of water.

Vegetables

Throughout the Italian peninsula vegetables are good, with considerable variety but, above all else, they are seasonal. No one wants asparagus in winter, or chestnuts in summer. One waits with gastronomic patience (also because it is cheaper) for a favourite vegetable to appear in the markets, then to eat it contentedly until its season is over. If one vegetable does predominate over all, it could be the tomato, found everywhere in all shapes and sizes, red and green in colour and used in cooking, in salads, and in sauces.

Vegetables in Italy, like the climate, vary from the top of the boot to the toe, influenced by the sun. In Piedmont and other northern regions are found the hard vegetables, turnips, potatoes, celery and cardoon, the latter not much known in Britain but which grows to an enormous size in Piedmont where it is often eaten raw. It is also used in *bagna cauda*. Other local vegetables, such as forest mushrooms or *funghi* are also eaten raw, with a lemon dressing. Artichokes and asparagus are plentiful and so are truffles when in season. There are also extra large yellow, red and green sweet peppers, hard white cabbages, cauliflowers and courgettes. Such vegetables are served not so much as something to go with a meat dish but as a course on their own, either as part of an antipasto or with a main course.

Over the border into Liguria, a narrow 'rainbow' strip of coast along the Mediterranean with a mild and sunny climate, almost everything appears in the markets during the course of the year and, like Piedmont, the area is rich in mushrooms and *funghi* of all kinds. Italians will never understand the British diffidence towards wild *funghi*. Here, wild or otherwise, they are extremely expensive but quantities are dried for winter use. Also dried are the local chestnuts which only have a short season when fresh.

Lombardy, on the other hand, is so busy producing cheeses, which are some of the finest in the country, that their range of vegetables is not so great as that of other regions in Italy; but their Savoy cabbages, turnips, locally called *rape,* and beans are all good; the latter are also eaten in great quantities by the Tuscans, so much so that Tuscany has even been called the home of the bean-eater. In the Emilia-Romagna region the people are great meat-eaters, but they also grow

A vegetable market in Rome photographed early in the twentieth century

162

potatoes, cardoon and other varieties of hard vegetables, as well as asparagus.

Travelling in the hinterland of Veneto to Treviso you find red chicory, *radicchio rosso*, which is served raw as a salad, braised and stuffed. It has a slightly bitter flavour. One has the impression that the only vegetables which interest the Venetians are their tender peas and asparagus. The cold climate of Trentino-Alto Adige produces a varied but limited number of vegetables. However, it makes up for this in its use of potatoes. A fair quantity of hard, firm cabbages are grown, as well as turnips, pumpkins and courgettes.

Moving southwards towards the centre of Italy we discover that Lazio is the home of broccoli where it is put to good use. This is a region rich in vegetables, with plenty of salad vegetables and herbs. Umbria, 'modest and green' as one writer put it, has olives, *funghi* and tender wild asparagus which, when in season, is more popular than the cultivated variety. Abruzzo-Molise, a fertile region with a mild climate, grows considerable quantities of vegetables which are exported both inside and outside Italy, but the giant cardoon, fennel, sweet and hot peppers, tomatoes, aubergines and courgettes are also popular here.

According to Italian vegetable connoisseurs, Apulia is the real home for vegetables, fresh in the summer but also dried in the sun for winter use. It is this drying in the sun which gives Italian dried vegetables such a good flavour. In Liguria the plum-shaped tomatoes are dried in the sun and preserved in oil to be used as a winter antipasto.

Sicily is the place for the fennel lover, and great lorries laden with the large white bulbs of this aromatic vegetable pound along the roads of the island. Other vegetables are highly rated as well, including aubergines, sweet peppers, broccoli and, of course, tomatoes. As far as Sardinia is concerned, the quality and variety of vegetables are good but one has the impression they are eaten, or served, rather as an afterthought, with one or two exceptions, like artichokes, especially the small chokeless type, which are eaten raw with a salad dressing; wild asparagus is collected avidly during its short season, and so is wild fennel. But the Sardinians prefer to concentrate on meat.

A traditional sight in southern Italy, and still occasionally seen today, was the vegetable seller with his mule

Barbabietole gratinate

Beetroots au gratin

TO SERVE FOUR

INGREDIENTS
675 g (1½ lb) cooked
   beetroots
butter
575 ml (1 pint) béchamel
   sauce
50 g (2 oz) Parmesan
   cheese, grated

In Italy most of the greengrocers and some vegetable-market vendors sell large beetroots which have been baked in cinders until their skins are thick, black, ashy and like a volcanic crust. The flesh is sweet and very tender and no boiled beetroot tastes as good as it is when baked.

Instead of Parmesan cheese, any other strongly flavoured cheese such as Pecorino may be used.

Preheat the oven to 180°C, 350°F, Gas Mark 4. Peel and slice the beetroots fairly thin. Lightly grease a baking dish with butter, add a layer of sliced beetroot, spread this with béchamel sauce and cheese and continue until all the ingredients are used up. The top layer should be of sauce, cheese and slivers of butter. Bake in the oven for about 20 minutes, or until the top is a golden brown. Serve hot.

Carote in salsa uova e limone

Carrots in an egg and lemon sauce

TO SERVE FOUR

INGREDIENTS
450 g (1 lb) carrots
50 g (2 oz) butter
salt and pepper
1 egg
juice of ½ a lemon

A very pleasant way of cooking carrots; this dish marries well with chicken, veal, or even alone.

Wash, trim, peel or scrape the carrots and cut into thin rounds. Put into cold salted water, bring to the boil and cook until the carrots are almost tender. Drain, reserve their liquid and leave the carrots until tepid. Heat the butter in the same pan, add the carrots, salt and pepper and stir until the carrots are coated with butter. Add 1 cupful of the carrot liquid and

continue cooking until the carrots are quite tender. Beat the egg and gradually add the lemon juice, stirring all the time. Take the carrots from the stove, gradually add the egg and lemon mixture, gently stirring all the time, return the pan to the heat and continue to cook over the lowest possible heat until the sauce thickens, but do not let it boil or it will curdle.

Carote al Marsala

Carrots in Marsala

TO SERVE FOUR

INGREDIENTS
450 g (1 lb) carrots
50 g (2 oz) butter
salt and pepper
1 teaspoon sugar
150 ml (¼ pint) dry Marsala

This is a speciality from Sicily, which is the home of Marsala.

Wash, trim and peel or scrape the carrots and slice into thin rounds. Heat the butter, add the carrots, stir well and let them cook gently until they begin to change colour. Add salt, freshly ground white pepper, sugar and Marsala. Continue cooking gently until the carrots are tender and all the wine has evaporated.

This dish is served hot and recommended with roast meats and poultry, also with grills.

Top : carote al Marsala;
centre : carote con panna e prezzemolo;
bottom : carote in salsa uova e limone

Carote con panna e prezzemolo

Carrots with cream and parsley

TO SERVE FOUR

INGREDIENTS
900 g (2 lb) young carrots
50 g (2 oz) butter
1 egg
150 ml (¼ pint) single cream
1 heaped tablespoon finely chopped parsley

This is a dish which can be served on its own. If young tender carrots are not available, large ones can be peeled and sliced into thin rounds.

Wash and trim the carrots. Cook whole in enough boiling salted water to cover and with half the butter until tender but not soft. Stir from time to time and take care the liquid does not evaporate. Soften the remaining butter and beat into the egg. Then mix with the cream and add the parsley. Take the pan from the stove and stir this mixture into the carrots, mixing thoroughly but gently. Return the pan to the stove and gently reheat, but do not let the carrots come to the boil again or the sauce will curdle. Serve immediately.

Cavolo al vino bianco

Cabbage cooked in white wine

TO SERVE FOUR

INGREDIENTS
1.5 kg (3 lb) hard white
   cabbage
25 g (1 oz) butter
1 tablespoon olive oil
1 medium-sized onion,
   very finely chopped
275 ml (½ pint) boiling
   water
pinch of salt
1 teaspoon sugar
1 tablespoon capers
150 ml (¼ pint) dry white
   wine

Cut the cabbage into four, discarding any wilted leaves and cutting out the hard core. Leave in iced salted water for 30 minutes, drain and shred. Heat the butter and oil together in a large pan, add the onion and fry until brown. Add the cabbage and stir thoroughly until well coated with oil and onion. Add the remaining ingredients, stir again, cover the pan and cook over a low heat for 20–25 minutes until the cabbage is tender.

Serve as a main course with fried bacon, tomatoes or sausages, or with cold ham.

Crauti

Sauerkraut Tyrol style

TO SERVE FOUR–SIX

INGREDIENTS
150 ml (¼ pint) olive oil
1 small onion, chopped
2 cloves garlic, chopped
900 g (2 lb) sauerkraut
stock
freshly ground black
   pepper
a few juniper berries,
   crushed
2 bayleaves

Tinned sauerkraut can be used in this recipe, although if sauerkraut loose in a tub is available, this obviously is better.

Heat the oil in a pan, add the onion and garlic and, when the onion begins to change colour, add the sauerkraut, stir well, then add enough stock to thoroughly moisten it. (The recipe calls for gravy from some roast pork but stock may be substituted for this.) Add pepper, the crushed juniper berries and bayleaves and continue cooking for 30 minutes.

A peeled and chopped apple sometimes is added to the sauerkraut during cooking.

Top: cavolo al vino bianco; *bottom:* crauti

Involtini di verza

Stuffed Savoy cabbage
leaves

TO SERVE FOUR

INGREDIENTS
1 small bread roll
milk
1 Savoy cabbage
225 g (½ lb) cooked minced
   meat
2 tablespoons grated
   cheese, preferably
   Parmesan
1–2 strips lemon rind,
   finely chopped
1–2 cloves garlic, crushed
2 whole eggs
salt and pepper
grated nutmeg
pinch of flour
1 egg, beaten
4–6 tablespoons olive oil
50 g (2 oz) butter

Break the roll into pieces and soak in enough milk to cover until they are soft. Drain, squeeze dry and crumble. Heat plenty of salted water in a wide shallow pan. Wash and carefully pull off all the leaves of the cabbage and select the largest and the best. You need 16–20 leaves. Plunge one by one into the boiling water and cook for about 2 minutes. Take from the pan with a perforated spoon and spread out on a cloth to dry. Prepare the filling. Put the meat, cheese, lemon rind, garlic, eggs, roll, 2 tablespoons of milk, salt, pepper and nutmeg into a basin. Mix thoroughly. Put a little of this mixture on to each of the leaves. Wrap each leaf firmly around its stuffing to completely enclose it. Gently dip each cabbage roll in flour and beaten egg. Heat the oil and butter together in a frying pan and fry the cabbage rolls until lightly browned and crisp. Serve hot.

These cabbage rolls usually are served with tomato sauce (*see page* 184) or with warmed cream.

Top : cavolo rosso;
bottom : cavolini di Bruxelles
con pancetta

Cavolo rosso

Red cabbage

TO SERVE FOUR

INGREDIENTS
1 hard red cabbage, about
 900 g (2 lb)
40 g (1½ oz) butter
2 tablespoons olive oil
50 g (2 oz) bacon, chopped
1 medium-sized onion,
 chopped
275 ml (½ pint) red wine
salt and pepper

This is a recipe from the Alto-Adige
region. Red cabbage can be served with all
types of meat and its flavour is even better
if reheated the following day after cooking.

Discard any broken or wilted leaves and
cut the cabbage in fine strips. Wash and
drain well. Heat the butter and oil in a pan,
add the bacon and, as this begins to cook,
add the onion and fry until it begins to
change colour. Add the cabbage, stir it well
into the fat, onion and bacon, then add the
wine, salt and pepper and cook over a
moderate heat, uncovered, for about 1½
hours, stirring from time to time, or until
the cabbage is tender.

Cavolini di
Bruxelles con
pancetta

Brussels sprouts with
bacon

TO SERVE FOUR *10*

INGREDIENTS
900 g (2 lb) Brussels sprouts *5*
100 g (4 oz) fat bacon   *10*
 rashers
50 g (2 oz) butter   *5*
salt and pepper
2–3 sprigs parsley, finely *5*
 chopped

Brussels sprouts are not all that often seen
in Italian vegetable markets, as their
season is short and they can be expensive.
Therefore, when the Italian housewife
buys them she makes a main dish of them.
Sometimes they are boiled first and then
lightly fried and served with thick wedges
of lemon; or they are boiled, drained and
tossed in a mixture of melted butter,
grated cheese and single cream, or they are
cooked together with shelled and skinned
chestnuts.

Trim the Brussels sprouts, discarding any
spoiled leaves, make a slit in the bottom of

each one and drop into lemon-flavoured
cold water. Drain and put the sprouts into
a pan with plenty of lightly salted boiling
water. Cook until *al dente*, which should
take 10–15 minutes.

 In the meantime chop the rashers into
short lengths. Heat the butter in a large
frying pan, add the bacon and cook it over
a moderate heat until fairly crisp. Drain the
sprouts, add them to the pan, mix well,
add salt and pepper (test before adding salt
for the bacon may have enough) and
immediately before serving add the parsley.
Serve at once.

167

Cavolfiore alla siciliana

Cauliflower Sicilian style

TO SERVE FOUR

INGREDIENTS
900 g (2 lb) cauliflower
5–6 salted anchovies,
  filleted
olive oil
1 large onion, finely sliced
100 g (4 oz) large black
  olives, pitted and halved
50 g (2 oz) Caciocavallo
  or Gouda cheese, thinly
  sliced
pinch of salt
275 ml (½ pint) red wine
finely chopped parsley for
  garnishing

Although red wine is stipulated for this recipe, white wine is usually more suitable when using white cauliflower; also green olives are better than black.

Cut off and discard the outer leaves and hard stalks of the cauliflower. Wash well and slice the curd. Wash the anchovies: if salted anchovies are not available, use those in oil but without washing. Cut into slivers. Put 2 tablespoons of oil in the bottom of a casserole, cover with a layer of sliced onion, a few olives, anchovy fillets, slices of cheese, a little salt and then a layer of cauliflower. Repeat this until all the ingredients are used up. Add the wine and several tablespoons of oil. Cook on top of the stove for about an hour and do not at any time stir. When the cauliflower is cooked, all the liquid should have evaporated but even so the dish will not be dry. Serve hot sprinkled with parsley.

Top : cavolfiore alla siciliana;
bottom : cavolfiore dorato

Cavolfiore dorato

Fried cauliflower

TO SERVE FOUR

INGREDIENTS
1 large cauliflower
1 slice of lemon
flour for coating
1 egg, well beaten
50 g (2 oz) butter or
  margarine

Wash the cauliflower and divide the curd into sprigs. Cook in boiling salted water with a slice of lemon until the sprigs are tender. Drain them well. Lightly coat the sprigs with flour and then dip in beaten egg. Heat the butter in a pan, add the sprigs and fry until brown.

Cipolline in agrodolce

Onions in a sweet-sour sauce

TO SERVE FOUR

INGREDIENTS
675 g (1½ lb) 'button'
  onions
25 g (1 oz) sultanas
50 g (2 oz) speck or fat
  bacon (*see page* 213)
50 g (2 oz) butter
1 tablespoon sugar
150 ml (¼ pint) wine
  vinegar
pinch of salt

If the small, flat 'button' onions are not available, then choose small mild ordinary ones. If possible, all the onions should be of the same size.

Peel the onions and drop them into boiling water to blanch for 5–6 minutes. Drain, cool, slice thickly if not using 'button' onions and dry well. Steep the sultanas in warm water to plump out. Dice the speck and put together with the butter into a shallow wide pan and fry until the fat runs freely. Add the sugar, stir well, then add the vinegar and an equal quantity of hot water, salt and finally the onions. Cover the pan and cook for 15–20 minutes, or until the onions are tender. Stir carefully from time to time to prevent sticking. Just before serving, drain the sultanas and add to the pan.

Serve hot with triangles of crisply fried bread or toast, or cold with antipasti.

Cipolle ripiene
Stuffed onions

TO SERVE FOUR

INGREDIENTS
4 large onions
1 stalk celery
1–2 cloves garlic
2–3 leaves sage or
  ½ teaspoon dried
2 tablespoons olive oil
2–3 sprigs parsley, finely
  chopped
4 heaped tablespoons
  breadcrumbs
salt and pepper
4 heaped tablespoons
  grated cheese, such as
  Parmesan
25 g (1 oz) butter or
  margarine

Peel off the outer leaves of the onions carefully to retain their shape. Cut a slice off the top of each, make a few gashes around the onions and pierce each one through the centre with a large fork. Put the onions into a large wide pan with plenty of boiling water and cook until just tender. Drain, cool slightly and then carefully push out the centres. Preheat the oven to 220°C, 425°F, Gas Mark 7. While the onions are cooking, finely chop the celery, garlic and sage. Heat the oil, add the chopped ingredients, including parsley, cook for about 5 minutes, then add the breadcrumbs, salt, pepper and the grated cheese. Cook this mixture for 2–3 minutes, mixing it well to a paste. Stuff the paste into the onions. Place in a generously buttered baking dish, preferably one which can be brought to the table, top each one with slivers of butter and bake in the oven for 30–45 minutes. Serve hot.

Cipolle di Napoli
Onions baked in Marsala

TO SERVE FOUR

INGREDIENTS
8 large white onions, all the
  same size
salt and pepper
150 ml (¼ pint) olive oil
8 cloves
1 sprig thyme
150 ml (¼ pint) dry
  Marsala or sherry
1 tablespoon capers

This dish comes from the south, and is generally attributed to Naples. Serve as a separate course.

Preheat the oven to 180°C, 350°F, Gas Mark 4. Peel the onions, prick them all over with the prongs of a fork and place in one layer in a shallow baking pan. Sprinkle with salt, pepper, oil, cloves and thyme. Cover the pan and bake in the oven for about 1 hour, or until the onions are tender. Sprinkle the Marsala over the onions and cook uncovered until this has evaporated. Arrange the onions on a serving dish, discard the cloves and thyme, sprinkle with capers and serve hot.

Top left : cipolle ripiene; *right* :
cipolle di Napoli; *bottom right* :
cipolline in agrodolce

Fagiolini in padella or alla napoletana

French beans cooked with tomatoes

TO SERVE FOUR

INGREDIENTS
450 g (1 lb) French beans
450 g (1 lb) ripe tomatoes
25 g (1 oz) butter
2 tablespoons olive oil
1 medium-sized onion,
    finely chopped
1–2 cloves garlic, finely
    chopped or crushed
salt and pepper
2 hard-boiled eggs,
    chopped
grated Parmesan cheese

Although this recipe calls for the small crisp French beans, ordinary runner beans may be cooked in the same way but they must be trimmed and broken into lengths of about 8 cm (3 in), not finely sliced. If the French beans are very small, leave them whole or snapped into half. Instead of fresh tomatoes, tinned ones may be used.

Trim the beans, wash and leave for about 30 minutes in iced water; if they have come straight from the garden this is not necessary. Peel and coarsely chop the tomatoes. Heat the butter and oil in a deep frying pan, add the onion and fry gently until a golden colour and soft. Add the garlic, then the tomatoes, stir well and let

Top left: fagiolini in padella;
right: fagiolini rifatti;
bottom left: fagiolini al sugo
di limone; *right*: fagioli
all' uccelletto

the tomatoes come to a slow boil. Add the beans, salt and pepper, cover the pan, lower the heat and cook gently for 45 minutes, until they are very soft. Serve hot, garnished with the eggs and sprinkled with the grated cheese.

The beans also can be served warm or cold, as an antipasto.

Fagiolini rifatti
Twice-cooked green beans

TO SERVE FOUR–SIX

INGREDIENTS
900 g (2 lb) green beans
4 tablespoons olive oil
2 cloves garlic, crushed
450 g (1 lb) tomatoes,
   peeled and chopped
2–3 fresh basil leaves
salt and pepper

French beans are the usual type of bean used in this recipe but tender young runner beans may be used instead.

Wash the beans and chop off the tops and tails. If using runner beans, do not slice but cut them into 2 or 3 largish pieces. Cook in boiling salted water until tender. Meanwhile heat the oil in a pan, add the garlic, cook for a minute or so, then add the tomatoes and basil. Add salt and pepper and cook over a brisk heat for 10 minutes, crushing the tomatoes to a thick pulp with a wooden spoon. Drain the beans thoroughly, add them to the pan and stir well into the sauce to coat them and continue cooking for a further 20–25 minutes, by which time the sauce will be thick and the beans very tender.

Fagiolini al sugo di limone
French beans with lemon

TO SERVE SIX

INGREDIENTS
900 g (2 lb) French beans
1 clove garlic
150 ml ($\frac{1}{4}$ pint) olive oil
salt and pepper
1 teaspoon sugar
575 ml (1 pint) vegetable
   stock or water
juice of 1 lemon
1 tomato, peeled and
   chopped
1 hard-boiled egg, chopped
1 tablespoon finely
   chopped chives

Top and tail the beans. Crush the garlic. Heat the oil in a medium-sized pan, add the garlic, salt and sugar, stir well and cook over a low heat for a minute or two. Add the beans, stir well until they are coated with the oil and garlic, then cook for 5 minutes over a low heat. Add the stock, cover the pan and cook until the beans are tender, even brown, and all the liquid has been absorbed. Add pepper to taste, lemon juice and serve, either hot or cold, garnished with the tomato and hard-boiled egg and sprinkled with chives.

Fagioli all'uccelletto
Dried beans cooked in sage

TO SERVE FOUR–SIX

INGREDIENTS
450 g (1 lb) white dried
   haricot beans
a few sprigs of fresh
   parsley and marjoram to
   taste
1 carrot
1 stalk of celery
3–4 tablespoons olive oil
3 cloves garlic
3–4 leaves sage or
   1 teaspoon dried
1 tablespoon tomato
   concentrate
red wine vinegar (optional)

The reference to *uccelletto*, meaning a small bird, in this Tuscan recipe is because of the sage, which is always used when cooking small birds.

Soak the dried beans overnight, drain and put into a large pan together with fresh water to cover, add the parsley, marjoram, carrot and celery, and cook over a moderate heat until the beans are tender. Drain well. Heat the oil in a large pan, add the garlic, sage and tomato concentrate, diluted with about 275 ml ($\frac{1}{2}$ pint) of water. Stir well, then add the beans while they are still hot and let them cook gently for 15 minutes.

The beans are served hot as an accompaniment to main dishes, especially sausages. A dash of good quality wine vinegar can be added to the beans just before they are served.

Parmigiana di melanzane

Baked aubergine

TO SERVE FOUR–SIX

INGREDIENTS

900 g (2 lb) aubergines
salt
225 g ($\frac{1}{2}$ lb) Mozzarella
  cheese
2 tablespoons olive oil
900 g (2 lb) tinned
  tomatoes, peeled and
  chopped
2–3 leaves fresh basil, finely
  chopped or $\frac{1}{2}$ teaspoon
  dried
1 teaspoon sugar
salt and pepper
olive oil
50 g (2 oz) grated
  Parmesan cheese
fine breadcrumbs (optional)

This dish is popular throughout the south of Italy. In Bari there is a similar dish called *Parmeggianne* which uses Pecorino cheese instead of Parmesan. In Britain, Cheddar cheese allowed to get a little dry can be used.

Peel the aubergines and cut into medium-thick slices. Sprinkle with salt and leave covered and weighted down on a tilted plate for about an hour to let the bitter juices drain away. Thoroughly rinse and wipe dry before using. If working against time, this procedure can be dispensed with. Slice the Mozzarella cheese. Heat 2 tablespoons of oil, add the tomatoes, basil, sugar, salt and pepper and cook until the tomatoes have formed a thick sauce for between 20–30 minutes. Preheat the oven to 220°C, 425°F, Gas Mark 7. Heat a good quantity of oil in a large frying pan. Add the aubergine slices a few at a time and brown on both sides. Take from the pan with a perforated spoon and drain on

kitchen paper. Spread a layer of aubergine on the bottom of a deep casserole, sprinkle with Parmesan cheese, add a layer of sliced Mozzarella, then spread this with the tomato sauce. Continue in this way until all the ingredients are finished, making the top layer one of aubergine. Sprinkle with breadcrumbs if using. Bake in the oven for about 30 minutes. This dish can be served either hot or cold.

Parmigiana di melanzane

Patate alla triestina

Triestan baked potatoes

TO SERVE FOUR

INGREDIENTS

900 g (2 lb) medium-large
  potatoes
3 tablespoons cooking fat
  or dripping
2 large onions
100 g (4 oz) smoked bacon
50 g (2 oz) butter
salt and pepper

Bring plenty of cold salted water to a bubbling boil in a large saucepan. In the meantime wash, peel and slice the potatoes, not too thinly. As soon as the water is boiling, plunge the potatoes into the pan and boil for 3 minutes. Drain in a colander and let them dry. Preheat the oven to 200°C, 400°F, Gas Mark 6. Heat the fat in a large baking pan until it is very hot, add the potatoes and fry until they just begin to change colour, then put the pan into the oven and bake the potatoes for about 1 hour. In the meantime thinly slice the onions and cut the bacon into strips. Heat the butter in a frying pan, add the bacon and onions and cook until the onions are soft. Add this mixture to the potatoes, mix carefully, add salt and pepper and continue cooking until the potatoes are tender, a further 30–40 minutes in all. Serve hot.

Top left : patate alla triestina;
right : patate alla pizzaiola;
bottom : crocchette di patate

Patate alla pizzaiola

Potatoes in a tomato sauce

TO SERVE FOUR

INGREDIENTS
900 g (2 lb) floury potatoes
salsa alla pizzaiola
    (*page* 184)

This is a very Neapolitan rustic dish to be served as a main course.

Wash the potatoes and cook them in their skins until tender. While they are cooking, prepare the sauce. As soon as the potatoes are tender, take from the stove, drain, cool slightly and peel. According to their size, either keep them whole or cut into thick slices. Add the potatoes to the sauce, continue cooking until they are reheated and serve hot.

Crocchette di patate

Potato croquettes

TO SERVE SIX

INGREDIENTS
150 g (5 oz) Mozzarella or
    Bel Paese cheese
900 g (2 lb) floury potatoes
50 g (2 oz) butter
4 egg yolks, well beaten
pinch of grated nutmeg
flour
olive oil
1 egg, well beaten
fine breadcrumbs

Cut the cheese into 12 cubes. Peel and cook the potatoes in boiling salted water until soft. Drain thoroughly and, while still hot, rub them through a ricer or mash until smooth. Add the butter, beat well and when this is completely amalgamated, add the egg yolks and nutmeg, beating well all the time. Turn the potato on to a floured board, smooth it down and leave until cold. Take off small pieces with floured hands – you should make 12 croquettes – and mould the pieces into fat, shortish sausages. In the middle of each put a cube of the cheese and cover it well. Prepare a frying pan with hot oil for deep frying. Drop the croquettes first into beaten egg, then into breadcrumbs and fry for about 5 minutes until a golden brown all over. Serve with a green salad.

Piselli al prosciutto

Peas braised with ham

TO SERVE FOUR

INGREDIENTS
900 g (2 lb) fresh peas, shelled weight
50 g (2 oz) butter
1 small mild onion, finely chopped
½ cup hot water or white meat stock
salt and pepper
100 g (4 oz) smoked bacon or Parma ham, diced

This is a very popular Italian dish.

Shell the peas and put them into a pan with the butter, onion, water and seasoning and cook gently until tender. Just before the peas are ready, add the bacon and simmer for a minute or so until this is hot. This can be served as a separate course.

If fresh peas are not available, use frozen ones but defrost them thoroughly before using and add them to the onion and butter in the pan without adding any liquid. Cook the peas uncovered for about 5 minutes, then add the bacon, heat through and serve.

Piselli alle noci

Peas with nuts

TO SERVE FOUR

INGREDIENTS
50 g (2 oz) small carrots
150 ml (¼ pint) hot stock or water
100 g (4 oz) butter
¼ teaspoon sugar
450 g (1 lb) peas, shelled weight
salt
12 walnuts

Frozen peas, not *petits pois*, may be used in this recipe. This is a dish to be served as a separate course, and is delicate in flavour.

Scrape and dice the carrots. Put the stock into a pan, add the carrots, half the butter and the sugar. Cook gently for 10 minutes, then add the peas and salt and cook for about 15 minutes, or until the peas are tender and all the liquid has evaporated. Meanwhile crack the walnuts and break the kernels into halves, but do not remove the skin. When the peas are cooked, take from the stove, stir in the rest of the butter and serve hot, garnished with the walnuts.

Piselli con il riso e il pollo

Peas with rice and chicken

TO SERVE FOUR

INGREDIENTS
25 g (1 oz) butter
100 g (4 oz) onion, thinly sliced
350 g (12 oz) boned chicken breast
2 sprigs parsley, finely chopped
2–3 teaspoons pine-nuts (optional)
425 ml (¾ pint) boiling meat stock
450 g (1 lb) peas, shelled weight
2–3 chicken livers, chopped
225 g (8 oz) fine grain rice
2 egg yolks
juice of 1 lemon

Large frozen peas, not *petits pois*, may be used instead of fresh ones if necessary.

Heat the butter in a pan, add the onion and fry it until soft but do not let it brown. Cut the chicken breast into strips about 3 cm (1 in) wide. Add to the pan with the parsley and pine-nuts, if using. Cover with the meat stock, then add the peas and cook over a slow heat for about 20 minutes, or until the peas and chicken are tender. Just before the end of cooking time, add the chicken livers. While the peas are cooking, boil the rice until tender – any method may be used for this. Beat the egg yolks, add the lemon juice, plus 1–2 tablespoons of the hot stock. Take the chicken breast from the pan but keep it hot. Add the egg and lemon sauce to the sauce in the pan and mix well over a slow heat, stirring quickly all the time to ensure that the egg and lemon is well amalgamated into the sauce. Drain the rice. To serve, put the rice on to a hot serving dish, add the peas with the sauce and finally the chicken breasts. It is important that all the ingredients are kept hot and the dish served as hot as possible.

Porri brasati

Braised leeks

TO SERVE FOUR

INGREDIENTS
4 leeks, about 450 g (1 lb)
200 g (7 oz) carrots
1–2 stalks celery
100 g (4 oz) onions
butter or other fat for
    greasing
2–3 sprigs parsley, finely
    chopped
1–2 bayleaves
salt and pepper
275 ml (½ pint) meat stock
2 eggs
275 ml (½ pint) milk

Preheat the oven to 180°C, 350°F, Gas Mark 4. Cut off the green parts of the leeks, and thoroughly wash under cold running water. Cut each leek into lengths about 8 cm (3 in). Wash, slice or dice the remaining vegetables. Rub a shallow casserole with butter. Add the sliced and diced vegetables, parsley and bayleaves. Sprinkle with salt and pepper. Arrange the leeks neatly on top, add the meat stock, cover, put into the oven and cook for 40–45 minutes, or until all the vegetables are tender. After 30 minutes, beat the eggs into the milk, add a little salt and pour this mixture over the leeks. Return the casserole to the oven and continue cooking, uncovered, for 15 minutes.

Porri con sugo di pomodori

Leeks in a tomato sauce

TO SERVE FOUR

INGREDIENTS
900 g (2 lb) leeks
25 g (1 oz) butter
25 g (1 oz) fat bacon, diced
1 small onion, sliced
225 g (8 oz) ripe tomatoes,
    peeled and chopped
2–3 leaves basil, chopped
    or 1 tablespoon chopped
    parsley

Leeks, if young, are milder than onions in flavour. For this recipe the leeks should be of medium size.

Cut off most of the green part of the leeks. Discard any coarse outer leaves; thinly slice off the base, leaving enough to hold the leeks together. Slit the leeks about a third of the way down and wash them under running water, opening the tops to ensure all dirt is removed. Drain upside down. Put the leeks into boiling, salted water and cook for 15–20 minutes. Drain thoroughly in a colander but reserve the liquid. In the same pan heat the butter, fry the bacon and add the onion. When this starts to brown, add the tomatoes and cook until they are soft. Add the basil, return the leeks and continue cooking in the sauce for about 5 minutes. Add a cup of the leek liquid and cook until the leeks are quite tender, adding more of the leek liquid if required. Serve with the sauce in a shallow dish.

Top left : piselli al prosciutto;
top right : piselli alle noci;
bottom left : piselli con il riso e il pollo; *bottom right :* porri con sugo di pomodori

175

Sedano al forno

Baked celery with bacon and tomatoes

TO SERVE THREE–FOUR

INGREDIENTS
1 large head celery
juice of 1 lemon
olive oil
4 rashers streaky bacon, diced
1 medium-sized onion, sliced
salt and pepper
225 g (8 oz) tomatoes
2–3 sprigs parsley, finely chopped

In this recipe tinned or fresh tomatoes may be used but, if using the former, they must be well drained. The best choice for tinned tomatoes in an Italian recipe are Italian peeled ones. Fresh tomatoes must be peeled, seeded and chopped; tinned ones need to be pulped.

Separate the stalks of celery, wash well, drain, discard any badly bruised stalks and cut the rest into 15 cm (6 in) lengths. Bring a large pan of water to the boil, add the lemon juice and celery and boil rapidly for 5 minutes. Take from the pan and drain well but keep the water. In a large pan heat 4 tablespoons of oil, add half the bacon, and all the onion and fry until the onion changes colour and the fat runs freely from the bacon. Add the celery, raise the heat and cook briskly for 5 minutes. Add salt, pepper and the celery liquid. Cover the pan and cook until the celery is tender, 10–15 minutes, depending on the quality of the celery. Preheat the oven to 180°C, 350°F, Gas Mark 4. Transfer the celery, bacon, onion and oil to a baking dish, sprinkle the remaining bacon over the top, add the tomatoes, parsley, more salt and pepper and a few drops of oil and bake in the oven for about 10 minutes. Serve as a main course.

Finocchi gratinati

Fennel au gratin

TO SERVE FOUR

INGREDIENTS
900 g (2 lb) bulb fennel
50 g (2 oz) butter
salt and pepper
grated nutmeg
50 g (2 oz) grated cheese, preferably Parmesan

There are several varieties of fennel, both a herb and a vegetable of ancient lineage. The type used in this recipe, and generally in Italy, is the bulb fennel, often known as Florentine fennel. Fennel is a digestive and, according to some authorities, useful when slimming.

The fennel bulb is large, with a faint aniseed flavour and can be used for celery in almost all recipes.

Preheat the oven to 220°C, 425°F, Gas Mark 7. Wash the fennel, discard any bruised leaves, cut off surplus stem and cut the bulbs into halves horizontally. Cook in lightly salted water until tender. Drain well, then place in a buttered shallow gratin dish. Sprinkle with salt, pepper and nutmeg to taste, cover with grated cheese, dot with slivers of butter and bake in the oven until just browned.

Top : sedano al forno;
bottom : zucchini in salsa
al Marsala

Zucchini in salsa al Marsala

Courgettes in a
Marsala sauce

TO SERVE SIX

INGREDIENTS
900 g (2 lb) courgettes
salt to taste
Sauce
4 egg yolks
150 ml (¼ pint) dry
   Marsala or sherry
salt
2 tablespoons water
40 g (1½ oz) butter, cut into
   slivers

This dish can be served as a hot antipasto.

Wash the courgettes, trim both ends and slice into thick rounds. Cook gently in a little salted water until tender, about 15 minutes. In the meantime prepare the sauce. Beat the egg yolks, combine with the Marsala and beat again until the mixture is fluffy. Add salt and water and pour this mixture into the top of a double boiler. Cook over hot but not boiling water, stirring constantly until the mixture thickens. Take from the heat, add the butter and stir until it is dissolved into the sauce. Drain the courgettes, place them in a hot serving dish and pour the sauce over the top. Serve at once.

   The sauce goes equally well with green beans and white cabbage.

Sauces

Sauces of all kinds are an essential part of the Italian kitchen and it is not surprising that Italian cooks have been experimenting with them since the days of the Romans. They learned much of the art of sauce making from the Greeks and later imparted some of their knowledge to the French, who continued the good work. A great deal has been written on the ancient Roman sauces, in particular *garum* which was as much a marinade as a sauce. Modern writers have been wont to liken it to the British Worcestershire sauce which has its origins in India.

The Italians have gone a long way in the art of making rich exuberant sauces, with plenty of variety and originality, although, oddly, their sauces are much simpler to prepare than those of the French, less subtle and certainly less demanding. Often it does not matter if an odd ingredient cannot be found, or if the cook changes a little of this or that to suit his own taste. What is important to the Italian cook is that his sauces have a freshness of flavour.

Italian cooking, and in particular the preparation and eating of pasta, has always relied heavily upon varied and original sauces. The photograph shows a spaghetti-eating contest in Naples at the turn of the century.

Many of the popular sauces which we associate with Italy today originated in the ruling houses of Venice, Florence and Milan, in the days when ships returning from long voyages were laden with rare, unknown spices, like cinnamon, cloves and saffron and cooks began to experiment with these aromatic flavours. However, it must not be overlooked that many of the best known Italian sauces, such as *agliata*, *pesto* or *bagna cauda* are of peasant origin, while the tomato sauces, without which no Neapolitan could exist, are all of very recent origin.

Slightly confusing are those sauces labelled *ragù*, a word which is derived from the French *ragoût*, meaning stew, but which in Italy is nothing like a stew. While a *ragoût* has meat cut into pieces, a *ragù* is a sauce of minced meat, and any type of meat can be used, it is a matter of taste and local tradition. The best known of the *ragù* sauces is that from Bologna which uses a mixture of meats, but not all recipes give the same mixture. In Naples there is the *ragù alla napoletana* in which beef is the only meat used. These *ragù* sauces are given long, slow cooking and can be kept, covered, for several days in the refrigerator.

There is also the *sugo* which can be anything from the gravy or the pan juices from cooked meat, juice from tomatoes and fruit, or a thick vegetable or meat sauce not unlike a *ragù*.

Exceedingly interesting and definitely full of imagination are the *agrodolce* sauces which can include candied fruits, pine-nuts and raisins, vinegar and sugar, wine, bitter chocolate and prunes. These are generally used with game, rabbit or hare, and not, naturally, with delicately flavoured meat or poultry.

Bagna cauda
Garlic and anchovy sauce

TO SERVE FOUR

INGREDIENTS
100 g (4 oz) butter
5 cloves garlic, finely sliced
225 g (½ lb) anchovy fillets
275 ml (½ pint) olive oil

This sauce, one of the oldest in Piedmont, belongs to a medieval trio of sauces, with the Ligurian *agliata* and the *aïoli* of Provence. All are peasant sauces, heavy in garlic and only suitable for strong stomachs.

There are variants in the *bagna cauda*, but two elements are always there – plenty of garlic and anchovies from brine, never a paste from a tube. Some recipes add cream and truffles but, as one Italian culinary writer remarked, 'this inclusion changes the sauce from a rough and ready, happy sauce into a hybrid'. The *bagna cauda* is served in much the same manner as the now well-known Swiss *fondue*. It is prepared in a small earthenware pot and

kept hot on an earthenware chafing dish, heated with a candle providing a minimum of heat. The chafing dish is set in the middle of the table around which sit the family or friends. On the table are dishes filled with prepared raw vegetables such as cardoon, celery, cauliflower, sweet peppers, and strips of fennel, and also a basket of coarse country bread. The bread is speared on to a fork and held with the left hand. In the right hand you take a strip of vegetable, dip it into the sauce and convey it to the mouth holding your chunk of bread under it to avoid oily spots on the cloth.

The *bagna cauda* is not usually served at meals but whenever the Piedmontese feel hungry and also curiously traditionally on Christmas Eve. It is accompanied with plenty of good strong local wine. It is pretty indigestible but for those who can take it, and who like convivial meals with plenty of garlic, then it is a delightful feast. Anchovies in brine in Britain might be something of a problem, but I feel it is permissible to substitute anchovies in oil, well drained. For those who like a fondue evening with friends, this recipe could make a change and the fondue utensils could easily be used.

When using anchovies in brine, they must be washed free of all salt, slit into halves and filleted – not a difficult operation. Heat the butter in a small earthenware or similar pot. Add the garlic and cook gently until it just begins to change colour; add the anchovies, stir well, then add the oil and continue stirring (with a small wooden spoon) until the anchovies have disintegrated. Cook over the lowest possible heat for about 10 minutes, then take the pot to the table, and place on the chafing dish in the centre of the table with a small heat below. The *bagna cauda* sauce is always prepared for use immediately, it cannot be made in advance and then reheated. All the vegetables must be absolutely fresh and, apart from being thoroughly washed and trimmed, should be sliced into suitable pieces for using as dips.

Agliata
Garlic sauce

TO SERVE FOUR

INGREDIENTS
soft part of a small white
  bread roll
white wine vinegar
5 large cloves garlic
150 ml (¼ pint) olive oil
salt and pepper

This is the Ligurian version of the Provençal *aïoli* used with hot or cold meats, vegetables and salt cod dishes. Traditionally it is made in a marble mortar with a wooden pestle but it can be made much more easily in a liquidizer and, indeed, this is done today in Liguria.

Soak the bread in vinegar until soft. Squeeze fairly dry. Put the bread, garlic, oil, salt and pepper into a liquidizer and

whirl to a sauce of mayonnaise consistency.

For those with no liquidizer but with patience, use a mortar and pestle. Peel and chop the garlic and pound in the mortar until it is soft to the point of being almost runny. Gradually add the oil, drop by drop at first, then in a gentle stream as for mayonnaise, pounding all the time. When the oil is finished, add the bread (which must be squeezed dry as for the liquidizer sauce), mix well and add salt and pepper.

Pesto

Basil sauce

TO SERVE FOUR

INGREDIENTS
12–15 sprigs fresh basil
1 clove garlic
sea salt
2 tablespoons grated
    Parmesan cheese
2 tablespoons grated
    Pecorino cheese
5 tablespoons olive oil

There are several recipes for Genoese *pesto*; this one comes from a Ligurian book of traditional recipes, appropriately called *Odor di basilico* with a cover the exact green and fresh colour of basil. The type of salt should be sea salt because this helps to keep the colour of the basil.

Wash the basil well, pat dry and strip the leaves from the stems. Put the leaves together with the garlic in a mortar and work to a smooth paste adding, as you pound, a little salt. Always pound in a clockwise direction and when the leaves are soft, add the two cheeses. Continue working to a smooth paste. Gradually add the oil, stirring well until the mixture is the consistency of a thick mayonnaise. Instead of using a mortar and pestle, the sauce can be made in a liquidizer. Put the leaves, cheeses, salt and oil in a liquidizer and whirl for a few seconds. When you are serving the sauce with pasta, and in Liguria a flat noodle called *trenette* is used, dilute the sauce with a small cup of the hot liquid from the pasta.

In recent years it has become usual to add a tablespoon of pine-nuts to the sauce when pounding, but these are very expensive today.

Salsa di panna

Savoury cream sauce

TO SERVE FOUR

INGREDIENTS
75 g (3 oz) butter
275 ml ($\frac{1}{2}$ pint) single cream
100 g (4 oz) grated
    Parmesan cheese
salt and freshly grated
    nutmeg

Heat the butter until it just melts, add the cream, beat well, then add the cheese, salt and nutmeg to taste. Continue cooking and stirring until the sauce is hot.

To serve, pour immediately it is cooked over hot, drained pasta or gnocchi.

Salsa alla cacciatora

Hunter's sauce

TO SERVE FOUR

INGREDIENTS
175 g (6 oz) mushrooms
4 tablespoons olive oil
100 g (4 oz) butter
1 fair-sized onion, finely
    chopped
275 ml ($\frac{1}{2}$ pint) dry white
    wine
150 ml ($\frac{1}{4}$ pint) hot stock
pinch of salt
100 g (4 oz) tomatoes,
    peeled and chopped
2–3 sprigs parsley, finely
    chopped
fresh tarragon (optional)

This is another sauce for which there are several versions. This recipe produces an excellent rich, dull red sauce used in particular with pasta and polenta.

Wash the mushrooms and slice thinly, caps and stems. Pat dry. Heat the oil and half the butter together in a pan. Add the onion and mushrooms and cook over a good heat for 5 minutes. Add the wine and continue cooking until this is reduced by half. Add the stock, salt and tomatoes, crushing them lightly with a wooden spoon or fork. Stir well and continue cooking for 15–20 minutes. Add the remaining butter, continue to cook and stir until this is melted, then add the parsley and tarragon, if using, and continue cooking gently for about 10 minutes.

Top : salsa di panna; *bottom :* salsa alla cacciatora

Salsa ai capperi

Caper sauce

TO SERVE FOUR

INGREDIENTS
2 tablespoons capers
6 anchovy fillets
1–2 sprigs parsley
150 ml ($\frac{1}{4}$ pint) each red
    wine vinegar and olive oil

This sauce comes from Sicily where capers grow in abundance and are greatly in demand in Sicilian cooking. I remember while in Sicily being awakened morning after morning at dawn by the loud chattering of the local peasants as they climbed the slopes of the hill on which my house was literally perched to collect the capers early in the morning, as they reached their peak. Their season is very short as an edible plant and the flowers bloom only for one day.

Chop the capers, anchovies and parsley finely. Mix with the vinegar, then cook in a small pan over a good heat for 8 minutes. Rub through a sieve or liquidize, return to the pan to slightly reheat, then add the oil, stirring all the time. Serve with boiled meats, grilled or fried fish, and vegetables.

Salmoriglio
Oil, lemon and garlic sauce

TO SERVE FOUR–SIX

INGREDIENTS
juice of 2 lemons
125 ml (scant ¼ pint) water
275 ml (½ pint) olive oil
2–3 sprigs parsley, finely
   chopped
3 cloves garlic, crushed
1 tablespoon finely
   chopped fresh oregano
   or marjoram or
   1 teaspoon dried

This is a simple and ancient sauce from Sicily where it is called *salamurigghiu* or *sammurigghia* and used mainly with grilled swordfish (*see page* 95). It can also be served with other grilled and baked fish, also with grilled chicken and other meats. It is served either hot or cold, also as a salad dressing and it goes well with fresh sliced aubergine.

Strain the lemon juice; scald but do not boil the water. Put the oil into a small pan (preferably one which can be brought to the table), add the scalded water, beating vigorously all the time with a metal whisk.

Still beating, add the lemon juice, parsley, garlic and oregano. When all these ingredients are thoroughly mixed, put the pan on top of a double boiler and cook over hot but not boiling water for 5 minutes, stirring all the time.

Salsa verde
Green sauce

TO SERVE SIX

INGREDIENTS
Method 1
1 tablespoon soft
   breadcrumbs
1 hard-boiled egg yolk
1 tablespoon finely
   chopped parsley
1 tablespoon anchovy
   paste
salt, pepper, olive oil and
   vinegar
Method 2
1 tablespoon soft
   breadcrumbs
milk or water
1 hard-boiled egg yolk
4–6 anchovy fillets
1 large bunch flat-leaved
   parsley, finely chopped
1 clove garlic, finely
   chopped
olive oil
salt and pepper

Method 1
Soak the breadcrumbs in a little water, then squeeze dry. Pound the yolk until soft, mix with the parsley and breadcrumbs and rub through a sieve. Add the anchovy paste, very little salt but plenty of pepper and gradually enough oil to make a thickish sauce, then enough vinegar to dilute it. Spread on thickly sliced tomatoes.

Method 2
Soak the breadcrumbs in a little milk, then squeeze dry. Chop the egg yolk together with the anchovies. Mix with the parsley, breadcrumbs and garlic and either pound in a mortar with a pestle, or whirl in a liquidizer. Add the oil, drop by drop as for making mayonnaise, to make a sauce of a fairly liquid quality. Test for seasoning, adding salt and pepper as required. Serve with boiled meats.

Salsa verde (Method 2)

Salsa agrodolce
Sweet-sour sauce

TO SERVE SIX

INGREDIENTS
100 g (4 oz) prunes
3 tablespoons sugar
3–4 bayleaves, fresh
   or dried
275 ml (½ pint) wine
   vinegar
75 g (3 oz) sultanas
75 g (3 oz) plain dark
   chocolate, grated
½ teaspoon freshly grated
   nutmeg or cinnamon

This recipe comes from Sardinia but throughout Italy such sauces are served with game, wild boar, venison and, in particular, hare. Recipes vary slightly from region to region, some recipes use bitter chocolate, others prefer sweet cocoa. Small dry prunes will require fairly long soaking before they can be used. The large, plump prunes can usually be cooked without soaking.

Pit and chop the prunes. Put the sugar into a small pan, adding the bayleaves and vinegar. Cook over a moderate heat until the sugar has dissolved. Add the sultanas,

prunes, chocolate and nutmeg. Stir well and cook gently until the sauce has thickened, 10–15 minutes.

Salsa di pomodoro
Tomato sauce

TO SERVE FOUR

INGREDIENTS
Method 1
450 g (1 lb) ripe tomatoes
1 small onion, coarsely
    chopped
1 each carrot and stalk
    celery, chopped
2–3 basil leaves, chopped
2–3 sprigs parsley, chopped
salt and pepper
Method 2
900 g (2 lb) tomatoes
2 tablespoons olive oil
25 g (1 oz) butter
50 g (2 oz) fat bacon, diced
1 small onion, finely
    chopped
garlic to taste (optional)
2–3 sprigs parsley, finely
    chopped
chopped thyme to taste
1–2 bayleaves
1 tablespoon flour

Salsa di pomodoro (Method 1)

Method 1
Peel and chop the tomatoes, put into a pan and let them cook until mushy without oil or other fat. Add the chopped vegetables and herbs. Cook gently for 30–40 minutes until the sauce is thick. Rub through a sieve and add salt and pepper. This is one of the simplest forms of home-made tomato sauce.

Method 2
Blanch, peel and coarsely chop the tomatoes. Heat the oil and butter together in a pan, add the bacon and fry until the fat runs and the bacon starts to crisp. Add the onion, garlic (if using) and herbs and continue frying until the onion is a golden brown. Add the flour, stir this well into the fat and cook until it begins to brown. Add the tomatoes and cook gently for 30–40 minutes. Stir well and rub through a sieve.

Salsa alla pizzaiola
Neapolitan tomato sauce

TO SERVE FOUR

INGREDIENTS
3–4 tablespoons olive oil
2–3 cloves garlic, chopped
675 g (1½ lb) ripe tomatoes
salt and pepper
1 sprig of fresh oregano or
    marjoram or ½ teaspoon
    dried

When fresh tomatoes are not in season, this sauce can be made with tinned, peeled tomatoes, preferably the Italian peeled plum-shaped variety. If fresh oregano is not available, then either basil or parsley may be substituted; if none of these, use dried oregano or marjoram.

Heat the oil, add the garlic, fry until it begins to change colour, then add the tomatoes, peeled and coarsely chopped, and cook for about 15 minutes until soft but not a complete pulp. Add salt and pepper

(some cooks also add sugar), a generous quantity of whatever herb is being used, stir well but gently and serve hot.

This quantity of sauce should be sufficient to dress 450 g (1 lb) of pasta or rice. It is also used in *bistecca alla pizzaiola* (*page* 121) and *patate alla pizzaiola* (*page* 173).

Salsa alla boscaiola
The woodcutter's sauce

TO SERVE FOUR

INGREDIENTS
25 g (1 oz) dried
    mushrooms
150 ml (¼ pint) dry white
    or red wine
1 large onion
1 medium-sized carrot
1 stalk celery
2–3 sprigs parsley
1–2 bayleaves
225 g (½ lb) pork sausages,
    preferably Italian
50 g (2 oz) butter
450 g (1 lb) tinned tomatoes
salt and pepper
275 ml (½ pint) single cream

In this dish Italian tinned, peeled plum tomatoes give a more authentic and stronger flavour than fresh British tomatoes. This sauce is particularly adapted for use with *tagliatelle* (wide noodles), gnocchi and polenta, and also with grilled steaks.

Soak the mushrooms in the wine until soft. Drain and chop. Finely chop the onion, carrot, celery, parsley and bayleaves. Skin and crumble the sausages. Heat the butter, add the chopped vegetables and herbs, let these lightly brown, then add the mushrooms and crumbled sausages. Fry these until they begin to colour, then add the wine in which the mushrooms were soaked and continue cooking until this has almost evaporated. Rub the tomatoes through a sieve and stir into the sauce. Cover the pan and cook over a low heat for about 1 hour,

adding a little hot water from time to time if the sauce appears to be too thick. Add the salt, pepper and cream, stir well and cook for a few minutes longer.

Salsa di noci

Walnut sauce for pasta

TO SERVE FOUR–SIX

INGREDIENTS
soft inside of small bread
  roll
a little milk
450 g (1 lb) walnuts
1 clove garlic
3–4 tablespoons grated
  Parmesan or Pecorino
  cheese
pinch of salt
olive oil

Sugo di carne

Meat sauce

TO SERVE FOUR–SIX

INGREDIENTS
25 g (1 oz) dried
  mushrooms
50 g (2 oz) butter
450 g (1 lb) lean beef,
  coarsely minced
$\frac{1}{2}$ a small onion, thinly
  sliced
1 clove garlic, crushed
1 stalk celery, chopped
1 fairly small carrot, finely
  chopped
275 ml ($\frac{1}{2}$ pint) red wine,
  beer or stock
3–4 ripe tomatoes, peeled
  and chopped
salt and pepper
275 ml ($\frac{1}{2}$ pint) water

Il ragù

Bolognese meat sauce

TO SERVE SIX

INGREDIENTS
50 g (2 oz) butter
3 tablespoons olive oil
1 each onion, celery stalk,
  carrot, all finely chopped
1–2 cloves garlic, finely
  chopped
2–3 rashers fat bacon
225 g ($\frac{1}{2}$ lb) each pork and
  beef, coarsely minced
3–4 chicken livers, chopped
  (optional)
2–3 Italian sausages,
  skinned and the meat
  crumbled
150 ml ($\frac{1}{4}$ pint) dry white
  wine
225 g ($\frac{1}{2}$ lb) ripe tomatoes,
  peeled and chopped

This sauce can either be whirled for seconds in a liquidizer or pounded for a somewhat longer time in a mortar with a pestle.

Using a liquidizer
Soak the bread in a little milk until soft, then squeeze dry. Shell the walnuts and crush finely. Chop the garlic. Put the bread, nuts, garlic, cheese and salt into a liquidizer, whirl for a second or two and gradually add enough oil to make a thick paste. Dilute with some of the liquid left over from cooking the pasta or some hot water but do not whirl again.

Steep the mushrooms in warm water for 20 minutes. Squeeze dry and drain. Heat the butter in a pan, add the meat and cook gently, stirring from time to time until it is brown all over. Add the onion, garlic, celery, carrot and mushrooms. Stir well, add the wine and cook for 15 minutes, or until it has evaporated. Add the tomatoes, lower the heat, add salt and pepper, cover the pan and cook gently for about 1 hour until the meat is very soft. Add the water, a

As far as the Italians are concerned there is no one *ragù*, known in England as Bolognese sauce, but many versions. The recipes may fundamentally agree but with differences between every cook, whether in a restaurant or family.

Heat the butter and oil in a wide shallow pan. Add the chopped vegetables, except the tomatoes, the garlic and bacon and cook over a low heat until they begin to change colour. Add the pork and beef, chicken livers, if using, and the sausage-meat. Cook until this mixture begins to brown. Add the wine and continue to

Using a mortar and pestle
Pound the walnuts and garlic together to a paste, add the bread, cheese and salt and continue pounding, adding the oil as you pound. Dilute with pasta liquid.

When serving this sauce with pasta, it is usual to serve grated Parmesan cheese and melted butter. Walnut sauce is also served with boiled turnips and with braised celery.

little at a time, to prevent burning. When the sauce is ready, rub it through a coarse sieve or mouli-légumes or liquidize.

In Liguria a similar sauce is made, adding such herbs as bayleaves, thyme and basil, as well as a couple of cloves. The herbs and cloves are removed and the sauce is served without being sieved.

Serve with spaghetti and other small pasta shapes.

Left: sugo di carne; *right*: il ragù

cook until it has almost evaporated. Rub the tomatoes through a sieve or mouli-légumes, add to the pan, stir well and cook gently for 1–1$\frac{1}{2}$ hours. Stir from time to time adding, if necessary, a little stock or water.

Now for some of those variations. Some cooks add dried mushrooms, soaked and finely chopped, to the above ingredients. Others say no pork, only beef, or add a few tablespoons of cream towards the end of cooking time, or a sprinkling of freshly grated nutmeg and sugar, and also finely chopped marjoram.

Dolci

Italians usually prefer to finish a meal with a bowl of fruit and a platter of cheese, or maybe a combination of both such as Gorgonzola and pears. Puddings as such are made on special occasions and the vast array of *torte* (tarts or pies) are usually made by the local confectioner or pastrycook who produces them in the kitchen behind his shop. Such pastries are wisely considered by most Italians as belonging to the province of the expert and, therefore, are not included in the pages of this chapter.

When the great Italian culinary writer, Luigi Veronelli, talks of *l'Aristocrazia dei dolci* he is referring in the main to the hundreds of biscuits, small and large cakes, which have been traditionally made in Italy for centuries. Many are distinctly rustic in origin and have remained so. Others, such as the Milanese *panettone*, are mass produced today and sold not only throughout Italy but also abroad where Italians have emigrated. He even includes the Turinese *grissini* which bear little resemblance to the general conception of *grissini* for these traditional 'sticks' should be hand made, long and uneven, crisp and yet melting in the mouth. They are still made by some bakers in Turin in the old-established manner and are sought out by *grissini* connoisseurs.

Christmas always brings out a welter of cakes which are rather more breads than cakes as we in Britain know them. Most are made to keep for a considerable time and usually they are rather dry, hence the custom of dunking them in red wine. The best known of the Christmas breads is, as I have already mentioned, the *panettone* which in Milan is followed up at Easter with a loaf in the shape of a dove which commemorates a famous battle fought in the neighbourhood. Siena has a pleasant *panforte* which looks like a round slab of nougat, while Verona feels it can lay claim to gastronomic fame with its *pandoro*, rather lighter and more delicate in flavour than most. Genoa has a fruitier *panettone*, almost in fact a cake, and Perugia for festive occasions produces a fruit cake in the shape of a fish from Lake Trasimeno.

When not producing cake-breads, the Italians are intent on biscuits which are more like the American cookies, and many of which are extremely good. Favourite is the macaroon, invented by the Turinese but now reproduced throughout the country, from the large *brutti ma buoni* (ugly but good) macaroons made with pride

A girl selling fritters and other pastries in Naples at the turn of the century. Fritters are still very popular in Italy today and are cooked in the local market places or on the roadside in spotlessly clean conditions.

in Borgomanera in the Novara province, to the tiny 'buttons' of Salsomaggiore in the Parma province.

Festivals bring out a heady crop of fritters and biscuits. Noted are the Tuscan *brigidini*, delicious aniseed wafers taking their name from the Convent of Santa Brigidini, and some rustic, crunchy biscuits called *biscottini di prato* (meadow biscuits). These are served with a bottle of red wine and once you get started on a plate of these there is no stopping.

Fritters are as popular as biscuits, cooked in the local market places or on the roadside in spotlessly clean conditions, and all worth a trial. In Liguria there are not only fritters, locally called *bugie* (lies), but also a festival of fritters. Among the annual fritters are the variants of *zeppole,* or St Joseph's fritters, and these appear in the delicatessens as well as in the markets and at village fairs. And, while still on the subject of fairs, there are the sugar floss men with their red and white sweet floss which they make up in front of the children.

Further south, in the country, the sweets get sweeter and sweeter. Apulia has an impressive collection of almond and honey cakes, while the island of Sardinia is positively oriental in her sweet touch, with Ricotta-filled pastry ravioli, *sebada*, sprinkled with sugar and hot bitter honey, which are very palatable. Another local favourite are *sospiri*, or angels' sighs, light and airy, and a variety of biscuits flavoured with mastic, a sticky substance which comes from the lentisk tree.

Sicily favours Ricotta-filled cakes and puddings, ice-creams and, if this is possible, the Sicilians are even more generous with the distribution of sugared almonds at weddings, christenings and confirmations than are their fellow Italians. Throughout Italy at all times of the year the confectioners are busy preparing small pink, white or blue gauze bags of sugared almonds which they arrange in their windows to look like fairy bouquets.

Naples is full of sweet-toothed Italians and here we find really richer than rich cakes, cream-filled pastries and streams of clients who keep the pastrycooks busy all day long.

The recipes given in this chapter are indeed Italian, they are family recipes, traditional and perhaps even somewhat on the rustic side. None is difficult.

Sardinian girls in traditional costume at the turn of the century are using the small igloo-shaped ovens then used in both Sardinia and Sicily to cook fancy pastries and breads.

Torta di pane e amaretti

Bread and macaroon pudding

TO SERVE FOUR–SIX

INGREDIENTS
175 g (6 oz) 2-day-old
  bread, crustless
425 ml (¾ pint) milk
200 g (7 oz) macaroons
50 g (2 oz) butter
1 tablespoon flour
100 g (4 oz) sugar
75 g (3 oz) sultanas
chopped candied fruit to
  taste
2 eggs
butter for greasing

This pudding is exceptionally good to eat and simple to prepare but much depends on the strong flavour of almonds, both sweet and bitter, which are used in the Italian *amaretti*. If such quality macaroons are not available, I suggest implementing the flavour slightly with almond essence. Chopped candied peel may be used instead of the usual candied whole fruits, for which the Ligurians are well known, and I also add some chopped dried but not soaked apricots.

Cut the bread into cubes and put into a mixing bowl. Scald the milk, pour this over the bread and leave for 2–3 hours. Crush the macaroons until they are like fine breadcrumbs. Rub the soaked bread through a coarse sieve back into the mixing bowl. Preheat the oven to 180°C, 350°F, Gas Mark 4. Melt the butter over a low heat, add to the bread and stir well. Add 175 g (6 oz) of macaroons, flour, sugar, sultanas, chopped fruit and finally break in the eggs. Mix well to a paste. Rub a round cake pan generously with butter, add the pudding mixture and sprinkle the top with the remainder of the crumbled macaroons. Put into the oven and bake for about 1 hour. Take from the oven and leave the pudding in the pan until it is quite cold before serving.

Fave dei morti

'Dead men's beans'

INGREDIENTS
50 g (2 oz) butter
50 g (2 oz) sugar
1 egg, well beaten
225 g (½ lb) flour
15 g (½ oz) baking powder
100 ml (4 fl oz) brandy,
  rum or sherry
egg for brushing

These morbidly named biscuits are traditionally eaten in many parts of Italy on All Souls' Day, 2 November. Their origin is obscure, although in ancient times beans were connected with death, providing comfort for the departed souls. In Sicily they eat on All Souls' Day similar cakes or biscuits but made in the shapes of arms, legs, ears, and noses, even more morbidly named *ossi dei morti*, bones of the dead. These are hidden in the house together with presents for the children, who are told the biscuits and presents have been sent by the spirits of the departed members of the family.

Preheat the oven to 180°C, 350°F, Gas Mark 4. Cream the butter with the sugar until smooth, add the egg and continue beating until this is completely amalgamated into the butter. Gradually sift in the flour and baking powder, work to a stiff dough, slowly adding brandy and just enough cold water to make a pliable dough. Roll out on a floured pastry board to a thickness of about 1 cm (¼ in). Break off small pieces and mould into shapes like large butter beans. Brush each one lightly with a little beaten egg and bake in the oven for about 15 minutes, or until a golden brown.

Amaretti d'Oristano

Almond macaroons

MAKES FOURTEEN–SIXTEEN

INGREDIENTS
100 g (4 oz) sweet almonds
100 g (4 oz) bitter almonds
225 g (½ lb) castor sugar
1 egg white
icing sugar

The Italians are reputedly the inventors of the irresistible *amaretti* or macaroons, which are to be found throughout Italy, varying considerably in size, shape, and texture. Some, like those from Salsomaggiore in the province of Parma, are exceedingly tiny, like small buttons, while in Liguria they tend towards quite a large but soft version, almost gooey. In Perugia, in Umbria, a similar type of cake called a *pinoccate* is made from pine-nuts which are served at Epiphany and Christmas.

Blanch all the almonds in boiling water for a minute or so, take from the water and pull off their skins as soon as possible. Dry in a warm oven for a few minutes, taking care they do not brown. Pound in a mortar or grind in a liquidizer together with the sugar until very fine. Pass through a sieve. Beat the egg white until stiff but not dry and fold into the almonds and sugar. Pipe in small blobs on to a greased or floured baking sheet, sprinkle lightly with icing sugar and leave for several hours before baking in a moderate oven (180°C, 350°F, Gas Mark 4) for about 15 minutes, or until they are very lightly browned.

The macaroons may be served immediately or kept for a short while in an airtight container.

Top : torta di pane e amaretti;
bottom left : fave dei morti;
bottom right : amaretti d'Oristano

Torta paradiso
Paradise cake

TO SERVE FOUR–SIX

INGREDIENTS
225 g ($\frac{1}{2}$ lb) butter
225 g ($\frac{1}{2}$ lb) sugar
2 eggs (size 3)
2 egg yolks
100 g (4 oz) flour, sifted
100 g (4 oz) potato flour
grated rind of 1 lemon
butter for greasing
icing sugar

Preheat the oven to 180°C, 350°F, Gas Mark 4. Soften the butter and whip it until creamy. Add the sugar, little by little, beating well between each addition. Whisk the eggs and egg yolks together until light and beat, a little at a time, into the creamed butter. Continue beating until the mixture is smooth and thick. Carefully fold in the two flours. Finally add the lemon rind.

Rub a 20-cm (8-in) cake tin with butter and lightly sprinkle with flour. Add the cake mixture, smooth it over and bake in the oven for about 1 hour. Take the cake from the pan and sprinkle with icing sugar.

It is recommended that a paradise cake should be eaten the day after it has been cooked. It keeps best if it is wrapped in foil when cool.

Zuppa inglese

'Tipsy' cake

TO SERVE SIX

INGREDIENTS
350 g (¾ lb) sponge cake
rum or sweet Marsala to
taste
½ quantity *zabaione*
  (*page* 196)
250 ml (½ pint) double
  cream
chopped glacé fruits

This very sweet pudding originated in Sicily, although the *zabaione* is a Piedmontese speciality. Why it was called *zuppa inglese*, or English soup, no one can quite explain. It became a popular sweet in the late nineteenth century, about the time the British were visiting Italy in really large numbers. Maybe some British cook produced a somewhat runny version of our traditional trifle and the Italians quite rightly dubbed it an English soup. There are several versions of this dish, but the following is perhaps the most usual. Instead of using *zabaione*, a rich egg custard or chocolate cream may be used.

Cut the sponge cake into three equal layers. Place one at the bottom of a glass dish in which the pudding is to be served. Sprinkle it with enough rum to evenly soak it but not too well, otherwise it will not only be the sponge which is tipsy. Spread with half the *zabaione* and cover with a second layer of sponge. Soak this in rum and spread with the rest of the *zabaione*; add the final layer of sponge and sprinkle this with rum. Chill and before serving whip the cream until very stiff, coat the top and sides of the pudding, and garnish the top with the glacé fruits.

Cassata alla siciliana
Ricotta cream cake

TO SERVE SIX

INGREDIENTS
450 g (1 lb) Ricotta cheese
100 g (4 oz) sugar
100 g (4 oz) plain dark
    chocolate
1 teaspoon vanilla essence
pinch of salt
4–5 tablespoons rum or
    brandy
chopped candied fruit as
    required
450 g (1 lb) sponge cake
icing sugar

Rub the Ricotta through a sieve, add the sugar and beat well. Grate the chocolate and beat three-quarters of it into the cheese. Add the vanilla, salt and rum and beat the mixture until fluffy. Add the candied fruit. Cut the sponge horizontally into three slices, the shape should preferably be square but round does as well. Put one slice into a mould which it fits exactly. Spread with half the Ricotta filling. Cover with a second layer of sponge, spread with the remaining Ricotta and cover with the last slice of sponge. Press this down lightly, put a weight on top and leave in the refrigerator overnight. Turn out to serve, sprinkled with icing sugar and the rest of the grated chocolate.

Ricotta al caffè
Ricotta with coffee

TO SERVE SIX

INGREDIENTS
675 g (1½ lb) Ricotta cheese
100 g (4 oz) sugar
2 tablespoons finely ground
    coffee beans
3–4 tablespoons rum or
    brandy
coarsely grated bitter
    chocolate

Rub the Ricotta through a sieve and beat until fluffy. Beat in the sugar, then the coffee and finally the rum. Mix well, put into glasses and chill for several hours. Serve sprinkled with grated chocolate.

Budino di ricotta alla romana
Cheesecake Roman style

TO SERVE FOUR–SIX

INGREDIENTS
450 g (1 lb) Ricotta cheese
2 egg yolks, well beaten
100 g (4 oz) sugar
25 g (1 oz) chopped
    candied peel (optional)
150 ml (¼ pint) rum or
    brandy
grated rind of 1 lemon
pinch of salt
butter
flour or fine breadcrumbs
½ teaspoon mixed ground
    cinnamon and castor
    sugar

Preheat the oven to 230°C, 450°F, Gas Mark 8. Rub the Ricotta through a sieve. Add the egg yolks, sugar, candied peel, rum, lemon rind and salt, beat well until the mixture is smooth. Rub a 20 cm (8 in) cake tin with butter and sprinkle with flour. Add the cheesecake mixture and bake in the oven for 10 minutes, lower the heat to 180°C, 350°F, Gas Mark 4 and continue to bake for 30 minutes, or until the cheesecake is set and a toothpick inserted into it comes out dry.

To serve hot, take from the oven, cover the top of the pan with a flat plate, turn it over firmly but carefully and ease out the cake. Serve sprinkled with cinnamon and sugar. To serve cold, turn off the oven heat, leave the door open and the cake in the oven until it is cold before taking it out.

A similar version of this pudding comes from Tuscany and includes sultanas and raisins but dispenses with the rum.

Top : cassata alla siciliana;
centre : ricotta al caffè;
bottom : budino di ricotta alla romana

194

Zuccotto

Pumpkin-shaped cream pudding

TO SERVE SIX

INGREDIENTS

50 g (2 oz) almonds
50 g (2 oz) hazelnuts,
    shelled weight
1 litre (1¾ pints) whipping
    cream
75 g (3 oz) icing sugar
100 g (4 oz) cooking
    chocolate, grated
450 g (1 lb) sponge cake
3 tablespoons brandy
sweet liqueur
butter, icing sugar and
    chocolate or cocoa

A traditional pudding from Tuscany which has nothing to do with pumpkins, except in its shape. It is moulded in a flattish, round pudding mould so that when it is turned out it has something of the shape of half a pumpkin. It is then coated with chocolate and sugar in alternate strips, and manages to look like a beach ball with a brown and white motif.

Blanch, peel and chop the almonds. Put the hazelnuts into a hot oven and leave for 5 minutes. Rub off the skins and chop coarsely. Whip the cream with the sugar until very stiff. Fold in the chopped nuts and the measured quantity of chocolate. Cut the sponge into slices about 1 cm (¼ in) thick and sprinkle each slice with brandy and liqueur. Line a round pudding mould generously with buttered paper and add half the sponge slices. Top the mould with cream to the brim, smooth it over with a knife and then add the remaining sponge slices. Cover, add a weight and leave for at least 3 hours in the refrigerator, longer if possible.

To serve, turn out on to a round flat plate and garnish. This is done by mentally dividing the pudding into large segments (like orange segments) and sprinkling one segment thickly with icing sugar, the next with powdered chocolate, and so on, white and brown all around, making sure of course that the segments are equal and you do not finish up with two brown or two white together.

Zabaione

Egg punch

TO SERVE THREE–FOUR

INGREDIENTS
6 egg yolks
6 tablespoons sugar
12 tablespoons dry Marsala
   or sherry

The old spelling of this well-known Italian sweet or punch was *zabaglione* but today this is regarded as archaic. The usual proportion for a *zabaione* is 1 tablespoon of sugar and 2 tablespoons of Marsala to each egg yolk.

Whisk the egg yolks until they are frothy. Add the sugar and continue beating all the time until the mixture is frothy and a pale yellow colour. Dribble in the Marsala and continue whisking until it is all mixed in. Pour into the top of a double boiler and cook over almost boiling water, stirring all the time until the mixture thickens sufficiently to form small mounds. On no account let the water under the pan boil or even touch the bottom of the top section or the mixture will curdle. Scrape round the sides of the pan continuously. As soon as the punch thickens, pour it into shallow glasses and serve hot, warm or cold sprinkled lightly with grated nutmeg.

Zabaione is recommended by Italian doctors as a restorative. Very rich, very sweet, it is best served with 'cats' tongues' or wine biscuits; or can be poured over stewed fruit. A layer of strawberries soaked in brandy can be placed in a long glass before adding either hot or cold *zabaione*; it can also be used in *zuppa inglese* (see page 193).

Left : zabaione with strawberries;
top right : zabaione;
bottom right : crema alla uova e Marsala

Crema alle uova e Marsala

Marsala egg custard

TO SERVE FOUR

INGREDIENTS
50 g (2 oz) flour
575 ml (1 pint) milk
4 eggs
50 g (2 oz) sugar
275 ml (½ pint) dry
   Marsala or sherry

This pudding comes from the Friuli-Venezia Giulia region which is full of Austrian influenced recipes and has nothing to do with a British custard. It is similar in flavour to a *zabaione* but less rich or sweet. It is served cold.

Sift the flour into a mixing bowl and gradually add the milk, stirring all the time to prevent lumps forming. In another bowl beat the eggs, then add the sugar and continue beating until the mixture is thick. Stir this into the flour and milk mixture and mix thoroughly. Finally add the Marsala, stir well then cook over a moderate heat, stirring with a wooden spoon all the time until the mixture is smooth and very thick. Rinse a glass dish with Marsala, add the custard, cool and put into the refrigerator to set and chill.

Serve either with very thin wine biscuits or 'cats' tongues' and with whipped cream.

Busecchina

Dried chestnuts cooked
in white wine

INGREDIENTS
450 g (1 lb) dried chestnuts
425 ml (¾ pint) white wine
2 tablespoons sugar
pinch of salt
150 ml (¼ pint) double
   cream

Dried chestnuts are usually available during the autumn and winter months in Italian delicatessens. In this recipe either dry or sweet wine may be used, but if the latter, use less sugar, otherwise the dish will be too sweet.

Soak the chestnuts in the wine plus enough water to cover or, if preferred, use only wine. Leave for 12 hours, then put them with their liquid, sugar and salt into a pan and bring slowly to the boil, lower the heat and cook slowly until all the liquid has been absorbed and the chestnuts are tender, 20–30 minutes. Cool, chill and serve with cream.

Top : busecchina;
bottom : torrone al cioccolato

Torrone al cioccolato

Soft chocolate and
nut nougat

INGREDIENTS
175 g (6 oz) butter
175 g (6 oz) finely grated
   bitter chocolate
175 g (6 oz) nuts, shelled
   weight
175 g (6 oz) sugar
1 egg plus 1 extra yolk,
   well beaten
2–3 tablespoons brandy or
   rum
175 g (6 oz) plain,
   unsweetened biscuits
   such as Marie or Petit
   Beurre

The variety in the Italian nougat or *torrone* repertoire is vast. This recipe produces a mixture rather more like a firm fudge as shown in the photograph, although it can be served in a glass bowl as a firm chocolate pudding. Whichever way it is served, it is excellent and curiously not too rich. The types of nuts usually used are walnuts, hazelnuts or almonds, all shelled and coarsely grated, or whirled in a liquidizer.

Heat the butter until soft, add the chocolate and continue beating until the mixture is smooth and absolutely dark brown. Add the nuts. Dissolve the sugar in a few tablespoons of water over a low heat, stirring all the while. Take from the stove and pour at once into the chocolate mixture, stirring all the time. When the mixture is a smooth mass, add the eggs, brandy and finally the biscuits, broken into small pieces. Turn the mixture into a lightly oiled, shallow, square dish if you want to turn it out, cover the top with foil and keep in the refrigerator until the following day. It will keep at least for several days, if required.

Torta di riso
Rice cake

TO SERVE SIX

INGREDIENTS

1 litre (1¾ pints) milk
100 g (4 oz) sugar
rind of 1 lemon, grated
pinch of salt
225 g (½ lb) Italian short
   grain rice
100 g (4 oz) almonds
4–6 bitter almonds
4 eggs
butter for greasing
breadcrumbs

In northern Italy rice cakes are popular and many regions, whether rice growing or not, have their own version, some being extremely rich. The Tuscan version is one of the richest and perhaps also the most difficult to make; thus it is not surprising that in these busy days housewives prefer to buy rice cake from their local pastrycook, a professional who makes them in kitchens behind the shop, as good if not often better than the home effort. The Tuscan version is baked in a pastry casing, the top of which is pinched all round to divide it into portions, these pinches looking like the beaks of birds. Thus, when you go to buy a piece of rice cake in Lucca, for example, you ask for one or two 'becchi' and this often calls for some local ribaldry for, although the literal translation of *becchi* is beaks, it also means a silly fellow or a cuckold in the Tuscan dialect. The recipe I have given is not difficult and comes from Emilia-Romagna.

Preheat the oven to 180°C, 350°F, Gas Mark 4. Put the milk into a large pan, add the sugar and all the lemon rind. Cook over a moderate heat until the milk comes to the boil. Add salt and rice, stir well and continue to cook over a moderate heat, stirring from time to time, until the rice is tender and all the milk absorbed. Take the pan from the heat, leave until the rice is cold but stir well from time to time. Blanch, peel and chop all the almonds. Separate the eggs, beat the yolks lightly and the whites until they are stiff. Rub a cake pan, about 25 cm (10 in) in diameter, with butter and sprinkle lightly with breadcrumbs. Mix the egg yolks into the rice and finally fold in the egg whites. Turn this into the buttered cake pan, cover with foil and bake in the oven for about 30 minutes. Remove the foil and continue baking until the top is a golden brown. Cool before turning the cake out to serve.

Pesche al vino bianco

Peaches in white wine

TO SERVE FOUR–SIX

INGREDIENTS
4–6 large peaches
150 ml (¼ pint) sweet white wine
4–6 tablespoons sugar
3–4 tablespoons water
3–4 tablespoons rum or Maraschino

For this yellow or white peaches may be used, ripe but not soft.

Gently peel the peaches, cut into halves and remove the stones. Put the peaches into a shallow wide sauté pan. In another pan mix the wine with the sugar, put over a moderate heat, stir until the sugar is dissolved, then add the water. Stir this well and cook for 1 minute longer. Pour this syrup over the peaches and cook over a gentle heat until the peaches are soft, 6–8 minutes. Take the peaches from the pan with a perforated spoon, pour the syrup over them, cool, and then chill. Just before serving, pour the rum over them.

Top : pesche al vino bianco;
bottom : pesche ripiene al forno

Pesche ripiene al forno

Stuffed baked peaches

TO SERVE FOUR

INGREDIENTS
4 large peaches
6 almonds, blanched and chopped
a few small macaroons, crushed
1–2 tablespoons finely grated bitter chocolate
275 ml (½ pint) sweet wine
a little butter
sugar to taste

This is a recipe from Piedmont.

Preheat the oven to 200°C, 400°F, Gas Mark 6. Lightly rub the peaches with a cloth and cut into halves. Take out the stones. Scoop out a little of the pulp from each peach half. Combine the pulp, almonds, macaroons and chocolate, mix it well and, if the mixture seems a little dry, moisten it with some of the wine. Put some of the filling into each peach half, top with a good sliver of butter and place the peach halves in a well-buttered shallow baking dish. Add the wine, sprinkle lightly with sugar and bake in the oven for 30–40 minutes and serve hot.

199

Dolce italiana
Italian sweetmeat

INGREDIENTS
100 g (4 oz) each: candied
  cherries, sultanas, dried
  figs, dried apricots,
  stoned dates, blanched
  almonds, shelled walnuts
  or hazelnuts
2–3 tablespoons brandy or
  rum
icing sugar

It is no more possible to give servings for this sweetmeat than it is to give the number of servings in a box of chocolates. The combined weight is approximately 675 g (1½ lb). The sweetmeat can be eaten as soon as it has been made and shaped, but it is better if left for several hours, wrapped in foil in a refrigerator.

Mix the fruit and nuts together and push through the coarse blade of a mincer. Add the brandy. Sprinkle a board generously with sifted icing sugar, add the sweetmeat and knead to a thick paste. It can then either be shaped into a single block or into two 'salamis' about 30 cm (12 in) long and 4 cm (1½ in) thick. If not eating it immediately, wrap carefully but well sprinkled with sugar in foil and store in the refrigerator. It will keep for quite a long time.

Dolce italiana

Insalata di frutta
Fruit salad

INGREDIENTS
bananas, apricots or
  peaches, strawberries
castor sugar
Strega liqueur

Peel and slice the bananas and apricots. Hull and slice the strawberries. Arrange in layers in a glass bowl, sprinkle with sugar and generously moisten with Strega. Leave for several hours before serving.

Fette di arance al Marsala
Slices oranges in Marsala

TO SERVE FOUR–SIX

INGREDIENTS
6 large blood oranges
sugar to taste
150 ml (¼ pint) sweet
  Marsala
3 tablespoons any sweet
  liqueur

Sicilian oranges are among the best in the world, especially the *sanguinacce*, or blood oranges, and their juice is very sweet. Usually Sicilians do not drink orange juice in the early morning but prefer to drink a glass of it after a meal as a dessert.

Peel and slice the oranges and remove the pith. Discard the first and last slices as these usually have not enough flesh. Put the slices into a glass bowl, sprinkle generously with sugar, add the Marsala and liqueur, stir gently and chill before serving.

Fragole al vino
Wild strawberries in wine

TO SERVE TWO–THREE

INGREDIENTS
450 g (1 lb) wild
  strawberries
275 ml (½ pint) sweet
  white wine
castor sugar

Put the strawberries into a glass bowl, add the wine, a little sugar and leave for several hours before serving.

In Sicily Marsala is used. Wild strawberries are also served sprinkled with lemon or orange juice and a little sugar – seldom cream as this tends to drown their delicate flavour, although nothing can mar their aroma.

Top left: insalata di frutta;
top right: fette di arance al Marsala;
bottom: fragole al vino

Granite (Water ices)

Water ices have been eaten in Italy since the days of the Romans. It is recorded that Roman emperors sent their slaves to fetch ice from the Apennines, 'hills candied with snow' Horace called them. Nero had a fondness for snow or crushed ice flavoured with honey. Also popular at that time was a tumbler of crushed ice over which pomegranate juice was poured. This was called *malum granatum* in Latin and is today called *melagrana*; and the drink was therefore called *granita* or maybe *granatum*. Marco Polo is supposed to have brought back stories of slant-eyed men sitting on silken cushions toying with glasses of crushed ice flavoured with exotic fruit juices.

However, although the Romans may

Granita di caffè
Coffee water ice

TO SERVE FOUR–SIX

INGREDIENTS
225 g (½ lb) sugar
275 ml (½ pint) water
850 ml (1½ pints) freshly
made strong black coffee

Dissolve the sugar in the water over a low heat, stirring all the time. When it has dissolved, bring the liquid to the boil and boil rapidly for exactly 5 minutes. Cool, mix with the freshly made coffee and pour into an ice tray. Freeze in the refrigerator at the normal temperature without stirring until granular, about 3 hours. Serve in sorbet glasses or tumblers.

Granita di fragole
Strawberry water ice

TO SERVE SIX–EIGHT

INGREDIENTS
900 g (2 lb) fresh
strawberries
225 g (8 oz) sugar
150 ml (¼ pint) water
juice of 1 small lemon
whipped double cream
(optional)

The quantity of strawberries may seem high but they reduce considerably when puréed. This quantity will give about 575 ml (1 pint) of pulp. Instead of the juice of 1 lemon, half lemon and half orange may be used.

Wash, hull and purée the strawberries, either in a liquidizer or by rubbing through a coarse sieve. Dissolve the sugar in the water over a low heat, stirring all the time, bring it to the boil and boil for just 5 minutes. Cool, then mix with the strawberry purée and lemon juice, stir well, pour into an ice-cube tray and freeze in the refrigerator at the normal temperature without stirring until granular, about 3 hours. However, if a less granular mixture is desired, stir it from time to time. This ice can be served with whipped cream. Serve in sorbet glasses or tumblers.

Granita di limone
Lemon water ice

TO SERVE FOUR–SIX

INGREDIENTS
275 ml (½ pint) strained
lemon juice
grated rind of 1 lemon
100 g (4 oz) sugar
575 ml (1 pint) water

Combine the juice and lemon rind. Put the sugar and water into a pan and cook over a moderate heat until the sugar is dissolved, stirring all the time. Bring the liquid to the boil and, as soon as it bubbles, cook it for exactly 5 minutes. Take the pan from the heat and let the syrup cool. Mix in the lemon juice and rind, pour into an ice-cube tray and freeze in the refrigerator at the normal temperature without stirring until granular, for about 3 hours. Serve in sorbet glasses or tumblers.

claim to have created the water ice, the Sicilians can claim to be the largest consumers of them. When the local bars put out their sign to say they are serving *granite*, water ices, it is a sure indication that summer has arrived. And in Sicily the eating of *granite* has reached such a cult that many take a tumbler of coffee or lemon water ice, together with a piece of fresh bread and a brioche, at breakfast time. To my mind this is a better start to the day than either tomato or orange juice, neither of which the average Sicilian would consider drinking early in the morning.

Water ices differ from cream ices in that they are made from water, sugar and a flavouring. They are simple to make, with no demands on the refrigerator, nor do they require constant stirring.

From left to right : granita di caffè; granita di fragole accompanied by whipped cream; granita di limone

Cheese, bread, herbs, flavourings and coffee

Cheese

Italy produces a great variety of cheeses. Not all of them travel and not all of them have a specific name. In many of the cheese shops, usually called *Casa di Parmigiano* or *di Formaggio*, and also in the cheese stalls in the markets, one often sees a cheese labelled *nostrano* which simply means local, or 'ours'. These are the country cheeses still made by the farmers and peasants (although sometimes copied by the cheese manufacturers). They are made with goats' or ewes' milk, sometimes with cows' milk, depending on the region and local pastorage, or often a mixture of two or even three milks. Most of these cheeses must be eaten fresh, although some are matured to be used as grating cheese. Almost without exception they are good cheeses and worth the trouble of seeking out.

Pecorino (1,2)

Although a great number of Italian cheeses bear the same generic name, a cheese of the same name can vary tremendously from district to district. A good example of this is Pecorino, the generic name for cheeses made from ewes' milk and probably the oldest of the Italian cheeses – it was mentioned by Pliny. Basically they are not too difficult to recognize. Most of them look exactly what they are, robust country cheeses. They are usually made in wheels or cakes, but there are other shapes, square or oblong. The curd is usually the colour of straw, but there are some which have a truly chalky white curd. Even the rind of the many Pecorino cheeses varies. The Siena Pecorino has a mottled rind; Lucca, also in Tuscany, produces a cheese with a charcoal-coloured rind, while some areas produce almost coal-black rinds. Norcia, in Umbria, has a particularly piquant Pecorino with a dark, deeply ribbed rind, while many others have a soft rind, are white and shaped like squashed balls or are even quite round. Considered one of the best of this group of cheeses is the *pecorino romano*, produced at Moliterna in the Roman countryside, a hard, dry yet smooth cheese. Pecorino when fresh is used as a table cheese but it is also matured until hard enough to be used as a grating cheese. In some areas, notably Sardinia and Liguria, a mature Pecorino is often preferred to Parmesan for grating, not because it is cheaper but because of its flavour. Many cheeses coming from southern Italy are variants of Pecorino.

Ricotta (3)

This soft white curd cheese was originally produced only in the south but today is made throughout Italy. The name means 'twice cooked' for Ricotta is made with the whey of other cheeses, such as Provolone, Pecorino and Mozzarella. It has a mild but distinctive flavour and is used a great deal in cooking in Italy both in sweet and savoury dishes. In Sicily, in the small hill village of Santa Lucia, a baked Ricotta is produced, and all over the country there are excellent versions of smoked Ricotta; some of these versions, like the pyramid-shaped Zigar, dark and swarthy in colour, are smoked in the dark recesses of shepherds' huts and served locally with boiled potatoes and gnocchi, but which hardly ever reach urban markets. In other areas, notably the Marches, a salted or hard Ricotta which is preserved between aromatic leaves can be found and is often referred to as 'Ricotta with a rind'.

Gorgonzola (4,5,6)

This blue-veined cheese ranks with the finest blues in the world and, according to legend, its origin is the result of an accident. A peasant cheesemaker, having had a meal at a local trattoria, paid for it with several whole Stracchino cheeses. The proprietor put them one on top of the other in his larder and left them for a while. When he went to take his cheeses, on a wet night, he found they had all gone, as he thought, mouldy. Being a thrifty fellow he tried one first before throwing them all out: instead he found them excellent and this, they say, is how Gorgonzola was born. Be that as it may, Gorgonzola originally was probably made in the small village of that name in the province of Lombardy, but today it is produced in vast quantities in and around Milan, as well as extensively in neighbouring Piedmont. It is manufactured from cows' milk, is uniquely soft and buttery, with a sharp but never salty flavour. To obtain its characteristic mould it is stored in damp caves. It is not an easy cheese to imitate and, perhaps the Italians are right in claiming that it is unique. Generally the Italians prefer the so-called *gorgonzola dolce* which is rather bland in flavour, but it is the sharper flavoured *gorgonzola piccante* which seems to have cornered the foreign markets, certainly it would seem the British.

Belonging to the same family is Stracchino, a name given to a number of soft, slightly piquant cheeses which must indeed be eaten fresh otherwise they change from piquant to sour. These cheeses are made from the milk of 'tired' cows, or those who have spent a lazy winter on the Gorgonzola grazing grounds near Milan.

Piedmont has also developed the production of Gorgonzola cheeses with such additions as a white Gorgonzola, Pannerone, which has a decidedly sharp flavour although made in the same way as Gorgonzola, except it is not stored in caves to develop the mould. Another blue-veined cheese with a heavy alpine flavour, sharp and salty, is Castelmagno.

Grana cheeses

This is a group of hard matured cheeses produced in northern and central Italy of which the following are the three main types:

1. Parmigiano reggiano (7) The only grana cheese which may be thus labelled is that produced in a small but well-defined area in Emilia-Romagna, in the towns of Parma, Reggio Emilia, Bologna, Mantua and Modena. It is an exceptionally fine cheese and laborious to produce, requiring not less than three years to mature. It has a closely knit curd interposed with pinpoint holes. It makes a perfect table cheese eaten fresh and as a cooking cheese it certainly has no equal. It should always be bought by the piece and grated at home when needed.

2. Grana padano This term denotes all the grana cheeses produced in the extensive area between Cuneo and Ravenna, including Alessandria, Milan, and Pavia. The cheese manufacturers of these cities are responsible for at least half of the grana cheeses. At first glance it is difficult to distinguish between them and it is a matter of local opinion which of these two great grana groups produces the finest cheese.

3. Grana lodigiano This is the outsider of the grana cheeses. It is made in the Lombardy town of Lodi and is a fine-grained cheese, strong in flavour, verging towards the coarse. Its colour, almost yellowish, is deeper than the class granas mentioned above and its curd is more holed or pitted. To a certain extent it does outwardly resemble the great grana cheeses but it is not in the same league.

Goat cheeses

These vary from 'sweet' to 'ferocious'. Some are from pure goats milk and others from a mixture of goats' and cows' milk. They are usually cylinder shaped and often broken into segments. The sweet or mild cheeses, *caprini*, are very delicate in flavour; while the strong ones can be very salty, very mature (high if you prefer) and sometimes lightly blue or green flecked; they sear the palate as they go down, but even more so if they have been left in oil with herbs and spices for several months.

Mozzarella (8)

This is an important cheese, mainly used in cooking. It is southern Italian in origin where it is produced in vast quantities and still made from buffalo milk, especially around Capua and Caserta. Buffalo milk produces the best Mozzarella which has a soft, almost rubbery texture, snow-white in colour. It is made overnight and is ready in the morning. It must be eaten absolutely fresh, while the whey is still dripping from it. In Italy it is sold wrapped in paper and kept in a bowl filled with whey. Once a Mozzarella has been cut and the whey runs out, it is only fit for cooking. Mozzarella is also smoked and makes a good table cheese. There are also Manteca which is a Mozzarella stuffed with butter and Scamorza, not easy to find outside its southern habitat. Today Mozzarella is made in other parts of Italy but with cows' milk instead of the traditional buffalo milk, and described by one expert as pleasing as an ice-cream and as insipid. *Fior di latte* and *Fior d'alpe* are similar cheeses.

Robiola

This is a generic name for a group of outstanding sophisticated cheeses produced in northern Italy. They are fast ripening cheeses, alpine in character, each with its own distinctive flavour. There are two types, bland and piquant, and originally they were always encased in a red covering. There are round and square Robiola, eaten both fresh and matured, and some connoisseurs insist that a good Robiola from Piedmont has the flavour of truffles, which could be so, as this is the truffle area. In this same family there is also Bra, a hard, almost white cheese, sharp and salty, served fresh for the table and matured for grating. Another cheese is Pagliarini, rather on the periphery of the Robiola but nevertheless good, sold on straw mats, hence the name, and served sprinkled with fresh olive oil and freshly ground black pepper.

Not all Italian cheeses belong to a distinctive grouping. The following are more individual in character.

Alpine cheeses
It might almost be better to classify these as Camembert type cheeses since all the world knows this French classic. In the north of Italy we find the small discs of Alpin which, at their best, are a serious rival to Camembert. They are fairly seasonal cheeses, not widely available and only produced in the country areas. A similar but sharper cheese, but also splendid, is Soera di Viozene which has a blackish grey crust and is described by its fans as having a sensual flavour or perfume; another is the Caprino di Rimella, a goat cheese with a slightly piquant flavour which ripens into a cheese of the Camembert type or class.

Taleggio (9)
Although now made throughout northern Italy a true Taleggio is matured in caves and comes from the Valsassina, Ballabio, Premana regions. It is a cheese which has many imitators as the name has not been protected. It is a soft, fat, white, cream cheese with a thin, pinkish rind and must be eaten fresh, within a day or so of its cutting, otherwise it can become sour.

Mascherpone

It is a moot point whether this is a cheese or a cream, for it so closely resembles clotted cream and indeed can be used as a cream with fruit or as a cake filling. It is a light buttery-white colour, served chilled in winter, sometimes sprinkled with brandy or sugar, or mixed with ground coffee and rum. The best comes from Abbiategrasso, near Milan. There is also a smoked version called *mascherpone passato*.

Bel Paese (10)

Owing to some splendid publicity this cheese is among the best known of the Italian cheeses and the small town of Melzo, from which it originates, the best known since the manufacturers of the cheese gave it a map of Italy as a label, with Melzo larger than Rome. It belongs to a group of fast ripening, rather bland cheeses. Pastorella is almost identical.

Groviera

This is the Italian version of the Gruyère or Emmenthal. It can be eaten fresh or left to mature and be used for grating.

Crescenza

This is a winter cheese described as being butter and cream in one mouthful.

Dolcelatte (11)

This is yet another member of the Gorgonzola family and locally described as 'parsley and cream'.

Asiago

This is a truly fine cheese, firm of texture, well pitted with small holes and with a fine flavour. It is used mainly as a table cheese but when matured can be used for grating, as it becomes granular. There are several variations coming from the Veneto-Friuli, Venezia, Trentino and Alto Adige areas. Two good cheeses of this class are the Vezzena Stravecchio and the Formaggio di Dobbiaco which should appeal to lovers of farmhouse Cheddar, as indeed should the Alpentopfen and Montasio.

Caciotta

Under this generic name we find a number of smallish round cheeses made from a mixture of ewes' and cows' milk; probably the best known of the many Caciotta cheeses are those from Tuscany. It is so popular that manufacturers have stepped in but not always with such good results.

Fontina

This is one of Italy's most famous cheeses and comes from the Valle d'Aosta where it is produced in a rigidly defined area. The curd is firm, faintly ivory and broken with eyes. It combines the nutty tang of the Groviera with the sweetness of Emmenthal. It is said to be 'the cook's dream' and often used in cooking.

Toma

The dialect name for a cheese made from ewes', cows' and goats' milk. The number of fine country cheeses labelled toma or tomini is legion and some of the best are found in Piedmont. In Monferrato in the small neighbourhood farms a toma is made that is perfect but it is never marketed. Alba too is a great centre for these cheeses. The best have a fairly soft curd, a thinnish crust and are usually straw coloured. Some of the toma in the Langhe and Monferrato are so sharp they need an almost iron stomach for they go down the throat 'like a lighted torch'. One local toma, after many months of being preserved in oil, is beaten to a cream and spread on bread.

Caciocavallo

This is a splindle-shaped cheese with a neck and head coming from Sicily. The name means 'cheese on horseback' but there is no one explanation for its curious name. It is made from mixed buffalo, cows' and ewes' milk, its texture is sharp with a smooth sharpish flavour and a faint aroma of bacon. Butirri is a variety stuffed with butter.

Caso forte

This is an ancient Italian cheese served at the beginning of a meal to promote the taste buds.

Provolone (12)

This is a very important cheese produced in the south which comes in all shapes and sizes, such as little pigs, gnomes, pears, balls and melons, all strung up often by the neck as from the hangman's rope. The most popular and exported shape is an enormous oval entwined with cord which leaves its marks on the shiny rind when removed. When young the flavour is delicate, but as the cheese matures it becomes piquant, tangy and even spicy.

Burrata

This is a very southern cheese shaped like a jug into which is poured the soft curd of either Mozzarella or Provolone, cream is then added, the top sealed and the cheese left to hang wrapped in leaves.

Pepato

This is a series of cheeses produced in Sicily and well flavoured with peppercorns, usually black.

Bread

The Italians have had a love affair with bread since the days of the Romans when public bakehouses were established from which free bread was distributed. Eating bread became and has remained a way of life for the Italians who manage to consume enormous quantities by British standards.

Contrary to the often expressed belief that there is no good bread in Italy, and that Italians are not half as imaginative as their French counterparts, I find there is immense variety, both in the type and shape of the bread made in Italy. Every town, indeed every village, has its own bread specialities, and when travelling most Italians will take home a sample or two. Italian bakers are far from being sluggish in their bread designs, as anyone who takes the trouble to browse in the bread shops will soon discover. Throughout the country there are bakers who literally sculpt bread, an art which goes back to the sixteenth century when it was practised at the Court of Mantua. Ferrara, a city which has been famed for generations for its bread making and which is still noted for its dedicated bakers, produces, as one enthusiastic writer declared: 'the finest bread in the world', praise which the Ferrarese consider is merited; they can tell you the actual date of a particularly famous bit of local bread design, in 1536, when Giglio, a master baker, covered a table with plaited breads for the then reigning Duke of Ferrara. These sculptures are on the whole gay, merry reproductions of birds and beasts, horses and carts, and dancing figures, all designed to appeal to children, who adore them both to eat and to keep. This latter operation has been made possible by putting a coat of transparent lacquer over the breads that will keep them perfect for an indefinite period. But in Sicily it is not only the bakers who produce breads of such inspired designs, the housewives also do so on days of religious festivals. They are made as altar offerings to decorate the village churches, and lovely indeed are some of their designs. Others are made for the children; in Palermo the sexual symbols found in the pagan temples are recreated in bread, while in Verona it is the custom at Jewish weddings to have a loaf of bread, complete with tulle, butterflies and flowers, also made of bread. Milan is a city so devoted to bread that there is even a bread club, and there is one baker renowned there for his artistic sculptured breads; it was a

Milanese baker who described the art of bread making as a mathematical formula, or like a musical composition by Bach.

In Italy bakers bake six days a week in some areas, seven in others, and often twice daily. Their loaves vary from quite enormous ones to bridge rolls and *grissini*; these last seem to find a place both in the bread as well as in the biscuit lists. Bread ranges from crusty loaves to the delicate Sardinian bread which is lace-patterned and looks far too good to eat. Also in Sardinia a bread is made like large, crisp wafers which the shepherds take with them to the mountains. This is stored between damp cloths but must be soaked in water or broth before it is eaten. And in the Valle d'Aosta a particular bread is made once a year in December, in the last quarter of the moon, to last for one year. It never hardens, nor does it go mouldy, and it is made from what is locally called a 'bastard' dough.

A great deal of Italy's bread is still baked in wood-fired ovens, and driving along country roads the sign *Pane al forno di legno* is frequent; it is always worth stopping to buy a loaf, sometimes so hot you burn your fingers picking it up. In Umbria a curious flat bread is made called *torta sul testo*; this is a round unleavened bread baked on hot stones and split open for filling with mountain ham or salami. In the country areas it is possible to drop in at a small farmhouse-trattoria and buy one for consuming in the garden or to take away. Another Umbria and Marches speciality is the *piadini al prosciutto*, a brittle type of flat unleavened bread, toasted and spread with local ham which makes an excellent mid-morning snack. In Sardinia they have never lacked for bread, white, brown or fruit and with a dozen or more different shapes. As bread baking in Sardinia is still a ritual, both the housewife and baker mark the sign of the cross on the rising dough before baking. Sicily too has a variety of breads, but not matching those of Sardinia.

It is not possible to give all the names and shapes of Italian breads, they are all 'local'. Many are baked for special occasions, such as the *panettone*, which is more a cake than a bread. Apart from everyday breads made throughout the country, there are those which are flavoured with herbs, such as rosemary, basil, fennel, the last a particular favourite in Sicily, and with sesame seeds. In Liguria a bread is made filled with unpitted small black olives. There are pumpkin breads, mint, oregano and aniseed breads, and a heavy honey bread with sultanas, figs and even chocolate. You would be hard to please if you did not find a bread to your taste in Italy.

Herbs and flavourings

The Italians have been cooking with herbs for many centuries. That they have continued to do so until now is because much of their best food is based on peasant cooking using the recipes of yesterday, all of which made lavish use of herbs. Many of these herbs were once in favour in old British gardens and kitchens, and more is the pity that they have been allowed to disappear.

Herbs came into use for diverse reasons; they were used in religious and magic ceremonies and for their medicinal properties. As for magic, is it any more strange that the Emperor Tiberius put on a crown of laurel during thunderstorms as a protection, than it is for us to fear walking under a ladder, or hoping that a passing black cat will bring us luck – which in Italy it doesn't, quite the reverse?

Apart from herbs, since the days of the Romans Italian cooks have been occupied with many flavourings and aromas with considerable success.

Aceto (1, 2) Vinegar
The Italians use vinegar rather more than is perhaps usual in Britain and most of it is made from grapes, which no doubt produces the best and mildest vinegars. Also a number of housewives make their own vinegars, using traditional methods of distilling, etc. Herb-flavoured vinegars play also a large part in Italian cooking. These can be made in any kitchen by the simple expedient of putting whatever herb you want into the bottle of vinegar. In my own kitchen I keep a supply of red, rosé and white vinegars, as well as some flavoured with rosemary, garlic, mint and basil.

Aglio (3) Garlic
This bulb plays an important if not vital part in the cooking of Italy, from the top of the boot down to the heel, but Italians are justly peeved when their cooking is dismissed as all oil and garlic. They understand the use and power of garlic and,

although used in quantity, it is also used with discretion. It adds zest to vegetables, meat, poultry, game and fish and develops the flavour of most foods while reducing the richness of others. There are several varieties of garlic, some bulbs being covered with dead white skins and others with mauve or pinkish skins. Some cloves are enormous, others tiny. Also the number of cloves to a garlic bulb varies enormously. Instructions in a recipe for a particular number of cloves must be taken only as a guide-line and one's own taste consulted. The flavour and aroma of garlic is pungent and it blends well with meat, especially lamb or mutton, as well as fish and vegetables. It is a great herbal panacea.

Basilico Basil
An aromatic and even slightly spicy herb of which there are over 50 varieties. To grow it prefers a warm climate but is now widely cultivated in sheltered places in Britain, also it is obtainable from herbalist suppliers. It is a herb of magic and its aroma is said to be conducive to meditation – strange that the lively Italians should be so fond of it. It is widely used in tomato sauces, soups and salads and is essential in many Ligurian dishes.

Borraggine Borage
A small plant covered with irritating hairs which has sky-blue flowers and grows widely and profusely in the Mediterranean region. It has a pronounced cucumber flavour and the flowers are often candied. Ligurians include the leaves in their vegetable stuffings for ravioli and they are often cooked and served like spinach, or dipped in batter and deep fried. Also they can be added to salads but first the leaves must be chopped for their hairy texture can be very unpleasant.

Traditional Venetian wine goblets

Capperi (4) Capers
Capers are an essential ingredient in every Italian kitchen. They are the buds of a small bush with the palest and loveliest of flowers which prefers to grow on old walls amid ruins. They are also extensively cultivated. In Italy capers are sold loose in the markets, either in a brine or packed in salt. They are used with fish, in sauces, vegetables and pickles, also with veal and lamb.

Cicoria Chicory
There are several varieties of chicory. The chicory herb which grows wild is a perennial. It is a charming sky-blue flower and its flavour, which is slightly bitter, is a favourite with many Italians. There is also in Italy the so-called *cicoria di Treviso* or *radicchio* which is at its best in the town of Treviso. It is a small plant, purplish-red-pink, a little like a small lettuce with which it is often mixed to heighten the bland flavour of a salad. It is also braised and fried.

Dente di leone Dandelion
The leaves, considered as nutritious, are used in salads and also cooked like spinach. They have a strong effect upon the kidneys, hence their popular name in France, *pissenlit*. In Italy the name is derived from the deeply notched leaves, supposedly resembling a lion's teeth.

Dragoncello (5) Tarragon
This is a neglected herb as far as the Italians are concerned, except in the region around Siena where it grows.

Finocchio (6) Fennel
The cultivated bulb fennel, wild fennel and fennel seeds are important in Italian cooking. The bulb fennel is used as a vegetable on its own account, braised, stewed and baked au gratin, and served raw as a salad. The wild fennel, slightly bitter but without the characteristic aniseed flavour, is used with fish, especially red mullet, and a little is often added to mayonnaise to give it character. Fennel seeds are often a feature of Italian snail sauces.

Foglie d'alloro (7, 8) Bayleaves
The bayleaf is one of the best known herbs and used in fish, egg, meat and vegetable dishes, in marinades and roasts, stews, stock-making, brines, sauces, even sweet custards and béchamel sauce, as well as spit-roasted meat and fish. Its flavour is aromatic but also somewhat bitter. In Italian folklore, a withered baytree is the forerunner of bad luck.

Ginepro Juniper
The berries are used in most Italian game dishes, with pork and ham, also with rabbit and chicken. Junipers are evergreen and the berries take three years to ripen, thus you find berries on bushes in three stages of ripeness. The leaves are very prickly and gloves are needed to collect the berries. Those grown in the Italian hills are considered stronger in flavour than those from Britain or Sweden. To gain their full flavour and aroma they must be crushed before being used. Juniper berries marry well with most other herbs and flavourings and, in particular, they mingle magnificently with garlic, red wine or brandy and in a dish of venison or wild boar.

Lardo (9, 10) Firm pork fat
This product is sold in Continental shops and also in many supermarkets and delicatessens, usually under its German name of *Speck*. It is a thick chunk of very firm fat pork which can be sliced like bacon. It is sometimes streaked, like streaky bacon, which is the best substitute for *lardo* when this is not available. In Italy it can be bought plain or smoked and quite often it is thickly sprinkled with leaves of rosemary, thyme, both finely chopped, and salt and pepper which gives it a fine flavour. Smoked *lardo* is thickly spread with paprika pepper, rolled and thinly sliced for eating. For cooking it must be put into a pan and fried over a moderate heat until all the fat runs freely and any bits become scraps of crackling.

Maggiorana (11) Marjoram
This is a spicy, sweet-scented herb related to thyme with which it can be mixed or replaced. It is used with clams, sauces, vegetables such as carrots, courgettes and onions, and omelettes. Its flavour is so delicate that it is advisable to add it to a dish towards the end of cooking, otherwise the flavour disappears. All varieties of this herb will dry and freeze well.

Menta (12) Mint
This is not a popular herb with Italians, perhaps because it does not marry well with garlic. It is used occasionally with lamb, broad beans, fish and stews.

Mirto Myrtle
A handsome evergreen shrub which grows all over the Italian hillsides. The ancients used it in their cooking and made *myrtalum*, a kind of stew. The Sardinians like to stuff or wrap up meat with myrtle leaves, especially pork, before cooking, or to flavour dishes of small birds, considered so much of a delicacy in the Mediterranean.

Dandelion

Fennel

213

Noce moscata (13) Nutmeg
This is a very important flavouring for the Italians; it is extremely pungent and is always used in spinach and cheese dishes. Every Italian kitchen has its supply of whole nutmegs and a specially designed grater. Nutmeg, like pepper, should be grated straight into the dish it is to flavour.

Olio (14) Oil
As far as the majority of Italians are concerned, the only oil worth considering is olive oil, for this country is one of the great olive-oil producing countries of the world. But it is important to know what constitutes a good olive oil, allowing for the dictates of taste and local preference, for olive oil varies considerably from one region to another. However, on one point all Italians are agreed, the best and only oil worth using is of the first pressing, the so-called virgin oil, and preferably from a cold pressing. A less good oil can come from a hot first pressing, and an exceedingly nasty oil can be made from the left-over pulp, which often goes to the manufacturers to be sold to an innocent public under the perfectly honest but misleading name of refined oil.

In Liguria, where the olives are small but sweet, the oil is pale in colour, delicate in flavour and can be used with all kinds of food, in salads, as well as cooking. But there are those who prefer an oil like that from Tuscany – heavier, fruitier and stronger, both in colour and flavour. Those who are still able to pick and choose among the olive oils and are connoisseurs, take different olive oils for different dishes, but such connoisseurs are few and far between these days when oil, even in the producing countries, is extremely expensive. Like many of the locals, I go into the hills armed not with a bottle but with a 12-litre demijohn to a peasant family who produce an oil that is pure and from a cold first pressing. Many Italians have taken to using peanut or soya oil for dishes in which the flavour of olive oil is not absolutely essential; but for salads, never.

Origano Oregano
This is roughly the same as the plant called wild marjoram in Britain, but as the family ramifications of this herb are enormous it is a difficult one to classify. In the south of Italy a peppery flavoured oregano is preferred, while the north prefers a sweet oregano, pleasant and aromatic. Oregano is collected in the woods and fields and dries very well. If properly stored it will keep its full flavour for at least three years. It is used with abandon in Italian cooking.

Pepe (15, 16) Pepper
Good pepper is expensive and therefore is worthy of serious attention. It should be bought as peppercorns and ground freshly for everyday use. Today pepper mills are both decorative and reasonably cheap to buy. The difference between freshly ground pepper and that bought already ground is tremendous. Peppercorns keep for an indefinite length of time. White and black peppercorns grow on the same bush and it is merely in their later treatment that their paths divide. White pepper is usually more expensive than black and should be used in all recipes that are accompanied by white sauces.

Pepe forte (17, 18) Red pepper
This is produced from the seeds of red or chilli peppers and used in stews, sauces and soups. It is heavily used in southern Italian cooking. Also in this class come the small hot peppers, called *peperoncini*, or chillies.

Pinoli (19) Pine-nuts
Pine trees are a great feature of the Ligurian landscape. The pine-nuts should really be called pine kernels for they are extracted from the seeds which are found in the cones. Their flavour is extremely delicate and slightly nutty. They are used in Italy in game dishes, sweet-sour sauces and in some sweet dishes. Today they are used in the *pesto* sauce (*see page* 182) but this is a recent innovation.

Pomodoro (20) Tomato
This versatile vegetable has been adopted by the Italians and is as much used in their cooking as a flavouring as a vegetable in its own right. There are several varieties in current use in Italy. Very deep-red tomatoes are used both raw and cooked; plum-shaped ones, usually a paler red, sometimes even an almost yellowish red, are used for sauces, purées and preserving. Green ones are used for salads and also the comically misshapen varieties with the full flavour of sun-ripened fruit.

Italians always peel tomatoes for cooking, except when they are to be stuffed, and almost always press out the seeds, for both skin and seeds are held to be indigestible. To remove the skin is a simple operation. Immerse the tomatoes for 2–3 minutes in boiling water, and slightly longer if the skins are particularly tough. Italian tinned tomatoes make an excellent substitute for the fresh ones, mainly because, although preserved, they lose less flavour than most other varieties of tinned vegetables. Italian plum-shaped tomatoes are usually available in Britain.

Oregano

Prezzemolo (21) Parsley
The parsley used in Italy is the flat or plain-leafed type, less pungent than the curly parsley preferred in Britain. Parsley in Italy is finely chopped and added to most savoury dishes as instinctively as is salt. Also used is the so-called Hamburg parsley which is grown as a root vegetable, although botanically it is a true parsley. It has a flavour similar to celery or celeriac, as indeed has the Neapolitan parsley, a southern Italian species which is grown in the same manner as celery. Parsley is not regarded in Italy as simply a garnish, but is used for its definite flavour.

Rosmarino Rosemary
A very distinctive plant with dark spiky leaves and with a strong aroma. It is discreetly used in many Mediterranean countries but in Italy liberally. It is used with lamb, in stews and soups and to flavour poultry and game. Most Italian butchers and poulterers have sprigs of rosemary on their counters to present to customers. Rosemary is also used with some fish dishes.

Rucchetta Rocket
This pungent herb is widely used in Italy to give a bitter flavour to green salads. Combined with lettuce or other salad greens with the usual salad dressing it makes a welcome addition to what might otherwise be too bland a salad.

A grapevine

Sale grosso (22) Salt
In Italy bay or sea salt is generally used and can be bought in various degrees of refinement. As salt is sold as a government monopoly in Italy, it is sold in tobacconists, although today one also finds it in the larger supermarkets. Salt is important as it brings out the flavours of the food with which it is cooked. Many cooks consider that it should be added as close to the end of the cooking as possible. However, when added, care must be taken that the flavour is not overdone. Salt can be added but it is almost impossible to do much about a dish that has been over-salted.

Salvia (23) Sage
In Italy sage is used with game, veal, liver and in particular with eels. Curiously the Romans used it in their medicines but not in their cooking.

Sambuco Elder
The elder tree which grows along the country lanes throughout Britain is no stranger and country people brew the berries into wine. In Italy it is one of the main flavourings in a liqueur of the same

Root ginger

name, Sambuco. Elder flowers can be used in sweet dishes, giving them a distinct but pleasing flavour.

Timo (24) Thyme
One of Italy's most widely used herbs for it goes into almost all savoury dishes, stuffings, sauces, meats and salads.

Vino (25) Wine
As wine drinking is a way of life in Italy, it is not surprising that it is the inclusion of wine in Italian cooking which gives its characteristic flavour to so many Italian dishes. In a country where wine is expensive, it might often seem that the quantities called for in some Italian recipes are high, but it is a matter of relativity. Only a small quantity of wine is required to create a strong aromatic flavour in a dish, and the alcoholic content of the wine vanishes early in the cooking, since alcohol has a lower boiling point than water and soon evaporates, leaving its flavour behind. Italians add wine to their cooking as a matter of habit, probably without thinking of it at all, but knowing it is going to contribute a flavour to the dish.

Both red and white wines are used in cooking and although it is not necessary to use the finest quality wine, it must be of at least good table wine quality. Wine which has gone off is no more use in the pot than it is in the stomach.

Zafferano (26) Saffron
This is one of the most expensive of all flavourings and colourings, produced from the stamens of the saffron crocus. As it is so expensive, we should be happy that a pinch is sufficient for any dish. In Italy it is used mainly for risottos and bland dishes, both for its colour and its very faint flavour or aroma. Before using, saffron must always be steeped in a little warm water. As saffron can never be cheap – it takes 200,000 flowers to make 450 g (1 lb) of saffron – be very suspect when offered a 'bargain'.

Zenzero (27) Ginger
This is hardly used in Italian cooking except in the south, in Basilicata. It should be noted that in Tuscany the hot chilli peppers are called *zenzero*, although they are called *peperoncini* elsewhere.

1. White wine vinegar
2. Red wine vinegar
3. Garlic
4. Capers
5. Tarragon
6. Fennel
7. Bayleaf plant
8. Dried bayleaves
9. Streaked lardo
10. Lardo
11. Pot marjoram
12. Mints
13. Nutmeg
14. Virgin olive oil
15. White peppercorns
16. Black peppercorns
17. Fresh chillies
18. Dried chillies
19. Pine-nuts
20. Tomatoes
21. Parsley
22. Sea salt
23. Sage
24. Thyme
25. White and red wine for
    cooking
26. Saffron
27. Ginger

Coffee

The Italians were among the first Europeans to drink coffee, indeed to have coffee bars. This came about after a despatch from the Venetian Ambassador to Turkey in the sixteenth century which reported the coffee-drinking habits of the Turks. Soon after this report coffee shops where clients could drink coffee were opened up and, it would seem, have flourished ever since. One gets the impression that Italians drink more coffee than any other Europeans but this is far from the truth. In the coffee-drinking stakes the Swedes are well ahead of both the Italians and the French, with the Danes and Germans in between.

Generally speaking Italians prefer coffee with a dark roast, called Continental roast in Britain. It is argued that the longer roasting needed to acquire this dark roast retains the oils and caffeine longer and in larger quantities, consequently the coffee is stronger and also slightly bitter because of the higher caffeine content.

In most Italian homes coffee is made either in a pressure-style coffee pot, *caffettiera*, or in a drip-pot, usually called a *napoletana*. Both come in several sizes capable of making from one cup to as many as 16. Both are fitted with a round cup-like sieve which restricts the pot from producing more coffee than it should. Both types of coffee pot can be bought in Britain. There is another version of the pressure pot which has a small tray attached on which are placed small cups, bought with the pot, and this too works on the pressure system but has several funnels, one for each cup of coffee through which the coffee is forced out directly into the cups.

1. To make espresso coffee in the home is not difficult. Almost fill the bottom section of the *caffettiera* with water, pack ground coffee into the sieve, screw on the top section which has a funnel in the middle and put the pot on the heat. As the water in the bottom boils it is forced through the sieve and funnel to fill the top section, having absorbed the coffee on the way. When the top section is filled, take the pot from the heat and pour the coffee into cups. Serve either black or with milk and sugar.

2. To make drip coffee, called *caffè filtrata* or *a macchinetta* in Italian, the *napoletana* pot is used which, as its name suggests, is of Neapolitan origin and more generally used in the south. This has three cylinders, one with a spout, one without, and one which is the sieve. Fill the section without the spout with water to just below the small hole you will see on the side. Pack the coffee into the sieve and cover with the remaining section with the spout, the latter facing downwards. Bring the water

to the boil over a moderate heat and when steam begins to spout from the small hole or vent, turn the contraption upside-down at once so that the spout is facing upwards. Listen and you will hear the coffee begin to drip. When this stops, the coffee is ready. Serve it black, with sugar if liked or with milk.

Not all coffee in Italy is espresso, although this again is the general impression formed by foreigners visiting the country. There is a fair variety of coffee drinks, as the list that follows shows:

Caffè aposta This is not a frequent expression but it means coffee made expressly for each client.

Caffè cappuccino This is coffee with whisked, foamy, hot milk added and often topped with grated chocolate.

Caffè corretto col cognac This is espresso coffee laced with brandy.

Caffè corretto col grappino This is espresso laced with a tot of Grappa.

Caffè doppio This is also called **caffè alto** or **lungo.** This method produces a slightly less strong but longer cup of coffee than the espresso.

Caffè espresso This is prepared in a large electric urn in which steam under pressure is forced through the powdered coffee.

Caffè francese This French-style coffee is more likely to be found in the home or in hotels. It is served at breakfast and seldom at any other time.

Caffè freddo This is cold coffee.

Caffè latte This is hot coffee and hot milk in equal parts.

Caffè macchiato This is coffee with a dash of milk.

Caffè con panna This is coffee with cream; if you want whipped cream, it is called *caffè montana*, and is a popular drink.

Caffè ristretto This is even stronger than the espresso and is also called *caffè forte*.

(1) Making espresso coffee using a caffettiera
(2) Making drip coffee using a napoletana

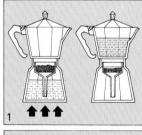

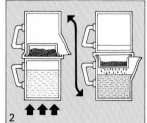

Preparing coffee using a caffettiera (*left*) and a napoletana (*right*)

Coppa dell'amicizia

The cup of friendship

TO SERVE FOUR

INGREDIENTS
4 small cups of strong
    black coffee
3 cups of Grappa
1 small glass dry red wine
sugar to taste
1 strip of lemon rind

One of the most interesting coffee drinks is the so-called *caffè valdostana* or *coppa dell'amicizia*, the cup of friendship. This drink is served among friends to drink a health or to show friendship. The coffee, mixed with other ingredients, designed no doubt to help promote friendship, is always served in a *grolla*, or grail, a relic of the Holy Knights of ancient days. These are still hand-made by local artisans in the Valle d'Aosta region, always of wood and carved with fruit or garlands of flowers. They are either in the shape of an altar chalice, a cup or a bowl, but all have a lid and spouts, usually four or more of the latter. The coffee is prepared in a separate pot and then poured into the *grolla*. Everyone drinks from the *grolla* but from a separate spout. The idea stems from the Knights of the Holy Grail who all drank from the same grail. These rather attractive hand-carved *grolle* are nowadays not only available in the d'Aosta region but in most household stores in northern Italy.

Prepare the coffee and mix all the ingredients together. Bring to the boil, ignite and then pour into the *grolla*. Serve at once.

219

The list that follows the regional map of Italy describes the very different attitudes to cooking throughout the country.

Piedmont and Aosta Valley (1)
A region of substantial dishes with the flavours of the mountains, forests and valleys, the penetrating aroma of truffles and mushrooms. The wines of Piedmont are among the finest in Italy.

Liguria (2)
Classical peasant cooking at its finest; the characteristic ingredients are olives, garlic, basil and pine-nuts, and also the mild, sweet olive oil of the region.

Lombardy (3)
A rice region where the risotto reigns supreme. Lombardians claim that their dishes are a subtle mixture of butter, cream and cheese.

Trentino-Alto Adige (4)
A world of gargantuan meals designed for cold days. A strong Austrian influence has produced smoked meats and salami, cabbage and potato dishes, plus an array of sweet dishes.

Veneto, Friuli, Venezia and Giulia (5)
The cooking of the city of Venice dominates the whole of the region with two contrasting styles, the one inherited from the former Doges, which is opulent and rich, and the second called *rustico*, which is simple and frugal.

Emilia-Romagna (6)
Food is taken seriously by the Emilians, who come to the table with a robust wholeheartedness, claiming that 'food is a hymn to the taste-buds, a triumph to the palate, and a sublimation of the best that man has to offer.'

Tuscany (7)
The Tuscans are very proud of their cooking which places a great emphasis on earthy dishes of peasant origin. Because of their predilection for beans, they are also called bean-eaters. However, Tuscany is also famous for the Florentine T-bone steak which is hardly a peasant dish and also Chianti wine.

Umbria and the Marches (8)
Although much of Umbrian cooking stems from its Etruscan heritage, it is famous for its pork products, as well as its confectionery. Its seaboard neighbour, the Marches, concentrates on splendid fish dishes.

Lazio (9)
The cooking of this region is based on that of its capital city, Rome. The Romans have purloined many of their dishes from neighbouring regions and blatantly labelled them '*alla romana*'. Lazio's authentic cooking is aromatic and makes use of light seasonings.

Molise and Abruzzo (10)
Lamb is so popular here that it is claimed to be 'the symbol of man and the divine'. There is widespread use of mountain hams and salami, and aubergines are the basic ingredients for most of the local dishes.

Campania (11)
The colourful cooking of Naples dominates this region and makes a plentiful use of olive oil, garlic, tomatoes, anchovies, olives and all forms of pasta.

Apulia (12)
The Apulians are champion pasta eaters. Meats are mostly cooked as ragoûts, with potatoes and white wine. A thrifty people, they see that nothing of an animal is wasted and their offal dishes are numerous.

Basilicata (13)
For the strong palate there is plenty to enjoy here, with game in abundance, thick soups and fiery sausages. The flavour of ginger permeates everything, from sausages to sauces.

Calabria (14)
Oranges, lemons, tuna, swordfish and giant peppers dominate Calabrian cooking, which is strong and hearty in the extreme.

Sicily (15)
Sicilian cooking is considered as the bridge between that of the eastern Mediterranean and Italy proper. The Sicilians never forget their island was once a seat of gastronomy and their cooks were in world demand.

Sardinia (16)
Sardinian food is rudimentary, historical and unspoilt. It is the cooking of a people who, through centuries of oppression, took refuge in mountain fastnesses, living on what the soil offered them and thus preserved their age-old cooking customs.

Index

223

Acknowledgments

The producers of the book would like to thank the following for their help:
Elaine Bastable, Carole Handslip, Joanna Percival and Brenda Sanctuary for testing and preparing the recipes for photography; Vicki Robinson for the index; Martin Newton for additional design; Fratelli Camisa, 1A Berwick Street, London W1 for allowing us to take the photograph on pages 26–27; Paolo Agnesi e figh S.p.A., Imperia, Italy, the pasta manufacturers, for their interest and encouragement as well as supplying the illustration on page 30; C.I.T. (England) Ltd., the Italian Holiday Experts, for their efficient travel arrangements; Trudi Petrassi of Windsor Wine and Food, Windsor, Berkshire for preparing the home-made pasta, ravioli and tortellini for photography and finally Jane Collins for researching black and white illustrations in Florence.

The producers would like to thank the following companies for the kind loan of accessories for the photography, and in particular Harvey Nichols, Knightsbridge, London, SW1 and Liberty and Co. Ltd., Regent Street, London W1 whose help was invaluable:
Casa Catalan, 57 Gray's Inn Road, London WC1
Casa Pupo, 56 Pimlico Road, London SW1
David Mellor, 4 Sloane Square, London SW1
Divertimenti, 68 Marylebone Lane, London W1
General Trading Company, 144 Sloane Street, London SW1
House and Bargain, 142 Notting Hill Gate, London W11
Imports from Tuscany, 38 Long Acre, London WC2
John Lewis, Oxford Street, London W1
Tile Mart Ltd., 151 Great Portland Street, London W1
Treasure Island, 81 Pimlico Road, London SW1
Way In Living (Harrods), Knightsbridge, London SW1

Also the following for advice and help with supplying Italian food and drinks for the photography:
Ambrose, 32 South Audley Street, London W1
Belloni's, Charlotte Street, London W1
Camisa and Son, 61 Old Compton Street, London W1

Black and white illustration acknowledgments
Endpapers: from Bartolommeo Scappi's *Dell'Arte del cucinare* (1643). The Bodleian Library, Oxford
Alinari, Florence pages **51, 91, 140, 162, 163, 180, 188, 189**
The Bodleian Library, Oxford pages **66, 80**
Museo storico degli spaghetti, Pontedassio, Italy pages **30, 210, 211**
The Rainbird Publishing Group Ltd pages **117, 119, 207, 212**

Porta di Guardia

Bottigliaria

Credenza

Corni

Ordine che si tiene in Sedia Vacante à seruire
gl'Illmi et Rmi Cardinali al Conclaue, si di
robbe di Cucina, come di Credenza, et
di bottigliaria